Reasonable People

Reasonable People

A Memoir

Kate Kasten

ISLET PRESS · IOWA CITY

BY THE SAME AUTHOR

Too Happy

Better Days

The Deconversion of Kit Lamb

Ten Small Beds

Wildwood: Fairy Tales and Fables Re-imagined

Foreign Ground: Stories

A Little Something for Everyone: Stories, Monologues, Dialogues and Observations

Islet Press, Iowa City
www.katekasten.com
Copyright © 2021 Kate Kasten
All rights reserved
ISBN: 978-0-9831959-6-2
Cover design by Cheryl Jacobsen
Typeset by Sara T. Sauers

In memory of

Elizabeth A. Kasten 1918–2002 & Carl A. Kasten 1915–1983
the reasonable people who raised me
&
Peter A. Kollman 1944–2001

AUTHOR'S NOTE

The excerpts from correspondence and college essay critiques are not the work of the book's author. They are verbatim quotations from the written words of the real correspondents and critics, whose names have been changed to protect their privacy.

Similarly, most locales, institutions and people go unnamed or have been given pseudonyms. For consistency, the author has given herself and her family pseudonyms as well.

I

Hotel

In 1950, when she is four, her family moves away from Chicago. During the long drive she is gray-faced and sick to her stomach. At the hotel room where they have planned to spend the first night in their new city, she stands in the doorway staring. Then she skips from bed to bed, the color returning to her face. She exclaims, "*This* is a hotel?"

Wallpaper

They move into a three-story, three bedroom house near the small private university where her father will be a business manager. Her older brother Nick has a room to himself. She shares the front room with her infant brother Teddy. His crib is against one wall, her bed opposite. The wallpaper has a colorful pattern of carriages and horses, ladies in hoop skirts, and gentlemen in top hats. At night she lies on her side facing the wall. When car headlights briefly illuminate the dark room, she watches the people and carriages and horses walk, roll and trot past her at a genteel pace. She doesn't remark on this phenomenon to her parents because she sees nothing remarkable in a wallpaper world going about its business.

Num num

Nick may have had a num num, but she doesn't remember it. By the time she's old enough to notice, he has discarded his. Teddy acquired a num num—a blanket—at around one year old. He held it to his cheek and sucked his thumb. Her first num num is also a blanket. But at four years old she trades it in for a saggy down-filled pillow with striped ticking, which she hauls around the house, sniffing one corner and sucking her right index finger. The pillow is too big to carry outside, but as soon as she comes indoors she goes searching for it again.

In order to hold her num num to her nose and suck her finger at the same time, she has to put her finger upside down in her mouth. This puts pressure on her two front teeth, but since they're baby teeth and will come out eventually, her mother doesn't fuss except to say, "Annie, isn't that uncomfortable?" The answer—no it isn't.

At five years old, she has traded the pillow for a pair of outgrown red cotton underpants. She sniffs the label while she sucks her finger. The underpants are small enough to accompany her outdoors. Her mother suggests she leave it behind when she goes to kindergarten. "I'm guessing none of the other kids will bring their num nums to school," she says. And that's true. But it doesn't stop her from carrying it everywhere else.

One day, at six years old, she comes home from playing with Dwight Anders on his front porch. She realizes she has left her num num at the Anders's and runs next door to retrieve it. It's gone. She knocks and Dwight's mother comes to the door. Mrs. Anders is a sour, gray-faced woman who spanks Dwight from time to time for no good reason.

She asks if Mrs. Anders has seen her num num. "Those underpants?" Mrs. Anders says, curling her lip. "I burned them."

"She shouldn't have done that," says her mother, with as much indignation as she's capable of. "It wasn't hers to burn." But she doesn't suggest a replacement, and that is the last of the num nums.

Wet pants

Her first grade teacher, Miss Rasmussen, is middle-aged and wears coke bottle glasses that give her the small eyes of a rodent. She doesn't like Miss Rasmussen because she is humorless, although that isn't the reason she would know to give. She just thinks of her as stern and strict, something she's not used to at home. Also, the kindergarten teacher, Mrs. Schneider, had been round and pink-cheeked and friendly, so Miss Rasmussen is a shock.

A small puddle of urine is found on a classroom chair, and Miss Rasmussen goes around the class feeling all the students' underpants until she finds the culprit—a shy boy—and in front of everyone sends him home to change. She will never forgive the teacher for this.

Mrs. Peeples

Mrs. Peeples, their elderly babysitter, is horrified to find her in the bathtub with her little brother. She, aged six, and Teddy, aged three, usually take baths together. From amidst the boats, ducks, squirt toys, and floating alphabet blocks, they are summarily yanked out of the tub and quickly wrapped in towels. In an ominous tone, Mrs. Peeples admonishes, "Little girls and little boys should *never* take baths together." She reports the babysitter's strange behavior the next morning at breakfast, and that is the last anyone sees of Mrs. Peeples.

Shins

She has Miss Rasmussen again the next year in second grade and has made the mistake of telling her classmate, Marlys Horner, that she hates Miss Rasmussen. She had no reason to believe that Marlys was a tattle-tale, so she's surprised when the teacher takes her into the cloak room at recess and asks her, "Did you tell Marlys that you wanted to kick me in the chin?"

She doesn't like to lie, and is glad that she doesn't have to because what she actually said was, "I'd like to kick Miss Rasmussen in the shins."

"No, I didn't," she says.

Miss Rasmussen puts her hands on her shoulders and looks her in the eye. "Annie, it isn't nice to hate people."

"I don't hate people," she replies. "I only hate *you*."

Miss Rasmussen keeps her in for the rest of recess. She sits alone feeling superior because Marlys didn't recognize "shin," a more sophisticated word than "chin." It doesn't occur to her how kindly Miss Rasmussen has treated her over the incident, all things considered.

Ambush

A black cat with thick matted fur habitually hides in the weeds between their house and the neighbors'. It ambushes the legs of unsuspecting passersby, sinking its teeth into their bare ankles and kicking them viciously with its hind legs, claws extended. She loves and respects cats, so she is not put off by this behavior. After a few such incidents she discovers that if she grabs the cat by the loose skin on the back of its neck and rolls and kneads the flesh, the cat will let go of its grip and become dreamy and placid long enough for her to make her get-away. She is rather proud of the punctures and scratches that she has endured.

Sonatinas and Minuets

A second-hand upright piano sits against the wall between the living room and the staircase leading up to the bedrooms. At night she is lulled to sleep by the soft trills of Beethoven sonatinas and Bach minuets, which her mother plays from the red book, *Classical Piano Pieces for Beginners*. Off and on throughout the day she replays the tunes in her head. Her mother tells her that when she was a child she longed to play the piano, but her parents couldn't afford either the instrument or lessons, so she made herself a paper keyboard and pretended to play. "Would you like to take piano lessons, Annie?" she asks.

She isn't sure. Her mother suggests she try it and see how she likes it. At her piano lessons and during practice she is aware of how haltingly she plays even on the easy drills, and she doesn't like doing things she isn't immediately good at. Within three months she has had enough and is allowed to give it up. Now, in bed at night she notices, as she hadn't before, that her mother's night time sonatinas and minuets are and have always been played with hesitations, wrong notes and a sluggish pace. They no longer lull her to sleep, but the tunes stay with her, and in later years when she happens to hear one, she feels a little tearful.

Army Surplus

Their summer vacations are spent in the Colorado Rockies or, in alternate summers, at Pentwater, Michigan within sight of the lake and the dunes. She sometimes wishes they could stay at motels but they can't afford it, so they camp, hauling their gear, painstakingly packed and held down by a tarpaulin in a two-wheel trailer hitched to the back of their car. All their gear is post-war army surplus, musty smelling and a dull green—tents, tarps, down sleeping bags, and inflatable mattresses and pillows. Even the entrenching tools and camp stove are army green. She wonders if their equipment ever saw combat. Her uncle Friedrich was in the Battle of the Bulge, got captured by the Germans and survived a POW concentration camp where he was brutally treated for betraying his German roots.

For the most part, though, the equipment has lost its war aura, becoming associated with the smells, sights and sensations of Norway spruce and icy rushing streams or fishy beaches and sand between the toes. At night, Nick goes off to his pup tent with a flashlight and a book while her mother tucks her and Teddy into their sleeping bags in the big tent. Their father follows behind to turn down the gas on the kerosene lantern that hangs from the tent's crossbar. Then he and their mother duck through the tent flap to sit together quietly for a while at the picnic table just outside.

It soothes her to hear through the walls of the tent her parents' murmuring voices, accompanied by an occasional snap of a burning log or the hiss of sparks flying off into the night. She and Teddy watch the glow from the lantern's filament dwindle to a tiny spot. She stays awake for that mysterious moment when the spot becomes so small it is swallowed up in the darkness.

Back yard

Her parents bought the house for the children because of its unusually long back yard. It is a series of distinct worlds.

In the area closest to the house there is a dilapidated detached garage covered in trumpet vine, a swing set that lifts out of its concrete footings when you swing too high, and an old-fashioned barbecue pit made of rocks and cement, which is fun to climb in order to shout into the iron chimney on top. This is the shady part of the yard. On hot summer days, her father puts the six-foot inflatable wading pool under the trees, fills it from the garden hose, and stretches out to read his *New Yorker*, his head propped on the soft edge of the pool. When he finishes the magazine, he gets up, his yellow cotton bathing trunks clinging to his thin white legs, and leaves the pool so she and her brothers can take turns running, leaping, sliding, and splashing on the slick plastic.

That's the first world. The second part of the lawn, except underneath an immature walnut tree and some elderly and stunted fruit trees, is mostly sunny. She and Teddy play in the large red-sided sandbox their father put together. They squat with their knees up to their chins, embellishing sand cities with flowers, walnut shells, twigs. The neighborhood cats frequent the sandbox, but she and Teddy are not bothered by the desiccated deposits buried there. They just scoop them up with their small shovels and toss them over the side into the weeds. There is a decaying wooden playhouse against the fence across from the sandbox, but they don't play in it because what can you do in a confined space outdoors except get out of it?

Finally, at the back, there's the garden. Her father plants it (sweet corn, beans, peas, radishes, onions); she and her brothers weed it (forced labor); and her mother harvests the fruits. A raspberry patch grows wild along the fence, providing bowls of ripe berries for breakfast throughout the season.

Decades later in the dead of summer she visits the yard, coming up from a path along the border at the back. Everything is gone. The lawn is a very small patch of brown, stiff grass. How did all those worlds fit into such a small space? She can't understand it.

Come Back Little Sheba

Next door lives a girl her age, Shirley Most, who is an only child. Shirley's parents are much older than hers, the mother in poor health. Heart trouble? Asthma? Shirley's back yard is contained by a chain link fence. Shirley and a German shepherd are the only ones to occupy it. The girl and the shepherd never play together. The dog barks frantically at any activity on either side of the fence.

Shirley's parents don't let her come over, and only once does Shirley invite her to visit their house. Her room has a canopy bed with ruffles and dozens of dolls arranged on the pillows and on shelves and in cradles on the floor.

Once, she has a conversation with Shirley from across their driveways. Shirley mentions a movie she has seen: *Come Back Little Sheba*.

"It's about a dog," says Shirley. "No it's not," she says, though she hasn't seen the movie, "It's about a sheep." "No," says Shirley, "it's about a dog." They argue back and forth. "I'll ask my mother," Shirley says and goes into her house.

She doesn't want to be standing there when Shirley returns, in case she's right, so she runs inside and up to her bedroom. When Shirley comes back and looks around for her, she sees her at her bedroom window. "My mother says it's about a dog," Shirley shouts. She shouts back, "I don't care."

Vocabulary

Because she reads a lot, her vocabulary tends to be more sophisticated than that of other children her age, which makes it amusing to her family when she gets words wrong.

At the swimming pool, she is trying to increase her stamina. She asks her mother to stand many yards away, where she can swim to her.

"You be my destiny," she says, not realizing how true the statement is.

Her mother, instead of laughing, tactfully corrects her. "'Destination,' you meant to say?"

And it *is* funny even to her because, on reflection, she does know the difference between destiny and destination.

For a while she insists that the first letter in the word "ballet" is a "v" and that everyone else has it wrong. A bulbous and bursting "b" is unthinkable for the representation of this most graceful and airy form of dance. When a look in the dictionary officially establishes her mistake, she can hardly accept it.

Foursome

There are four of them—Marilyn, Nancy, Peg and herself. From first through sixth grade they are together on the playground, at each other's houses after school and on weekends, at birthday parties and overnights. She doesn't remember how or why they became one inseparable group in the first place. In high school, they probably would have been labeled a "clique," but they're not conscious of excluding others, just that they include themselves.

In their younger years they explore their neighborhoods, scuttling through the culvert under Maple Street where they sing and make echoes. Or they jump rope and play hide and seek and tag. Sometimes they dress up in their mothers' cast off clothes and pretend to be mothers themselves, or teachers, or movie stars. In fifth and sixth grade they tape notes to each other's lockers and have slumber parties where they watch TV and rub each other's backs and bake and eat.

She and Peg are both middle children, between two brothers. Marilyn and Nancy have four siblings each. Otherwise, there is nothing to connect them. They don't talk deeply. Mostly they just do things together. And they have no particular skills or interests in common. Maybe it's a matter of similar temperaments. None of them breaks out in fits of anger or takes wild risks or is painfully shy or intimidates others. They all get good grades and are obedient in school. They seldom argue or compete. She is perhaps the most imaginative of the four, maybe a little bossy, but the others seem content to follow her lead.

They are a Marilyn, Nancy, Peg and Annie team, and this group identity seems almost as natural to her as her own individual identity; in fact, it is sometimes more comfortable, more predictable, and less troublesome.

Rules of Behavior

Her father has told the lettuce story several times at the dinner table, but it always amuses her. When he was a child, he was required to eat everything on his plate and to stay at the table until he did so. He could hardly bear to eat lettuce, and one day at lunch, when his parents weren't looking, he slipped his lettuce into his handkerchief and put it in his pocket. That afternoon, he was taken to a doctor's appointment by his mother. At the doctor's office, sweating at the prospect of getting an injection, he took out his handkerchief to mop his brow, sending lettuce flying in all directions.

Upon consideration, she finds this story surprising because although her parents had been brought up under conventionally strict table rules, they wouldn't dream of making her or Teddy or Nick eat something they found distasteful. For much of her childhood she has existed primarily on sweets, and Teddy went through a phase of refusing to eat anything but radishes.

Mealtimes aren't the only occasions when rules are conspicuous by their absence. She feels sorry for her friends, whose parents seem devoted to arbitrary and petty regulations: "Don't run in the house" "Keep your voice down" "Don't touch the china cabinet" "Get your elbows off the table" "Clean up your room, *now*!" When she is at their houses, she senses a constant undercurrent of parental disapproval and is never quite sure if she is transgressing some rule or other.

Housekeeping

Her mother puts a great deal of thought into the furnishings and décor of the house. Of necessity, much of their furniture comes from the Salvation Army, but she has good taste and a good eye, so the house is decorated with some distinction. She also likes tidiness and a minimum of clutter.

Yet her mother puts no restrictions on how she and Teddy and Nick keep their rooms. They're not required to make their beds or pick up their toys and clothes. As long as their doors are shut, who's to care? Consequently, their rooms are a bit of a mess, but they certainly could be worse. Not being forever nagged, she and her brothers set their own standards, which wouldn't do for downstairs, but work well enough for bedrooms. At least they can find whatever they're looking for. Nothing is absolutely buried.

The Facts

When she is seven years old, she asks where babies come from, and her mother gives her an abridged, but, as far as it goes, not inaccurate account of the facts.

"But how does the baby come *out* of the mother's stomach?" she asks.

"There's a small hole between a mother's legs that stretches very wide when it's time for the baby to slide out."

"But how does the baby get *into* the mother's stomach?"

Her mother hedges somewhat on this one. "An egg in her stomach starts to grow and after nine months becomes a baby."

"But where does the egg come from?" she persists.

"Well, women are born with many eggs inside them."

"Are they like chicken's eggs?"

"No, they're very tiny. You can only see them with a microscope."

"But why do they start to grow?"

Here is, literally, the moment of truth. Her mother explains the fertilization process.

"But that's his *pee pee* thing!" she exclaims. "That's yucky!"

"I know it sounds yucky now," her mother says. "But when you're much older, it won't seem yucky anymore. It will seem ... enjoyable."

She shakes her head vehemently. "No it won't. It will always be yucky!"

"Well, remember how you used to hate tomatoes? You thought they were yucky. But now you like them."

She isn't convinced.

"Anyway," her mother says, "it doesn't matter because it will be a long, long time before you feel different about it, not until—" here she feels obliged to fudge the truth "—you're all grown up and married."

That does sound like a long way off. She feels reasonably satisfied then and doesn't think much about it after that. After all, she did learn to like tomatoes.

Confession

She holds three tormenting secrets in her heart, which feels like an overinflated balloon in her chest whenever she thinks about these secrets. Then, one day in her eighth year, the agony of holding onto them outweighs the need to keep them to herself. Trembling, and with a flush that she can feel spreading across her neck and cheeks, she goes to her mother and blurts them all out at once.

"I swallowed a button, I stole a dime, and I told Marcia Addison that you liked the smell of skunks," she declares and bursts into tears.

Her mother, quite naturally attends to the button first, asking how long ago it happened.

"In kindergarten," she replies between sobs. "Will I have to have my stomach pumped?" Something of this nature happened to her when she was four and swallowed a whole bottleful of prescription cough syrup accidentally left on the kitchen counter.

Her mother keeps a straight face.

"No, honey. That button went right through you a long time ago."

The dime had slipped out of a classmate's pocket on the playground when she was seven and she had snatched it up.

"Well, Annie, you were very young. You wouldn't take something that didn't belong to you *now*, would you?" She shakes her head. "And the skunk?"

Her mother's tolerance for skunk odor she had imagined to be confidential, having recently learned the word confidential from her father when he inadvertently let slip a private, work-related matter at the dinner table.

"Skunks don't smell nice. I thought it was confidential."

"Well, I don't consider it confidential. I'm not ashamed of it if you aren't."

And the balloon in her chest collapses, all the air finally released.

She had kept the swallowed button a secret because of the earlier cough syrup trauma. The other two secrets she kept not for fear of punishment—she knows her parents better than that—but from the terrible embarrassment she would suffer at having to admit to them that she was not the upright and moral child they must surely believe her to be.

Witch Hunt

From April to June, 1954, her father races home at noon to catch the televised Army-McCarthy hearings and watch the liberal lawyer Welch take on the arch-villain Joe McCarthy. In the evenings he rehashes the highlights at the dinner table.

Then on June 9th, Welch takes McCarthy down for good. Her father quotes Welch gleefully, *"'Senator, have you no sense of decency, sir?'"* She has never heard such an exultant tone in his voice before. *"'At long last, have you left no sense of decency?'"* Her father slaps his thigh. "Welch *nailed* the bastard! The whole room applauded!" She is stirred. Her father has become Joseph Welch, a hero of the righteous.

Bedtime

Bedtime is eight o'clock. For as long as she can remember she has had trouble getting to sleep and staying asleep. The slightest noise wakes her. By the time she's nine she anticipates bedtime with dread. Night after night she does battle with herself. The biggest thing keeping her awake now is the fear that she won't be able to sleep.

In bed she lies on her side, tuned into the nuances of her wakefulness: a subtle vibration in her chest, her clenched jaw, thoughts that loop through her mind, mostly about the impossibility of shutting her thoughts off.

One night, after an hour, or what seems like an hour, of lying in bed monitoring her level of sleeplessness, she hears her mother coming up the stairs. She gets out of bed and goes into the hall, crying.

"I can't get to sleep!" she says.

Her mother appears surprised. "Oh, I'm sorry, honey. Do you feel sick?" She lays a hand on her forehead.

"No! I just *never* get to sleep!" She hasn't mentioned this before, and she realizes that her mother has had no idea.

They sit down on the top step together. "Well, Annie, if you can't sleep, why don't you just turn on the lamp and read?"

This option has not occurred to her. Her bedtime is eight o'clock. That's when she's supposed to go to sleep. She frowns. "But what about Teddy?"

"Oh, you know Teddy. When he goes to bed, he's out like a light."

"What if I don't get to sleep all night? I'll be so tired."

"Eventually your body will get sleepy if you're not thinking about it. Read a book you've read before so it won't be too stimulating. Read as long as you like."

This sounds reasonable. She chooses *Charlotte's Web*, which she has read three times. After two chapters, her eyes keep closing and she falls asleep with the light on. Sometime during the night her mother tiptoes in and turns it off.

Fractions

When she cheats on an arithmetic quiz, her guilt is more intellectual than visceral.

She gets Superior grades on her report cards in all classes until she is confronted with third grade arithmetic. What exactly are fractions? How do you add and subtract them? She tries to do the homework but can't hold on to the concepts. It does not enter her mind to ask her father, the accountant, to explain fractions to her. She is handicapped by the notion that she should be good at this naturally, without help.

There is a quiz. She has never gotten below 100% on quizzes in reading, vocabulary, and spelling. Now she stares at the paper. The questions make no sense. When Mrs. Healy's attention is diverted, she glances at the quiz of the girl next to her and copies the answers. She receives a score of 82%. It's a blot on her record but it could have been worse. She feels only a little guilty for cheating. She judges that it was wrong, determines never to cheat again, and closes the case.

Package

When she goes to the bathroom she notices in the wastebasket a strange little package wrapped in toilet paper. There appears to be a blood stain along the edge. She takes the package out, unwraps it and finds a white pad that, when opened up, is soaked on the inside with red and brown clots of blood. Surprised and repulsed, she quickly wraps it again and, holding the package at arm's length, takes it to her mother, who is in the bedroom putting away laundry.

"Mommy! What's this? It's all bloody. Is someone hurt?"

Her mother sits down on the bed. She says, "Let's see, Annie," takes the package from her and opens it. She pats the bed. "Come and sit down with me."

"Did someone get hurt?" she repeats.

"No, honey, no one got hurt. This is called a Kotex pad, and the blood on it is a special kind of blood that came out of me."

She studies the bloody pad and the trailing toilet paper intently as her mother explains about the pad's preventing the blood from leaking on her underwear and about the belt she wears to secure it, and what's special about the blood, and how it comes out for about five days every month. She tells her what the process is called and says that in a few years, when she's older, the special monthly blood will come out of her, too, and that she might feel a bit of discomfort the first day, called "cramps," but they shouldn't be too bad. Her own cramps are mild.

"So, Annie," her mother says, "do you have any questions?" But her mother has been quite thorough, so she can't think of any questions except, "Should I wrap it again and put it back in the waste basket?" "Sure," says her mother. "That would be very helpful."

Tickets

Karen Dungey lives in a big rambling house across the street. She and Karen occasionally play imaginative games in the side yard. One day Karen goes into the house to go to the bathroom. When she returns, she is holding a few tickets of the kind sold in movie theaters. "Do you want tickets?" she asks. "We can have a roll of them for free." Tickets, sold at a penny or a nickel apiece, would lend authenticity to their plays and puppet shows. "Uh huh," she says. "Come on, then," says Karen.

Karen leads her into the house and up the stairs to the second floor bathroom. Karen's brother is waiting there. He's quite a bit older, a teenager, maybe fifteen or sixteen. He closes the door. A roll of tickets sits on the edge of the sink.

The brother is tall and broad and his back is to her, blocking her view of her friend. She hears rustling of clothing but she can't see what's happening. Then he turns to her. Karen says, "If you let him do something, he'll give us the tickets." "Do what?" she says. And suddenly she feels his hand sliding down inside the front of her underwear. She jerks away. "I don't *want* tickets!" she shouts and pushes past them out the door. She runs down the stairs, outside, and across the street and doesn't stop running until she is in her own house. Out of breath, she tells her mother what happened. Her mother says earnestly, "Well, Annie, just don't ever play there again."

As if she needs to be told.

Chevy

The old round-shouldered '49 Chevy has clocked thousands of miles pulling their heavily loaded two-wheel trailer across the plains and into the mountains and back. It's time to trade it in. The '55 models have just arrived at the dealership, and the family is smitten with the sleek, sporty Bel-Air. The car will have to be red and white, that's a given, red being her mother's favorite color. But the sticking point comes when they leap on the notion of a convertible. Her father balks.

"No, Jane. It's not safe," he declares to her mother.

"Oh Erich, what do you mean, 'not safe'?" Her mother puts an arm around his waist. "How could it be unsafe with such a good driver at the wheel? In all the years you've been driving, you've never once had an accident."

He walks around the convertible, looking at it from several angles, kicks the tires, and runs his hand along the taut canvas top. He gets the salesman to show him how to get the top down and tucked away.

"Well, all right," he says, and closes the deal.

Sunday

For her, Sundays mean leisurely breakfasts, reading the funnies, and playing outside or lying propped against a sofa pillow with a book. It is inconceivable in her family to spend Sunday mornings sitting on hard pews and listening to someone give a lecture. She knows her friends and classmates have to do this, or attend something called Sunday school. She can't imagine choosing to take an extra half day of school. Five days a week is plenty.

Hell

Mary Lynn Pearsall, a Catholic girl down the street, asks if she has been baptized. "I don't think so," she says. Mary Lynn's mouth drops and her eyes widen with alarm. "If you aren't baptized, you'll go to Hell!" She knows about Hell, having, at nine years old, absorbed many religious ideas from the air around her, but she hasn't considered whether it's a real place. She runs home to ask her mother.

"Am I baptized?" she asks.

"No," her mother says, absently.

"But Mary Lynn Pearsall says if I'm not baptized, I'll go to Hell."

Her mother pays attention now, takes her hand, smiles gently. "Well, Annie, some people believe in Hell, but we don't." Which is good enough for her. She knows her parents are sensible people.

Exposure

Her mother thinks it may be unfair to impose an indifference to religion on her and her brothers without giving them a chance to make up their own minds.

Although there is a Unitarian "Fellowship" in the city to accommodate both believers and nonbelievers, the Unitarian Fellowship is on the other side of town. For the children's exposure to religion her parents choose the Episcopal Church, which is a half block from their house. Her mother accompanies them on the short walk to church one hot August morning.

She is wearing white patent leather shoes and a fluffy yellow dress. The boys are spruce enough in short-sleeved shirts and bow ties. Nick walks a little ahead, she and Teddy dawdle, engrossed in a game of not stepping on cracks. At the corner they turn left onto Maple Avenue and, the church being just at that corner, they arrive all too soon.

The church is a small dark-colored brick building with a high peaked roof, slender stained-glass windows and "St. Andrews Episcopal Church" in gold gothic letters on the facade. It looks very foreign to her, and she holds back, watching the dressed-up adults and children pass familiarly through the red double doors.

In the cool vestibule a woman and man are serving as greeters. Their mother steps forward and introduces herself.

"We're not members of this church," she says, "but we live just down the street. Is it possible for the children to attend Sunday school today? Nick here is twelve, Ted is seven and Annie is ten."

The greeters seem inordinately pleased and rather swoop toward them.

"I'll stay for the service and be here when your classes are over," their mother tells them.

Before they're escorted to the basement, she catches a glimpse through open doors of the large high-ceilinged room where her mother takes a seat facing a kind of stage with a podium draped in white. The light through the stained glass windows is pretty, but what catches her eye is the wooden statue of the man—Jesus (she knows enough to know that)—hanging in the center of the wall behind the podium where it is impossible not to look at it. The people will spend an hour facing that stage, and she wonders how they'll keep their mind off the tortured man hanging there with nails driven through his hands and feet.

Downstairs she feels a little fearful when she's separated from her brothers. She tries to see which rooms Nick and Teddy are being taken to, but the woman greeter leads her around a corner and out of sight.

About six or seven other children are seated at low tables and chairs in the Sunday school room. On the wall facing her as she enters is another image of Jesus—a painting of him hanging by his nailed hands and feet, his eyes gazing upwards. Nobody is paying attention to it. She takes a sidelong look. Like the girlie calendar on the inside of the closet door in her grandfather's study, it is shocking.

The teacher says, "Remember last Sunday we talked about the miracles that Jesus performed? Do you remember what they were?"

A girl raises her hand. "He walked on the water?" A boy chimes in: "He made a blind guy see!" "And a dead guy," exclaims another. "He made him alive."

"Yes, very good, children. And he fed five thousand people with only five loaves of bread and two fishes! So people were very impressed, but you know, he didn't have to perform miracles to impress people. Let's see how people loved him before they even knew what he could do."

On each table are coloring booklets and crayons. The woman guides them through their booklets, page by page. They will spend some time coloring the pictures and then take them home to finish.

"Who do you suppose this man in the boat is? Remember? We talked about him at the end of class last week."

"Jesus?" replies a boy, uncertainly.

"Not Jesus, but a very good friend of Jesus. He's bringing in his fishing net. Who was the fisherman, children?"

"Simon!" several of them assert.

"That's right! It was Simon."

Then she explains all about Simon—how Jesus had come up to where Simon and his brother were fishing and told them to put down their nets and follow him.

"'I will make you fishers of men,' he said, and 'Simon, I will name you Peter.' And off they went with Jesus."

She thinks about catching men as if they were fish. What if they didn't want to be caught? Fish certainly didn't. And she wonders about those nets. Did Simon and his brother just leave them there? Someone might steal them after a while, or they'd get washed away in the lake. And even if Simon didn't need the nets anymore, someone else might. They could at least have carried the nets along and given them to some fisherman they met on the way.

"Isn't it wonderful," says the teacher, "how much they loved Jesus even though they'd just met Him. See how they're smiling? They're so happy to be in His presence."

Her parents had cautioned her never to talk to strangers, especially if they offered you something. Simon and his brother, she presumes, were adults and could probably have defended themselves if they'd gotten in trouble, but it still seemed foolhardy.

And what about the fishermen's family? Did they ever find out what had happened to the men? Jesus gave Simon a fake name, so how could they find him?

The teacher uses words like "worship," "our heavenly father," "our lord." It sounds like fairy tale language, like games she and Teddy play: "You be the lord of the manor and I'll be the lady" ... "You're the servant. You bow down and worship me." They know it isn't real when they play such games, but this grown-up woman is not pretending.

After the Bible lesson, there is singing. Then, finally, the class ends with a preview of next Sunday's lesson and a prayer. The other children clasp their hands together and close their eyes, repeating after the teacher: "Our father who art in heaven..." The teacher closes her eyes, too. She keeps hers open.

In school she had studied about the Greek and Roman gods and goddesses who were worshipped by ancient people. "These people were afraid of the forces of nature and other things they didn't understand," said her fourth grade teacher, "so they created gods, built statues and made pictures of the gods, and told stories about them called myths to explain what they were afraid of."

"How was Sunday school?" her mother asks when they come back upstairs. She's waiting just outside the door.

"We had cookies," Teddy says, cheerfully.

"It was boring. I'm not going anymore," says Nick.

"I didn't like it!" she says, screwing up her nose.

"What didn't you like?"

She considers the question for a moment.

All she can think to say is, "It was kind of embarrassing."

Candy Man

All the kids in a three- or four-block radius around her street know about the Candy Man. At Halloween, they make the trip up College or Maple Avenues to ring his doorbell. She and Teddy only have to walk across the street and down three houses. She, in a homemade Lonely Little Petunia in the Onion Patch costume and he, in a store-bought Roy Rogers outfit, always get to the Candy Man's house early.

The Candy Man is a salesman for a candy distributor. His basement is lined from floor to ceiling with shelves containing boxes and boxes of every candy known to America: Milky Way, Mars, and Clark Bars, Reese's Peanut Butter Cups, Butterfingers, Lemon drops, M & M s, Candy Corn, Tootsie Rolls, Lik-m-Aid, Wax Lips, Bazooka Bubble Gum, Jaw Breakers, Junior Mints, Candy Cigarettes ... The list is exhaustive. The children are allowed to pick one of every type of candy they like. One each of *every*thing until the supply is depleted.

They line up on the front steps and along the sidewalk, waiting quietly. No jumping the line. No shenanigans. The Candy Man is a stickler about politeness, and the kids have only one thing in mind—being allowed into that basement. It's Trick or Treat night, but no tricks are required at the door. It would take too long to get kids through, and the Candy Man is dedicated to getting everybody in and out. No one wonders how he can afford to give all this candy away, or why he does it. He's not especially friendly or jolly—no Santa Claus.

He expects nothing in return.

I Go Pogo

She and Teddy sit on the sofa snuggled up to their father on Sundays as he reads aloud the comic strip Pogo. Pogo is a possum who lives in a Florida swamp. During Dwight D. Eisenhower's run for president (campaign slogan: "I Like Ike"), Pogo also throws his hat into the ring ("I Go Pogo").

Pogo is the only comic strip in the "funny papers" that takes on racism and McCarthyism and even pokes fun at Christmas ("Deck us all with Boston Charlie …"). Her father assumes the voices of the zany swamp animals—Simple J Malarky, Miss "Sis" Boombah, Churchy LaFemme, Howland Owl.

She sends a fan letter to Walt Kelly, the cartoonist, and receives a reply with his autograph at the bottom of the letter and three "I Go Pogo" buttons inserted. Proudly, she wears an "I Go Pogo" button to school, but is baffled and disappointed when her classmates fail to be impressed. She can't understand how anyone could be indifferent to Pogo.

From the Desk of …

Sometimes after school she and Teddy walk the four blocks to their father's office in the University's Old Main Administration Building, a stone Victorian topped by a clock tower. He has recently been promoted from Business Manager to Vice President for Business and Finance. When anyone asks her what her father does, she likes saying, "He is the Vice President for Business and Finance at the University." Not until much later, when she herself is choosing a college, does she learn that this small university, which she would have been able to attend tuition-free, is considered a solid but not first-rate institution.

He has a secretary and an assistant, who occupy outer offices. The assistant makes funny, clever jokes at her father's expense. Her father, laughing, quotes them at home. His secretary keeps his calendar and monitors his visitors.

She and Teddy climb to their father's second floor office at the top of a long, steep flight of stairs. When they arrive, out of breath, Mrs. Dawson says, "Well look who's here!" She gets on the intercom and announces, solemnly, "Mr. Lang, Annie and Teddy have honored you with a visit." They can hear him over the intercom and through his partly open door, exclaim, "Hey! Send them right in!"

She loves to look at the things on his desk, especially the neat little pile of notepads printed at the top with the words "From the Desk of Erich Lang." If her father has work to do, he sets her and Teddy on chairs at the big conference table and gives them a box of crayons he keeps in his desk, and paper to draw on while they wait. They aren't allowed to draw on "From the Desk of Erich Lang" tablets because these are paid for out of the University's budget, but he gives them the blank sides of discarded papers filled on the other side with figures.

Sometimes, when he's too busy to see them longer than to say hello and give them a hug, they go outside to chase each other around the thick old campus oaks and run up and down the wide sidewalks that head in every direction. They play until it's time for their father to come and find them, after which they all walk home together.

Life Guard

When they're out somewhere, her father always walks a little ahead and points out potential hazards. "Guys! Notice there's a branch sticking out here. Boy, that could put out an eye." "Janey," he warns her mother, "be careful, here's a patch of ice. Kids, do you see the ice?" "Hey, everyone, watch out, there's poison ivy growing by the trail here." "Don't trip on this piece of sidewalk. Jesus, that's an accident waiting to happen."

She mentions it to her mother. "He's always telling us watch out for this, watch out for that! Like we can't see it ourselves."

Her mother smiles. "Oh that's just Erich," she says. "He does that with everyone. I've been with him when he's walking with the president of the University or a board member, and he's warning them of every little thing."

She isn't really indignant about it. Her father's warnings are like the familiar music of his speech, his "Up and at 'em, Madam!" in the morning when he wakes her for school, or his "It's the berries!" when he's feeling content.

And the other thing is, he warns but seldom prohibits.

Camp Wells

Camp Wells swimming pool, used for training troops in the First World War, is one of the largest swimming pools in the world. In the ninety-degree days of summer, the family gather their towels, goggles, rafts and sunscreen every weekend and make the ten-mile trip through the countryside to Camp Wells.

She can hardly endure the wait as their car rounds the many curves past corn and soybean fields before finally climbing a steep hill where, at the summit, the huge turquoise rectangle of water glitters far below in the sunlight.

She and her brothers never fail to shout with glee at this glorious sight as if they had never seen it before. They jump impatiently on their seats as the car descends to the parking lot, where they pile out and run for the changing rooms. She wears her suit under her clothes so she can divest herself of them quickly and dash through the shower to get into the pool that much faster.

But then she halts in her tracks at an agonizing decision that confronts her every single time. Should she go directly to the pool and plunge right in? Or should she stop first at the concession stand to have the most delicious food in existence: a Camp Wells sloppy Joe made with lots of mustard, ketchup and onions? If she does the latter, her parents won't allow her in the pool for half an hour lest she be drowned by an attack of the infamous child-killing stomach cramps.

She sometimes doubts the reality of this danger. She's never seen anyone succumb to it, and after all, there's a life guard, the pool is full of kids and adults, and her parents will be sitting nearby on the grassy hillside keeping an eye on things; someone would be sure to save her.

But, as usual, her father isn't taking any chances, so the choice has to be made. As much as she yearns to get into that heavenly, cool blue water, more often she opts for the sloppy Joes first.

Zella Jane's

Halfway home from Camp Wells, sun-burned, tired and ravenous, the family keeps a look out for the hand-written, wind-worn sign that alerts them to Zella Jane's, a little roadside farm stand just around a bend, that sells only three things: fresh-picked ripe sweet corn, fresh-picked, ripe beefsteak tomatoes, and warm, home-made glazed doughnuts. It is all anyone can do to keep from devouring the lot before they pull into their driveway. Her mother keeps a firm hand on the paper bags. This will be dinner. And what more could anyone wish for?

Appropriate Gifts

She and Nick don't play together even though they're only two and a half years apart. She doesn't expect it. She's a girl. And in any case her older brother is stand-offish with everyone; he ignores Teddy, too, who of course is much too young. Teddy longs wistfully and hopelessly for Nick's attention.

But at Christmas, Nick and Teddy sometimes come together over gifts.

When all the wrapping paper has been whisked away, and she sits surrounded by her new Betty Crocker Baking Kit, or the Japanese doll with removable Geisha wigs sent by her rich Uncle Friedrich from the Philippines, or a red and green plaid shawl draped around her shoulders or the charm bracelet with little cats, dangling from her wrist, her brothers are sprawled on the living room floor playing with Nick's tin Spitfires and army green rubber soldiers equipped with rifles, bayonets and howitzers. There is no age difference between the two boys then as they "Pyew! Pyew! Pyew!" at each other across the battle lines and crash their planes together in mid-air. The following year, during those few days after Christmas, it's an electric train that equalizes them. Their father captures every holiday on 8 mm movie film.

Sugar Plum Fairy

She goes crazy for her record of *The Nutcracker Suite*. To the accompaniment of the Spanish, Arabian, Chinese and Russian dances, the Dance of the Reed Flutes, the Waltz of the Flowers, and the Dance of the Sugar Plum Fairy, played at maximum volume, she twirls and flings herself about the living room and dining room, leaps onto and off the sofa, runs partway up the staircase and makes grand gestures from the landing before tripping down again and ending her performance by sinking like a fallen soufflé in the middle of the living room rug. She does not require an audience.

Then, when they attend a family reunion at Opa's house at Christmas in Milwaukee, she notices a *Nutcracker Suite* record album in the parlor. Aunts and uncles and some of the cousins have been lounging around, enjoying the lights of the Christmas tree and nibbling on the gingerbread house that the aunts have made and decorated. Everyone has been singing carols to Aunt Trudi's accompaniment on the old upright piano, and now Aunt Trudi has gone away to bring out plates of cookies from the kitchen.

That's when *The Nutcracker Suite* album catches her eye. She pulls it from its sheath and plops it onto the record player, knowing exactly which groove to set the needle on.

Taking center stage in the cramped parlor, she glides sinuously to the Arabian Dance, tiptoes daintily to the Dance of the Reed Flutes, swoops—ONE-two-three, ONE-two-three—in the arms of an imaginary partner to the Waltz of the Flowers. At some point, she is aware that she may be getting tedious. The cousins go in and out.

Aunt Trudi sidesteps around her to dispense cookies. Teddy, in the doorway, is capering wildly in imitation of her. But most of all, she sees her mother wearing the smile that, if you could have seen only her eyes, would not give the impression that she is smiling at all. Nonetheless, she can't seem to stop herself until the last dance has played and she has made a deep Sugar Plum Fairy curtsy. The applause is desultory. Everyone's face is stiff.

Opa's House

She wishes she could live there year-round. Every room, every hallway, every niche, from attic to basement enchants her. It is a modest-sized four-bedroom Victorian, but to her it seems enormous and exotic in every way, from the laundry chute and attic tower room to the winding back staircase and the butler's pantry.

The spooky, moldy-smelling basement contains a coal-burning furnace and shelves of blackened jars holding unidentifiable preserves put up by some anonymous cook in the days when paid help was common in middle class homes, or perhaps by her own grandmother, who died of a stroke before she was born.

Once a year, either at Christmas or in July, the whole family gathers here in Milwaukee—her father's two brothers and two sisters and their spouses and children and, of course, Opa. Her grandfather is confined by arthritis for most of the day to his pallet mattress in the sunny cubicle off a room that has been converted to a library for his thousands of books in German, English and French.

In the large front bedroom, kept clean by the aunts and preserved as it must have looked when their mother was alive, she and Teddy are sometimes allowed to sink onto the soft goose down comforter covering the canopied bed that Opa and Oma once slept in. A faint lemony smell permeates the room. Aunt Eva says it is the scent of *Kölnisch Wasser* 4711, the cologne her mother had worn throughout her short life.

Most of all, though, the large finished attic is what draws all the cousins as soon as each contingent arrives—Aunt Trudi's and Aunt Eva's little girls, who live in suburban Milwaukee, and Uncle Karl's four boys from the East Coast—the feral twins, Kurt and Max, and their two younger brothers. The war hero, Uncle Friedrich, is unmarried as yet, but his World War II spoils—a German Luger, a bayonet—are the first things Nick and the boy cousins pounce on after they've bounded up the stairs and raced into the big room.

All along one wall bench seats with hinged covers hide a trove of Lang family artifacts: decades-old costumes from fancy dress parties, dolls and other toys, a set of fencing foils. In closets along another wall her grandmother's musty-smelling dresses hang, off-limits by order of the aunts. In a cramped space deep under the eaves sits a three-story, fully furnished dollhouse.

When the bad boy twins grow tired of examining the treasure trove, they entertain themselves by taking turns shinnying down the laundry chute. Somehow they manage to climb into the attic opening and press their backs and feet against the walls of the chute without falling, and then inch themselves all the way down to the basement, emerging black with dust.

At the dinner hour Opa is helped by one of his sons or daughters down the broad staircase like a grand pasha. He walks stiffly with a cane, wearing a threadbare silk kimono and straw slippers, his bright pink cheeks and gruff humor belying his poor state of health and chronic pain.

They all—adults and children together—eat by candlelight at a long table in the small dining room that's just big enough to accommodate them and no more. The grownups look glamorous with their deep-set eyes and high cheekbones, their slender limbs, their casual, easy-going presence. Afterwards, her mother and the aunts clear the table, her father and the uncles light up fragrant-smelling cigars and Opa has the glass of the sherry that keeps pain at bay and his cheeks pink.

She sleeps with Teddy in her aunts' old room. The big boys sleep on the narrow beds in the attic where her father and his brothers had slept in their youth. Before bed, though, she gets to take a luxurious bath in the deep, claw-foot tub. Even Opa's bathroom has its own smell—of Lake Michigan hard tap water and Ivory soap.

She always gets up in the morning while everyone else is asleep and goes down to the spacious kitchen. A set of canisters full of *pfeffernüsse* cookies baked by her aunts lines the top of the cupboards out of reach. Just knowing they're there she anticipates their spicy aroma of anise, cinnamon and molasses and on her tongue the soft texture of powdered sugar. After dinner, an aunt will lift a canister down for her and her brothers and cousins to reach in and take three or four for dessert. On the counter a round, red kitchen clock with big black hands stands on three legs. Its ticking punctuates the silence of early morning, resounding off the plaster walls and high ceiling. She sits at the kitchen table in her nightgown, swings her bare feet back and forth to the clock's rhythm, watches the second hand jerk forward on its circular path, and just listens.

The Other Cousins

She thoroughly enjoys all three brilliant children of her mother's sister, Aunt Dot and her husband, Uncle Cliff.

Maria, the one who is Nick's age, gets straight As in school, writes poetry, has perfect posture and sews some of her own clothes, of which, as this beautiful cousin grows out of them, she is the grateful recipient. A box in the mail from Aunt Dot means a treasure of carefully ironed and folded puff-sleeve dresses, navy blue wasp-waisted jumpers with deep pockets, smocked blouses and more.

Phil, her own age, tells sardonic, self-deprecating jokes in a deadpan voice and draws morbid Charles Addams-like cartoons depicting himself in various states of peril. She admires his intelligence and cleverness and doesn't understand how he can be so modest and unpretentious. When the families visit, she can't get enough of him.

The genius of Lila, younger than Teddy by three years, is camouflaged by the wispy white-blond bangs that hang into her white-blond lashes and sleepy, powder-blue eyes. At four years old, when her brother tries to pull her into the car as they're about to drive away, she unleashes her startling vocabulary, indignantly reprimanding him with, "Phil, you are strangling my arm!"

The family of five lives in a one-and-a-half story, 1920s suburban bungalow much like the one Aunt Dot and her mother grew up in. When her family visits there, they set up their big tent in her aunt and uncle's backyard to accommodate the overflow. Between her father's relatives and her mother's, she feels she has been born into the best of all possible families.

Four Eyes

Every summer there is a family reunion in Milwaukee at Opa's house near the lake. One afternoon when she is ten, she, Nick, and her cousins the twins Kurt and Max and their younger brother Marty are on their way back from the beach, a little drugged from the sun, barefoot and dragging wet, sandy towels. With their identical pairs of spindly legs, jutting collar bones and blue eyes glittering above sunburned cheeks, the five couldn't be taken for anything but a clan. The twins are undersized and skinny but ferocious as hyenas.

Half a block from their grandfather's house, they notice two boys loitering in front of Gruber's, the corner Mom and Pop store. One boy is tall, probably older than Nick or the twins. The other is short but stocky. They abruptly cross the street and come to a stop in front of Nick, blocking his way.

"Hey, Four-Eyes!" says the short one.

Nick stops walking and stands with his arms at his sides, a neutral, veiled look coming over his face. She moves to stand next to him.

He has worn glasses since he was eight and she knows he has been bullied for it repeatedly even though, to her, the glasses make him look handsome and distinctive. She feels that Nick should never have to fight. Better that angel-faced Teddy or even she herself fight if necessary.

At that moment her cousin Kurt pushes his way between them and shoves, not the short boy but the tall one, in the chest, causing him to stumble backward. "You shit! You're a shit!" yells Kurt and pushes the older boy to the sidewalk.

Her first thought is of Nick, that he can escape now, slip away home while he has the chance. But he continues to stand there a little removed, his expression blank. Kurt and the neighborhood bully roll on the hard cement and are soon locked in each other's arms. She and the rest stand watching, the short boy alternately yelling encouragement to his friend and insulting her cousin.

"Kill him, Jake!" he shouts. "Scream for Mama, Four-Eyes!"

She realizes that "Four-Eyes" for these boys is a generic insult. It isn't being used to single out her brother after all. Directed at her fierce cousin, who does not wear glasses, it has the ring of a military form of address, to provoke a fight. She hopes that Nick might now feel proud to have been included as one deserving of such a name.

The older boy throws her cousin off, pushes him onto his back and straddles him pressing his knees into Kurt's shoulders. Kurt pours forth a stream of swear words.

"You fuckhead bastard! ... Motherfucker! ... Piss whore!"

"Yell for Mama!" the boy taunts him again. At this, Kurt spits in his face.

In the next moment, the boy grabs Kurt by the hair and slams the back of his head on the sidewalk. She gasps at the sound of bone hitting concrete.

"Stop it!" she screams. "Stop it! Stop it!" Nobody seems to hear her. Grinning, the tall boy slams Kurt's head on the sidewalk again. The others all look on, Nick a little apart. Neither Max, Marty, nor the short boy interferes or gets into it himself. Maybe it's a rule of fighting, she thinks.

"Let go of him! Let go of him!" she cries.

The shrill pitch of her voice sets her cousins and the short boy to calling out a patter of random insults, mostly obscenities.

The third time Kurt's skull cracks against the pavement, a line of blood issues from one nostril. Amazingly, he continues to swear at full volume.

"I'll kill you, bastard!" Kurt yells, without irony, into the bully's face. The tall boy pulls Kurt's head up by the hair, but before he can smack him down again, she runs forward and throws herself on the boy, grabbing him by his own hair and pulling it as hard as she can, jerking his head back. He pays no attention whatsoever. He puts one hand on her cousin's throat and calmly begins to squeeze Kurt's neck.

"Say Uncle, Four-Eyes! Uncle! Uncle! Uncle!" he jeers.

Kurt's face is a deep red, almost purple, and blood is now coming out of his other nostril, but she can see by the mulishness in his blue eyes and the flexion of the muscles across his skinny chest that he is nowhere close to saying "Uncle." He will pass out before he'll say it.

At this she lets go of the boy's hair, jumps off his back and begins running the half block to Opa's house. She is crying so hard and is so out of breath by the time she arrives that she can't communicate to her father what is happening, as if she is in one of those dreams where you try to call for help but all that comes out is a puny ineffectual voice that doesn't speak comprehensible English.

But her father doesn't need her to go into detail. He sees the state she is in and the direction she is pointing, hears her semi-coherent utterance ("Boys! ... Kurt! ... Blood!") and goes into action.

That evening, Uncle Karl, her father's brother and father of the bad boy twins, referring to this incident when comparing his own and her father's approaches to parenthood, says, "To me, this would not have been such important news—Kurt's or Max's getting their brains knocked out or knocking someone else's brains out—that was like the newspaper delivery. You'd be a little surprised if they missed a day. But Erich's out the door so fast he forgets to put on his shoes. He's in such a hurry to get to the scene of the mayhem he jumps into the car, for Christ sake. The fight's just down the block, but he gets into the car, backs it out, drives over the curb, taking half of Oma's lilac bush with him in his goddamn haste to break up the fight."

When her father squeals to a stop and jumps out of the car, leaving the door standing open, the fight is over and Kurt, Max, Marty and Nick are walking toward the house still trailing their sandy towels. The two neighborhood toughs are nowhere in sight. Kurt is licking blood off his upper lip, swearing, rather cheerfully, she thinks, and Max and Marty are uttering excited, tense reminiscences of the fight's high points.

"Didn't do anything! ... Bastards started it! ... Tried to kill Kurt! ... Fuckheads better look out next time!"

Although she wonders, she doesn't ask Nick or her cousins how the fight got stopped or who won. There is no mention of her brother's not defending himself or Kurt's taking on the job for him. She understands that, to the fierce cousins, all that matters is kin.

Thwarted Ambition

The only sport she plays is backyard badminton with Teddy. Because Teddy is a very little boy, and she is not athletic, they spend ninety percent of their games picking the birdie out of the grass.

If she needs sunshine and outdoor occupation, she takes a book to the yard and reads in a lawn chair: *The Wind in the Willows*, *Alice's Adventures in Wonderland* and *Through the Looking Glass*, *Charlotte's Web*. All this reading gives her a permanent slouch and the aspiration to be a writer. When she does sit down with pen and paper, though, she's stumped. What can she write *about*? All that comes to her are plots that have already been taken. Even when she comes up with a semi-original story, she has only hackneyed phrases and overused words to express it.

She keeps trying, but then she reads *Huckleberry Finn* and that's the end of it. How pathetic her writing is compared to Mark Twain's. If by eleven years old she can't produce anything as good as *Huckleberry Finn*, she might as well give up the whole endeavor. There's no hope for her. She simply can't write.

Douglas Eggers

Back in second grade she first began to love Douglas Eggers, a smallish sturdy boy with rich black hair in a dense crewcut, deep brown eyes, and eyelashes so thick and long they cast shadows on his cheeks. He has a slightly husky voice, which she is always aware of across the playground. He doesn't notice her at all, and even when she was seven she knew that girls weren't supposed to pursue boys but must wait to be pursued. She waits. Sometimes she feels hurt that he pays no attention to her, but she consoles herself with the fact that he doesn't pay attention to any girl, not even Marilyn, with her delicate features and naturally wavy blonde ponytail.

She will love Douglas unrequitedly for four years until they both move on to different junior highs and she develops other infatuations. Looking back from the mature vantage point of high school, she will remember that the boys in grade school generally didn't love girls the way girls loved boys. It may have had nothing to do with her attractiveness or lack thereof.

George Morris

And yet, George Morris loves her. There couldn't be a greater contrast between George and Douglas. George is a skinny kid with ears that stick out at almost a forty-five degree angle. His cheeks perpetually glow a bright scarlet as if he has just finished a marathon race. He slurps his Ss so that there's always a little foam at the corners of his mouth and he tends to substitute W for R. Within his hearing, children sometimes recite a ditty: "Georgy Porgy puddin' and pie, kished the girls and made them cwy…"

He is an outcast, of course, and usually alone. She feels perpetually guilty about him, having heard and noticed that he loves her. From time to time he speaks to her shyly, with unmistakable adoration in his eyes. She senses that if she goes out of her way to be kind to him, his need for friendship will overwhelm her, so she keeps her distance, though she is never deliberately cruel.

In fifth grade, at recess, she hears Denny Addison, a nasty sixth grade bully, calling her name. "Hey, *An*—nie!" he sings, "Here's your lover boy." He has wrenched George Morris's arm up behind his back and is hauling him across the playground. When they come up to her, Denny pushes George against her chest, exclaiming so everyone can hear, "Kish her, Georgy. You know you love her. Kish her and make her cwy." George resists briefly, but Denny wrenches his arm higher. George kisses her quickly on the cheek and averts his eyes. Denny lets him go then and takes off, whooping in triumph.

"How *dare* you!" she shouts at George because, in the moment, nothing is more infuriating than being kissed against your will. "I'm going to tell the teacher, and YOUR NAME WILL BE MUD!"

"No," he pleads, "Don't tell the teachew! Please!" She stalks off, outraged.

She doesn't tell on George, though. When she has calmed down sufficiently, she recognizes that, to be fair, it wasn't his fault.

The next afternoon as children are crowding in the halls, getting ready to go home, she pounces on Denny from behind like a tiger, grabs hold of his ears and twists with all her strength. He cries out and tries to shake her off, but she slaps one arm around his neck and chokes him until he falls to his knees. Then she lets him go, knowing that he won't get up and hit her, now or ever, because boys never hit girls.

Dramatics

On Saturday mornings she takes a Children's Theatre class at Norman Hall, the University's Fine Arts building across from Old Main. A professor, Guinevere Desmond, teaches the class. She is in her forties, her prematurely white hair worn in a silky page boy. She wears cashmere sweaters with the sleeves rolled to three-quarters length, flowing skirts cut on the bias and ballet flats. The children call her Miss Desmond. Miss Desmond calls the class Dramatics.

She is eight years old when she starts taking Dramatics, and there is nothing she doesn't like about it. On the six-block walk to the venerable three-story Norman Hall she skips and runs and sings. From half a block away, she can hear through open windows the cacophony of scales being sung by sopranos and tenors, or played on pianos, flutes, and violins in the practice rooms on the first and second floors. Dramatics is hidden away on the third floor at the top of a narrow, winding wooden staircase that creaks with each step, like secret stairs in a fairy tale.

The classroom has a small curtainless stage with three steps leading up to it from each side, and an area with folding chairs facing it. Miss Desmond sits on the edge of the stage to give her instructions. "Today we're going to be in a forest. Let's get in touch with all our senses." Then she moves to the back of the room and sends several children onto the stage. "Choose an animal that you would like to be and show us how that animal experiences the forest."

She chooses to be a cat because she is enthralled by cats, and even though you don't find them in forests, she knows that Miss Desmond doesn't quibble over such details.

"What do I see? What do I hear?" the teacher calls to them. "What do I taste? Touch? Smell?"

She sharpens her claws on an imaginary tree, sniffs the air, prowls through imaginary underbrush and adds her realistic meows to the roars and grunts and bird calls emanating from the other animals onstage.

Once a semester, Miss Desmond directs a full-length children's theatre production, held in the vast Old Main auditorium, an extension of the Administration building. Two or three hundred children and their parents from all over the city fill the main floor and the sweeping wrap-around balcony to watch the performances.

Roles are cast from the Dramatics classes, and the scripts—printed in little blue booklets—are ordered from Samuel French, Inc. When the scripts arrive she immediately writes her name on the cover and, if she has a speaking part, circles all her lines and begins memorizing as soon as she gets home.

Rehearsals are in the classroom on Saturdays until the last week before the play, when they are held after school and into the evenings in the big auditorium.

Every square inch of the auditorium delights her. At the back entrance, there is an intriguing staircase that, to her surprise, leads up to a large airy meeting space on the second floor adjacent to her father's office. Behind the stage, tall flats left over from other productions—cityscapes, meadows, interiors—are propped against the wall. The children, laughing, hide in the scenery. In the dim light the thick red velvet curtains undulate whenever a child moves behind them. Sometimes the children are so noisy that Miss Desmond has to shush them from the back of the auditorium. In the small beige Green Room they wait until their scenes come up, or, at the dinner hour, they give their orders to a graduate assistant, who runs across the street to the

Varsity Café and brings back large paper bags of cheeseburgers, French fries and milk shakes.

Before the dress rehearsal, Miss Desmond's college drama majors teach the children to apply makeup in a room with lighted mirrors, and help them into colorful period costumes festooned with flounces.

She takes Dramatics through seventh grade. In the fall of the year she's twelve, she is given the coveted role of Becky Thatcher in *Tom Sawyer*, coveted because it's a romantic lead opposite a cute, if short, boy with a shy smile. They get to hold hands. Her friend Carla says, as if in passing but with a little smirk, "You get all the leading roles because your father is Vice President at the University."

"No, I don't!" she protests.

In the five years she has taken Dramatics, she has been cast in three other leading roles: Gretel, in *Hansel and Gretel*; Sarah, in *The Little Princess*; and Beauty, in *The Sleeping Beauty*. Each time she had considered herself lucky rather than favored. She can't imagine that Miss Desmond would take her father's job into consideration, and of course her father would never apply pressure. He won't even let her use his *From the Desk of*... tablets. How can Carla think such a thing?

But now, for the first time during rehearsals Miss Desmond has to call from the back of the auditorium, "Annie, pro*ject!* Big voice! Send it back here! I can't hear you!" She develops stage fright before the performance. Afterwards, the cast gathers outdoors with families and other audience members for picture taking. Marilyn and Nancy and Peg have come. She's aware that people are looking at her in her costume with her makeup on and that everyone knows she's the one who played Becky Thatcher. Later, when her father's photos are developed, she thinks, "That costume doesn't fit right. It makes me look scrawny. And the makeup is too orange."

In the spring semester, Miss Desmond asks her to play a child in a college production about a man who has to go to war and leave his young daughter. In the scene where he leaves her, the college boy who plays the father is supposed to look sadly into her eyes and take her hands in his. Instead of looking into her eyes, he looks at her forehead. His hands holding hers are limp and moist, and a rash of red pimples covers the hollows in his cheeks. Miss Desmond has to keep telling her to speak up.

When her mother asks if she wants to sign up for Dramatics again that summer, she says she'd rather have her Saturday mornings free.

Recreation Director

On weekends, when she isn't off playing with Marilyn or Nancy or Peg, Teddy brings his little friend Belinda over from the apartments behind their block, and the two of them stand in the kitchen awaiting instructions. She gives them minor roles in plays and puppet shows which she writes, stages and directs. Or she organizes daring escapes from convicts along the paths through the weeds next door. In winter, they stomp out complicated Fox and Geese mazes of her design in the snow, or if the weather is too cold, they go through the house with mirrors under their chins to see what it feels like to walk on the ceiling. Sometimes they flop down on the sofa in the living room and she tells them stories that she makes up as she goes along.

Belinda's mother, who usually sends her daughter out to play in patent leather shoes with straps and fluffy taffeta dresses puffed out by starched crinolines, asks her to stop telling Belinda ghost stories because they give her nightmares. She shouldn't have been surprised then, when after helping with the creation of a haunted house in the loft room of Folks's garage down the street, Belinda is too scared to enter it when it's finished.

Sulk

She knows that it distresses her mother when someone in the family is angry, sad, frustrated or in any other way unhappy. On such occasions her mother's voice gets high and chirpy. She tiptoes around the disgruntled one, offering distractions, expressing sympathy and cheer.

She doesn't want to distress her mother, but this vulnerability to other people's moods makes bullying her irresistible.

The family takes a vacation to Longboat Key in Florida. The two-day car ride is endless, hot and sticky, but it will all be worthwhile when they get to the Gulf. She has frolicked at Lake Michigan beaches, and this beach will be even better—transparent turquoise water, white sand and colored shells. She has seen the pictures in the brochure. A bridge has only just opened this year, so the island is virtually empty—just a few cottages and one paved road.

When they arrive at their little cabin, before fully unpacking they all run eagerly to the beach and fling themselves into the water. Inflatable rafts are brought out and blown up. She and Teddy ride theirs like horses and engage in splash battles.

Then she looks down into the shallows and sees a flash of something scuttle along the sandy bottom. It has a long thin tail and is flat like a pancake. She screams and paddles toward shore.

"It's a sting ray," her father says after she describes it. "Just keep an eye out and splash around before you put your foot down so they know you're coming and they'll get out of your way. They're more afraid of you than you are of them."

Her over-cautious father would have been very unlikely to say this if he thought there was real danger, but she cannot be persuaded to get back in. She sits on the beach hugging her knees. The more her family swims and floats and shouts and plays, the more resentful she feels. Everything is ruined.

For the whole week she will not smile even once, and takes satisfaction in rebuffing her mother's upbeat exhortations to come join them, her periodic attempts to sit with her and to put an arm around her shoulders and reassure her, cheer her up. She shakes off the arm and notes with bitterness when, finally, even her mother backs off and leaves her to her sulk.

She spends the time beachcombing, which is small compensation for what she is missing. She realizes she is doing this to herself, but she can't help it, she can't stop; she is compelled to punish her family, and especially her mother, for her disappointment.

Taffy

She's had Taffy since she was seven. Taffy is a small, short-haired cat of a pale cream color, hence the name. Every six months or so Taffy has kittens. Altogether she has had eight litters. Somehow, once they're weaned, homes are always found for them.

No one else in the family is especially interested in cats in general or Taffy in particular, so it is conceded that Taffy is her cat. She's the one who feeds her and cuddles her and changes the litter box. She always makes up a basket for the kittens in the entryway between the back porch and the stairs to the basement.

She is very strict about how others may handle Taffy and the kittens. No one is to disturb a cat while it's sleeping, or pick it up roughly or, when carrying it, fail to support it under its feet. In fact, she would rather no one handle the cats but herself.

She finds it endlessly fascinating to watch them. If Shirley Most's German shepherd comes bounding into the yard next door, Taffy can nimbly shinny up to the highest branches of a tree and get herself down again. In the living room, she can leap to the top of the tall bookcase in one graceful bound. She sharpens her claws on trees, arching her back to get power into it. The kittens tussle and attack each other in the grass before exhausting themselves and falling asleep together in an adorable little heap.

Taffy's most recent litter is just old enough to eat solid food when Taffy doesn't come home one night. It's not completely unusual for her to stay out overnight, but not when there are kittens to attend to. The next day she still has not come back. The family fans out to search for her in the neighborhood. They don't find her, and none of the neighbors has seen her.

"She wouldn't have run away," she asserts to her mother. "She wouldn't leave her kittens." Maybe, she thinks, the cat got hit by a car or a dog killed her. After a week, she concludes that Taffy is dead.

She finds homes for the four kittens, and then that's the end of having cats. At first she misses Taffy, and she shuts out disturbing images of her possible last moments on Earth. Within a few weeks, though, she doesn't think much about Taffy. It is just a fact that pets live a short life. They die and that's all. She has other things to think about. In a couple of months Taffy is just a memory.

Meanwhile, she hasn't cured herself of the sulkiness that plagued her and her family on their Florida beach vacation. In fact, she doesn't even try to cure herself. Somehow, little disappointments and deprivations send her into fits of pouting and she perpetually glowers.

One evening, after being gloomy at dinner because she wanted to go to the library that afternoon to replenish her supply of books but her mother didn't have time to take her—"I don't have anything to *read*!"—she goes up to her room and her mother follows soon after.

"Knock knock," her mother calls at her door. "Can I come in?"

"Okay," she says, grudgingly. She is on her bed paging through a book that she read a long time ago, *Babar at the Circus*.

Her mother sits alongside her and looks into her eyes. "Honey," she says, placing a hand on her arm, "are you missing Taffy?"

Even at eleven, she knows how to read her mother, who has just handed her an excuse.

"Yes," she says, lowering her eyes mournfully.

Her mother pats her. "That's natural," she says. "You loved her. I know it's hard to imagine, but someday you'll feel better."

She nods glumly and goes back to looking at her book. Her mother pats her again, gets up and leaves, shutting the door behind her.

Vaguely she senses that not only she, but her mother, too, has been handed an excuse: her sulking is natural and it's nobody's fault.

Outside-Inside

In October and early November the family rakes the leaves fallen from the old oaks that grow close to the house. The leaves are piled onto the army surplus tarps their father lays on the grass. He wields the heavy iron-toothed rake while everyone else uses the rakes with flexible prongs spread out like fans.

Her father lets her and her brothers flop backward onto the leaves and jump in them before he reconstitutes the piles and, with Nick's and their mother's help, drags the tarps to the back garden to dump the leaves. He has plowed the garden with a rented rototiller to prepare it for spring planting, so it's a safe open place for the burn. They all stand around watching the bonfire dance and send sparks into the blue autumn sky. Sometimes her mother brings marshmallows to roast. When the ashes have cooled, everyone spreads them over the garden and works them into the soil.

Leaf raking is the only exception to the implicit outside-inside gender rule for chores.

Once a year, before they take off on vacation, the car gets a thorough cleaning outside and inside. It's the boys' job to hose off the exterior, suds it with the chamois, hose it off again and polish it. Much of the chore involves spraying each other, adjusting the pressure on the hose nozzle to create dazzling rainbow effects, and generally horsing around.

She, meanwhile, is inside the car. It's July. Even with the doors open it's sweltering. The only outside part of her job is to pull out the floor mats, hose them down, scrub them with a brush and lay them on the hot driveway to dry. Her primary task is to collect and discard candy wrappers and other detritus, vacuum all inside surfaces, and scour a year's accumulation of grime collected in the tiny pits of the Chevy's white vinyl seats and seat backs.

She cleans in sections using SOS pads and Babo, stopping now and then to wipe with a clean sponge the dirty swirls she's worked up. The sponge has to be rinsed from a bucket that needs frequent dumping. Her brothers oblige her by filling the empty bucket from the hose while she sits in the car. It never occurs to her that there's no good reason why she should always be assigned the inside task. She knows only that she hates it.

Exhibit

She, Marilyn, Nancy and Peg are ambling down College Avenue and swinging their lunch buckets on their way home from school. A half a block ahead, a man is walking toward them. He draws near, and as he steps onto the grass alongside she does a double take, not sure she can believe what she is seeing. The man passes and continues on his way. The girls turn to each other, their mouths agape.

"His thing was hanging out!" she says.

"Maybe he went to the bathroom and forgot to zip," says Marilyn. They giggle at the thought and turn to stare at his receding back. He was an ordinary-looking man, wearing an ordinary beige rain coat.

"You'd think he would've felt it and looked down at himself," she says and feels a little bad for him, imagining how embarrassed he'll be when he finally notices.

When she gets home, she tells her mother about the man. "He didn't even know it was sticking out!" she exclaims. Her mother hesitates a moment.

Then she says, "He did know, Annie. This kind of man is called an exhibitionist. He was trying to shock you. If you ever see anything like it again, change your route and take another way home."

She isn't so much shocked as she is puzzled. How could the man not have been embarrassed?

Drink

Her parents' friends come over in the summer, bringing their young children, and sit on lawn chairs in the big yard, chatting and drinking beer and ice tea while she and her brothers and the other kids play.

She wants to know what her father's beer tastes like. "Can I try it?"

Probably knowing what will ensue, he holds it out. "Just a very small sip," he says.

She takes a swallow. "Ew!" She screws up her face and hands back the bottle. "That's awful! How can you drink that?" He smiles.

Her parents and their friends and colleagues are almost contractually bound to reciprocate parties. Despite her mother's insecurities about cooking and meeting the imagined standards set by the rich people of her childhood, she ends up having to give a dinner or cocktail party on a monthly basis.

Afterwards, she and her brothers scavenge the leftovers. They head for the bowls of potato chips and her mother's clam dip (onion soup mix, canned clams and sour cream), her favorite. They go at it until it's all gone. Usually several half-finished drinks in funnel-shaped glasses with cherries at the bottom are left sitting on the coffee table and end tables. The cherries suggest that the drink might be sweet. One evening she takes a big gulp.

Gasping, she pushes the glass away. "Oh, that's horrible!" she says. "Don't drink that!" Teddy trustfully complies. Nick doesn't seem to mind the taste. He finishes off the other half-full glasses.

Shame on You

She and her mother are at a shopping center that encloses a block of indoor retail stores, something of an innovation in 1957. The wide central aisle is bustling with shoppers. She notices a little boy of about six who has wandered a few yards from his mother, attracted by a colorful display. The mother lunges at the boy, grabs him by the arm and jerks him backward, shouting furiously, "You get back here. *Shame* on you!" The little boy shrinks into himself.

Her mother, without taking a beat, strides over to the woman and in a voice that seems to have come from an entirely different person says, "No! Shame on *you*!"

She catches a satisfying glimpse of the woman's stunned face before her mother returns to her and they continue their shopping without comment. But it is a wonder, her mother in this avenging light. How did she, so mild-mannered, so averse to conflict, have the nerve? She understands dimly that she has just seen the depth—or height—of her mother's empathy with children.

Sickly

It seems she is always getting colds and sore throats. She finally gets over one—they sometimes last for a week or more—and another comes along. Maybe it's something to do with frequently having her fingers in her mouth. She can't seem to keep from biting her nails. Her mother has a similar problem. She chews on her cuticles until her fingertips are red and swollen.

She and her mother both try to cure themselves by painting a bitter-tasting solution on the ends of their fingers, but it keeps getting washed off and they go right back to their bad habits. Unlike her, though, her mother never gets colds or any other ailment. Her mother is most amazingly healthy, while she perpetually coughs and drips.

Reading in bed has helped her get to sleep these days, but nothing prevents her from waking at the slightest sound or at any irregularity in sleeping arrangements. She invariably gets a cold after a slumber party. She and Marilyn and Nancy and Peg stay up late, finally turning in for good at one or two a.m. when the mother makes them stop their giggling and get to sleep.

The other girls soon drift off, but she lies awake tossing and turning on an unfamiliar bed or thinly carpeted floor, listening to the others' breathing and the sounds of the house around her. After only two or three hours of sleep, she wakes pale and haggard with circles under her eyes. She always fears she will get sick, and indeed the next day she comes down with a cold. She would just as soon forgo slumber parties for this reason, but if she did, she would feel left out.

Winners and Losers

Sitting in the bleachers at the Field House, she's in a world of sound—the slap and squeak of rubber-soled shoes on the glossy floor, the metallic *poing* of the ball bouncing off the rim, the referee's shrill whistle, the harsh buzzer for fouls and time outs, the roar of the crowd and its synchronized cheers.

Her father doesn't listen to sports on the radio or read the sports page in the newspaper, but as an administrator he feels duty-bound to show up for at least some of the University's sporting events. She doesn't much like the football games—they last too long, it's always too cold, and nothing much happens except the piling up and separating of the boys, whose identities are camouflaged by their thick padding.

Basketball, though, is another thing altogether. The boys race back and forth across the court, leap into the air, and spin around each other like dancers in a sped up ballet. When they fall, they fall with grace and jump up again as if oblivious to the resounding crack of an elbow or knee against the hardwood. Every season she screams the players' names to drive them forward and develops crushes on half the team.

As the game goes on, however, her enjoyment is replaced by her exquisite pity for players on either team who miss a free throw or lose the ball or are called back to the bench after too many fouls, and she cringes to hear opposing fans crow over these blunders. How must that boy feel, with his parents and friends probably in the stands, watching his humiliation? And at the end of the game, when the losing team, red-faced, glum, and covered in sweat, has to shuffle by the winners and shake their hands before trudging off to the locker room, she can hardly bear it.

In the spring, the University hosts a national collegiate track event, which the family always attends. Here, along with the exciting long jumps, pole vaulting, hundred-yard dash, and hurdle relays with baton hand offs, she must endure the agonies of long distance runners who finish all alone a whole lap, or even two, behind everyone else, staggering to the finish line and collapsing on the grass. It seems cruel that they should be made to feel they have to finish the race. How they must long to peel off and limp away out of sight.

Every time she gets in the car with her family and heads off enthusiastically to these events, she always forgets that it will end with her almost in tears.

Knee Slapper

They get a television a little later than other people—neighbors and kids at school—and they don't watch it much because her mother dislikes most of the shows and the loudness of the commercials. But one show they all enjoy is "You'll Never Get Rich" with Phil Silvers as Sergeant Bilko. When Bilko puts one over on the disgruntled Colonel Hall or includes the hapless Private Doberman in one of his schemes ("But, *Sarge!*"), her father throws back his head and laughs uncontrollably and soundlessly as if he's suffocating (the Lang silent laugh, as Nick calls it) and slaps her knee. She makes sure she sits next to her father on the sofa because she loves it when he slaps her knee. It's as if he can't contain his abundance of hilarity and has to spill it over to include her.

Art

She and Nick and their mother can draw. She draws swans, fairy tale princesses, castles, horses, squirrels, dogs, and cats. Nick draws battles, forts, soldiers, and weapons with fiery blasts bursting from muzzles. Their mother draws and paints landscapes and still lifes. Teddy doesn't draw, but he can make anything in three-dimensional space. He builds elaborate structures from Lincoln logs and later from balsa wood. Their father takes exceptionally fine photographs capturing family life. On vacations, there is always at least one camera hanging from a strap around his neck—an 8 mm home movie camera and a camera loaded with slide film or film for prints. In her family, the necessity of making art is a given.

Back to School

Her mother doesn't have much time to draw or paint, however, because when Teddy starts first grade, she goes back to school, resuming the college education that stopped when she got married. As the wife of a University employee, she can attend tuition-free.

She decides on a BA in psychology, having become interested in the subject when she became a parent. "I want to understand children better."

"Understand us, you mean?" she says.

"Well, yes. And myself, too."

During the semester that her mother takes Psychometrics, she and Nick and Teddy are administered personality and IQ practice tests. They get to take the Wechsler Intelligence Scale for Children (WISC), the Children's Apperception Test (CAT), and the Draw a Person Test (DAP), She likes saying these acronyms to herself: "I've taken the CAT, the DAP and the WISC."

When she and her brothers are older and their mother has gone on to pursue a Master's degree, she gives them the MMPI, the Rorschach, Sentence Completion and the Stanford-Binet IQ tests. No matter how much they ask, she never reveals the results.

Her mother takes coursework during the morning and early afternoon, before she and her brothers come home from school. She does her homework at night after they've gone to bed. It will take ten years for her to get her degree.

The best part of this back-to-school situation is that she gets to quiz her mother before exams. They sit at the table after dinner where she reads the questions from 3 × 5 cards. "Good job!" she says when her mother gets them right. Sometimes she prompts her with clues. By the time she graduates from high school, she herself will have earned what amounts to a four-year degree in psychology.

Asked what her father does for a living she tells people proudly; but now she also adds, "And my mother is studying to be a psychologist." She likes the ring of it.

Hero

They're at Pentwater on the Michigan side of Lake Michigan. It's a fine sunny day, with a few high clouds and a little breeze. The lake is choppy after a night of storms, and she is in the water next to the long pier, riding the waves on her plastic raft. Her mother is helping Teddy build a drip castle on the beach with wet sand from a bucket. Nick, as usual, has started to paddle as far from shore as he can, as if he could paddle his raft all the way across the lake to Milwaukee. He's already about to pass the end of the pier. Her father has noticed and hurries down the pier to intercept him. "No farther!" he yells. Nick pretends not to hear.

She slides off her raft to paddle on her own steam. Not an especially strong swimmer, still, she loves being immersed and weightless. She dog paddles for a while, rising and falling on the waves until a wave breaks over her head and she swallows water. It's too rough to float without a raft and she drops her legs down in order to wade back to shore, but where there had been a sandy bottom here yesterday alongside the pier, there's no bottom at all now, and she's in over her head. Her raft is floating toward the beach. She tries to swim toward it, but a current keeps driving her close to the concrete wall of the pier where the waves are slapping and crashing. Another wave submerges her. Panic weakens her arms as she flails to the surface.

She screams for her father, catching a glimpse of him kneeling at the end of the pier gesturing to Nick to come back in. She screams again, but he doesn't hear her over the sound of the waves. Her mother is too far down the beach to hear.

Uselessly she struggles to get clear of the current and find the sandy bottom. Her arms are getting weaker. More waves break over her head and she comes out of them gasping. But now before she can go under again, she gathers all her breath and screams louder than she has ever screamed in her life. She sees her father turn at the sound and catch sight of her. In an instant he is sprinting down the pier, shouting, "I've got you, Annie!" Halfway down, he takes a leaping swan dive into the water, and comes up by her side. He pulls her onto his back, folding her arms around his neck, and swims her to shore.

On the beach at last, she cries a little from relief. He takes her on his lap and holds her tightly. Nick brings himself back in when he sees what has been going on, and her mother comes running from down the beach.

The waves from the night's storm had scooped out a wide, deep trough all along the pier where yesterday she could have waded in up to her armpits. It had not occurred to any of them that the sands could shift so drastically. "Jesus, I should have thought of that!" her father exclaims.

The incident has frightened her, of course, but what she replays in her mind is not the waves crashing over her head or the moments of panic when it appeared no one would hear her and she would sink and drown. What replays in her mind is her father's magnificent flight toward her and his unhesitating dive off the pier, his plunging into the turbulent water, and swimming her to shore like a hero from a legend.

It is perhaps this image of her father's coming to her rescue that gives the incident an almost mythical aura of heroism, erasing any trauma, and allowing her to run down the beach a few minutes later to regain her raft and get right back into the lake. Her father's love has allowed her love of water to remain intact.

Looks

Her friends say she has a beautiful mother, and privately she agrees. Her mother has deep-set blue eyes, a long straight nose and high cheekbones. Her dark brown hair is worn off her forehead, smooth and parted down the middle. The ends are gathered in a long flat barrette at the nape of her neck. She perms and pin curls the ends to keep the barrette from slipping off her straight, fine hair and to fashion it in a curly bun-like fluff.

"Everyone says you're beautiful, Mom," she tells her.

Her mother dismisses the compliment. "That's just because I've found a look that works for me," she says. The look requires eye liner applied with a dark brown eyebrow pencil, a touch of rouge, the application of an eyelash curler to her thin lashes, and the glossy red lipstick that is fashionable throughout the fifties. Her mother leaves lipstick marks on glasses and cups and has to wipe them off their father's lips or cheek before he goes to work. The cosmetic routine is not as elaborate as it might be. She doesn't use mascara or eye shadow or base.

She wears blouses and sweaters tucked in, her waist encircled by a wide cinch belt, and hides what she sees as her too-short legs by wearing drapey skirts that end at mid-calf. Even on camping trips, unless it's very cold, she wears these skirts. She is self-conscious about her flat bottom and thinks pants make her look "stumpy."

She seldom sees her mother without her "face" and is not surprised when she tells her, privately, "I wear my make-up to bed," from which she concludes that her mother doesn't want their father ever to see her without it. Her mother removes and re-applies her make-up when he is in the shower or after he has left for work.

Would she want to do this when she gets married? Is it what you have to do to keep your husband's interest? What if you accidentally allowed your real body to be seen? Living with him day in and day out, could you ever let your vigilance slip? It seems exhausting.

A Room of Her Own

There comes a time when she wants a room of her own. She's eleven and too old to share a room with Teddy. She wants privacy.

Her parents move her bed and her belongings to the half-finished attic reached by way of a short staircase across from the bathroom. The staircase takes a bend part way up, which makes the attic seem especially hidden.

The unfinished back half of the attic has exposed floor joists with bats of insulation between them and a couple of plywood slabs laid down to allow access to the window that looks out on the backyard. The finished half has flooring with a register cut through to bring in heated air from the rooms below. They place her bed under the front window, in the middle so she won't bump her head on the sloping ceiling when she gets in and out. She wonders if it will be spooky being in the attic at night, in the dark. But even on her first night she immediately feels at home in her cozy domain. It is all hers.

The move takes place in summer when the temperature is in the nineties during the day and not much lower at night. Her parents put a fan in the back window and set it to pull air across her from the window at the head of her bed. In the heat, she takes off her nightgown and lies naked, her arms at her sides, feeling the humid breeze flow over her skin. She would never be able to do this if she were still sharing a room with Teddy. It gives her a luxurious sense of freedom.

She flutters her fingers lightly down her arms and chest to raise goosebumps and the illusion of coolness. Then she runs her hands along her sharp hip bones and over the taut valley of her stomach and pokes a finger into her belly button.

In the bath, it is always about water. She squirts it from her fists, heaps soap bubbles around her shoulders, sinks down and rolls over in a Dead Man's float, lifelessly suspended to see how long she can hold her breath. In the shower she pretends she's standing under a waterfall. But in her attic room, as she lies flat on her back in the dark she finds that this new nakedness is all about skin.

After passing her hands over her stomach she reaches down to stroke her thighs and the two plump little cushions that sit in the place where the thighs meet. As she touches here, her fingers lightly brush against a small nub of something, and suddenly she feels an odd thrill there, a twinge, but not of pain, and an acute spreading of the sensation inside her. She touches again and the twinge becomes more urgent, the spreading more intense. Now she rolls the little nub around under her finger. Within seconds, she is overwhelmed by a build-up of acute sensations. And then spasms come, deep within. She gasps. Her heart pounds. For at least a minute, maybe more, the spasms continue before gradually fading, leaving a swollen, delicate feeling in their place contradictorily like a mouth that is gaping open.

She lies there for some time astonished by her discovery. After a while, she touches the nub once more and experiences it all over again—that keen moment just before release and the exquisite throbbing to follow. And suddenly she realizes that this feeling is not new. It's very familiar. She has experienced it without touching herself, many times, in fact, throughout her childhood when it has wakened her in the middle of the night from sleep only to be forgotten in the morning.

Now, she can make it happen at will.

Somehow she knows that it's not something to talk about with anyone, not even her mother. Not because she thinks it's bad or wrong, but because it's just very, very private, an inexpressible intimacy with herself alone.

Something Borrowed

One afternoon, her mother climbs the stairs to her room and stands in the door.

"Annie," she says, "that was your Aunt Eva on the phone. She was wondering if you might have taken home one of the costumes from Opa's attic."

She hesitates for only a few seconds before replying.

"It's under the bed," she says. "I just borrowed it." Her mother folds her arms and continues to stand there silently as she pulls out her small suitcase from under the bed and opens it.

Upon reflection, she can see why her aunt suspected her. During the most recent reunion at Opa's in July, she swanned around the house and yard all day in the satin costume ball gown. The dress almost fits her now that she's eleven.

When it was time to leave Milwaukee, she packed it into her suitcase. Of course she planned to return it next year when the family would gather again. Why *not* borrow the dress? No one else would have a use for it or even miss it. If *she* didn't take it, it would just sit there in Opa's attic out of sight. There wasn't even any need to ask permission. It was just a costume anyway. And it fit her.

Her mother holds out her arms. "I'll mail it to Eva," she says.

She hands over the dress. "I was going to bring it back next year. I was only borrowing it. No one else wears it."

"Lucia and Patty went to play dress up and found it gone."

It takes a moment for it to sink in that the yearly family reunions aren't the only times her cousins visit Opa's. Lucia and Patty live in the area. Her aunt must go over regularly to look after her father, and sometimes she must bring the girls with her. It's unsettling to think that Opa's house has a place in the life of her relatives when she isn't there to be part of it.

"But ... they're too little to wear this dress."

"Don't you remember how you used to put on my old dresses and shoes when you were little?" Of course she remembers.

Her mother refolds the costume and takes it away.

She listens to her footsteps descending the stairs. Then she closes the empty suitcase and puts it back. At that moment, her mother's words return to her from three years ago when she confessed to stealing a dime: "You were very young, Annie. You wouldn't take something that didn't belong to you *now*, would you?" Does her Aunt Eva think she's a thief? Does her mother? But I was only *borrowing* it, she wants to tell her mother again. I didn't think it *mattered*.

Ethics

Her mother explains the reason the family moved to their city. Her father had landed a job as an accountant at a large national firm in Chicago, so at last they could afford to get married and start a family. Not long before Teddy was born, however, her father began to be uneasy about his boss's pressuring him to "cook the books."

It was her mother's idea then to apply for accountancy jobs at universities, where profits were not a priority and they would enjoy an academic environment with stimulating, intellectual friends. They sent out resumés to universities in alluring places like California, Colorado, and New Mexico as well as to less competitive ones in the Midwest. The first to give her father an interview was the first to offer him a position. He accepted and signed the contract immediately. If he waited any longer, he might have no choice but to accede to his boss's demands or quit his job. He had three children and a wife to support.

"Erich is not a risk taker, so we ended up here," her mother says, adding, as if to soften any implied criticism, "He wanted to do what was best for all of us. Well of course he was right, and it turned out to be a good decision." There is a slight wistfulness in her mother's voice. This medium-sized, Midwestern plains city and small unexceptional university are not, apparently, what she had hoped for after fantasies of an ocean, or mountain, or high desert home.

She finds the story a little tragic, even heroic—her father's ethics had led him to sacrifice money, prestige and possibly a more interesting life for the security of his family. She repeats the story proudly to her friends.

Long Legs

Her mother suggests she wear saddle shoes because they were so fashionable when she was in high school and are still fashionable for girls today. But at eleven she has become self-conscious about her legs. Her calves are too skinny for those big clunky shoes, she says. She would be embarrassed. She's worn dainty ballet flats since first grade and she will continue to wear them. "Oh, Annie," her mother protests. "You have lovely legs. They're so nice and long. What I wouldn't give for long legs like yours!" There's nothing wrong with her mother's legs. She's petite, so of course her legs are short.

Word

Teddy sees a Black person on the street and says, "Look. There's a nigger." He must have heard the word at school. Their mother turns around from the front seat of the car and says, "Teddy, honey, that's not a nice word. We don't use it. The word you should use is "Negro.""

Neighborhood

It's mid-August, a sultry, sweltering evening. They've gone to a movie to bask in the air-conditioning. When they come out, the heat is still heavy, but the sun is low, so her father and Nick fold down the Chevy's canvas top and tuck it into the boot.

She gets in the back seat with her brothers. Her mother says, "Let's run down to the Safeway on Governor and get a gallon of ice cream."

Her father pulls onto 28th Street and drives south. Her mother, as usual, gazes at the scenery. They're passing small, one-story houses built close together on postage stamp yards. In the heat, people have come out to sit on porches and stoops. Kids are playing in the sun-dried yards and on the sidewalks. Two boys are chasing each other with squirt guns.

She doesn't remember her father ever driving down this street before. They usually shop at the Safeway close to home, and it strikes her that all the people she is seeing are Black.

She feels a jerk as her father suddenly speeds up. He says, "Does that guy have a gun?"

Nick looks back eagerly. "What guy?"

Her mother says, "A gun? I didn't see a gun."

"I'm sure I saw a gun." His voice is tense. He is speeding down 28th Street now with fixed concentration on his driving. In the back seat, swiveling her head left and right, she looks for people with guns but doesn't detect any.

She senses her father's relief when he pulls into the Safeway parking lot on Governor Street, a main thoroughfare that runs east and west through the city. They're a few blocks west of the Governor's mansion.

Before they go into the supermarket, her father says to Nick, "Let's get this top back up," and they lift and secure the canvas top. When they finish, her father goes around the car and locks all the doors.

Prior to this, she has not been afraid of Black people.

Outrage

On television a lone fifteen-year-old Negro girl is hemmed in by a mob of screaming, cat-calling White adults threatening to kill her. She is wearing a short-sleeved blouse and a full, gathered skirt and holds a school notebook against her chest. Her eyes are covered by sunglasses, but it's obvious the girl, holding her lips together to keep them from trembling, is trying not to cry. The girl walks to a bench and sits down. A White reporter asks her questions, gingerly holding a microphone out at arm's length as if she might bolt if he comes too close. She stares straight ahead and doesn't, or can't, answer.

"Are they crazy? Who *are* these horrible people? How *can* they?" she asks her mother.

Her mother turns away from the television screen. "I don't know, honey. They're just bigots. It's sickening."

A White woman puts her arm around the girl's shoulder, gently helps her to a city bus, boards it with her and presumably accompanies her safely home. But will that girl ever feel safe after this? Will she ever get over it?

Disclosures

As she gets older her mother occasionally discloses bits of private information about herself. She likes to hear these confidences. As far as she knows, her mother doesn't reveal such things to her brothers.

Teddy has never indicated that he knows any of this inside information. She takes it for granted that it's just between mother and daughter.

For her birthday, her mother gives her a diary, locked with a little key, which she keeps hidden in a crevice in the plaster board under her bedroom window. She writes in the diary almost every day.

"Do you like your diary?" her mother asks, seeing it on her bedside table.

"I love it."

"I thought you might like having one. I kept a diary all through high school."

It turns out that her mother's diary still exists, tucked away in a drawer of her bureau under some sweaters. She pleads with her mother to see it.

"Oh, Annie. It's too embarrassing. All I wrote about was boys, boys, boys. And trying to be popular. I was a terrible social climber."

She thinks her mother should not blame herself. One piece of information she already knows is that her mother grew up poor in a one-and-a-half story bungalow. The house backed up to the El tracks a couple of blocks from the mansions and stately homes of her classmates in one of the very wealthy suburbs along Chicago's North Shore. The girls at her high school took piano and riding and drawing and tennis lessons and bought new outfits whenever they felt like going into Chicago to shop. Her father was a failed lawyer who was fired from his law firm in the middle of the Depression and had to scrounge up individual clients, who were few and far between.

There was romance to be found in her mother's story, like something in a novel. Why wouldn't she be a "social climber?" Who wouldn't feel the desire to fit in, coming from such a background?

Her mother has held onto the diary all these years, hiding it under sweaters in the bureau drawer. It's written in the strange, half cursive, half block script her mother improvised because cursive wasn't taught in her high school in the '30s. The diary is thick, with red leather covers. They sit on the bed and look at it.

"I'll read you a few entries, and that'll be enough. The rest of it will just be more of the same. Dreadful."

It's full of references to the glorious Duff Scranton, a boy she pines for but who won't give her the time of day. Another boy, Junior Graham, loves her but she has no use for him except when she needs a date and has no other options. This is reminiscent of her own adoration of Douglas Eggers and the unwanted attention of George Morris except that Junior wasn't an outcast. He simply wasn't Duff Scranton.

The diary describes her mother's strategy for gaining popularity. She reads, "'You ask people a lot of questions about themselves. You make your eyes big, and nod while they're talking. It works!! I'm getting the reputation of being a good listener'. Ugh! That's enough!" Her mother closes the diary and puts it away. "I was ghastly. Very good at living a lie."

Bottom Drawer

She honors her mother's privacy for several months until she can't anymore. One day when her parents are out, she goes back to that chest of drawers and goes looking for the diary. It's not to be found under the sweaters, nor in any other drawer. Clearly her mother has decided to put it out of reach or maybe, given her scorn for her youthful self, has destroyed it.

In the bottom drawer, however, she discovers the underwear. Black and red lace camisoles and garter belts, transparent, nippleless bras, crotchless bikini underpants. She immediately understands what she's seeing: this is what a woman does to please a husband. She carefully folds the garments and puts them back exactly as she found them.

Knowledge Shared

She, Marilyn, Nancy and Peg are at her house. They play jacks until they get tired of getting up and chasing the ball when it bounces across the floor. Then they divide themselves into pairs—she with Marilyn, and Nancy with Peg—and play Spit for a while, using two decks of cards. Her parents and little brother are out doing errands and buying shoes for Teddy. Nick is down the street at his pal Jimmy Folks' house. Jimmy has a Bee Bee gun, so they're probably shooting bee bees against the back of the Folks' barn. She's twelve years old now; her parents don't worry about leaving her and her friends at home alone.

Eventually they get tired of cards and look for something else to do.

"You want to see something?" she says.

She leads them upstairs to her parents' bedroom, where she opens the bottom drawer of the dresser. They crouch on the floor to examine the contents as she takes out each item, one by one. "Sexy underwear," she says, stating the obvious.

They have never seen anything like it. Where does her mother get them? they wonder, but she doesn't know. They're excited, suppressing their giggles, though there's no one in the house to hear. Carefully, she returns the articles to the drawer. "I'll show you something else," she says.

They troop up the attic stairs to her bedroom.

She sits down on her bed. "Do you want to play boy and girl?"

"Okay." Marilyn nods. The others nod, too.

She pulls off her corduroy pants and then her underpants and lies down on her back. "This place between your legs feels good," she says, touching herself in that spot that she discovered a few months before and has been revisiting ever since. They move in for a closer look. She spreads the lips. "You move your finger around on it, and it feels good." She demonstrates, and as she does, the intense sensation starts coming on. It comes on even faster than usual because of her friends watching. She shuts her eyes. She gasps.

"Look!" says Peg.

She opens her eyes and looks down at where Peg is pointing. A little bubble has formed. It's because she is so damp there, she realizes. The others don't giggle. They stare intently, fascinated. It doesn't seem strange to her that what had seemed utterly private a few months before, has become shared knowledge.

"Do you want to try it?" she asks Peg. She gets up from the bed and Peg lies down after pulling off her pants and underwear. To the others she says, "Peg will be the girl and I'll be the boy." They watch her touching Peg and Peg writhing a little, her eyes tightly shut. When she's finished, the others take turns being the girl or the boy until everyone has had a chance at both roles.

Afterwards, they all go downstairs and eat the chocolate chip cookies that she and Teddy made that morning. Soon the rest of the family comes back and her friends go home.

Once her mother had told her that when she was grown up and married, the idea of sexual intercourse wouldn't seem yucky as it did when she was seven. What she and her friends have done is not sexual intercourse as her mother explained it, but for some reason, she connects the excitement she has discovered with what happens between women and men. She couldn't say how she knows this. But she is far from wanting an actual boy to play a part in her solitary pleasure. It's one thing to play this game with her friends. With a real boy it would be frightening and dangerous. She remembers the brother of her friend Karen Dungey and the upstairs bathroom and the tickets.

Hands Off

Her mother thinks it's wrong to hit a child for any reason.

"You've never spanked us," she observes. "Dad hasn't either."

"No we haven't," her mother says, "but one time I did something I'm ashamed of to this day."

"Oh what?"

"I threw Nick across the room into the sofa. The sofa *cushion*" she adds.

"You *did*?"

"Poor Nick. The nursery school used to report that sometimes he had temper tantrums and hit other children."

"Nick?" She's surprised. "But he's always quiet. He never fights."

"Yes. Well, thank goodness he grew out of it." Her mother's brow furrows and she shakes her head. "You couldn't blame him, poor little guy. When he was only a year old he had that surgery on his eyes. He had to be in the hospital for ten days, and parents could only visit for one hour twice a week! Can you imagine?"

She can't.

"And he wasn't allowed to lie down. They had him strapped in a sitting position the whole time. It was terrible."

"But why did you throw him into the sofa?"

Her mother closes her eyes and grimaces for a moment.

"You were about six months old and he was three. He was very jealous. I caught him hitting you, and I grabbed him up and threw him. It was just a reflex. He wasn't hurt, but, oh, what a thing to do. I felt awful afterwards."

She imagines Nick plunging into that old gray sofa, how surprised he must have been.

"That was the one and only time I've ever laid a hand on any of you. And Erich never has."

"Did your parents ever spank you?" Her friends report spanking as a common occurrence.

"Yes. Sometimes. But it just seems like bullying. A big grown-up hitting a little child."

How did she get so lucky, she wonders, to be born to such reasonable people?

Ted

When he is nine, Teddy announces that "Teddy" is a baby name and from now on he wants to be called "Ted." They all agree to the new name, but "Teddy" is hard for her to relinquish. "Teddy" is a boy with round innocent eyes and a button nose, a boy who has barely taken off his coonskin Davy Crockett hat since receiving it on his seventh birthday. "Ted" would be a tall boy with square shoulders and a breaking voice. Nonetheless, she complies with his request and for the most part succeeds in retiring the old name.

Ted Dog

Nick's friend Jimmy Folks is moving away and can't take his three-year-old neutered shepherd-collie mix. Nick is allowed to have him if he promises to feed and otherwise take care of his pet. Coincidentally, the dog's name is Ted. Now, when someone asks "Where's Ted?" the reply is "Ted Boy? Or Ted Dog?"

Unfortunately, Nick acquires Ted just weeks before the city passes a leash law, so he has to walk Ted several times a day, a chore he neglects more often than not. No one else is keen on the task either, especially since Ted Dog strains at his leash. Either he goes un-walked until he gets frantic, or someone opens the door and illegally lets him loose in the neighbors' back lot, from which he returns covered in burs and ticks. It doesn't occur to anyone that the simple solution is to train him to heel. She feels sorry for Ted Dog, but she is just as guilty as the rest.

Weather, Birds, and The Story of Fur

Back in the fall of 1957, when she's ten years old, she is assigned to write her first report. The subject is Weather. Her teacher has handed out a modest checklist of topics to cover, after which students can add something more if they like.

Her report is thirty-six pages long and includes a table of contents, twenty-one chapters (charts clipped from the newspaper; pictures she has drawn herself; a list of songs about the weather; two original short stories—"Trip to the Weather Station" and "John and the Weather"); several poems, both original and traditional; and a list of vocabulary she has learned from her research.

This is nothing compared to her fifty-six page report, "The Story of Fur," in the spring semester when she's eleven. She contacts Dowdell Furriers, the supplier of coats, capes and stoles to the local elite, and convinces them to send her one-inch swatches of Beaver, Bear, Caracal, Fox, Muskrat, Mink, Persian lamb, Pony, Rabbit, Raccoon, Skunk, Seal, Squirrel, and Wolf fur. These she glues to the pages she has illustrated with drawings of the animals along with descriptions of their habits. Samples from Badger, Chinchilla, Ermine, Lynx, Leopard, Marten, Mole, Nutria, Opossum, Sable, and Weasel are not forthcoming, but each gets an illustrated page anyway. For the final page she pastes in a letter to her mother from the furriers' headquarters congratulating her on qualifying for an exclusive Dowdell credit card.

By sixth grade, when she's twelve, she outdoes herself with a ninety-page report on Birds. Sketching their shapes in pencil and coloring them in with crayons, she draws each bird (thirty-five in all) perched in some part of its habitat. On every following page is a lengthy description of the bird's size, calls, habits, nest, food, and territory. There are general sections on such topics as Encouraging Birds around the Home, How High Do Birds Fly? etc. and at the end of the whole report eight pages of questions with clues, entitled "What Bird Am I?"

No one seems to think this is a little excessive, she, least of all. Once started on a project, she simply cannot stop.

Civilizations

She and Ted are sprawled in the top row of bleacher seats beneath immeasurable clusters of stars. It is 1958, and they're staring up at the Colorado sky while Nick and their parents sit down below in the front row, attending to a lecture about the cliff dwellings they've seen that day and the way of life at Mesa Verde in the ancient past.

"That star is moving!" she says.

"Which star? Where?"

She points. "There! There!"

Her brother says it's probably an airplane. But there's no flashing light. And it's very high. For at least a half hour they watch its almost undetectable progress across the sky. It's as if a star has decided to take off and go calling somewhere else in the universe but is in no particular hurry to get there.

"It's not a plane," she says. "It's a satellite."

"A satellite!" Ted is excited. "Which one?" Six satellites have been in orbit since 1950; three Russian and three American. "If it's Russian, there might be a dog up there!"

She imagines the trapped, frightened, probably sick dog. If people are so hot to go up in space, she thinks, they should go up there themselves and not inflict their obsession on powerless animals.

Before the satellite disappears down the edge of the Earth, she can't stand to watch anymore, thinking of that dog. She joins the rest of the family in time to learn that the Pueblo Indians left Mesa Verde at the end of the 13th century because of drought and overpopulation but, most of all, because of too much dependence on corn crops. It seems that, not only today but throughout history, people in charge keep doing the wrong thing.

II

Twelve

In that summer of her twelfth year, the tight foursome of friends starts to fall away without any official parting, like autumn leaves in successive gusts of wind.

Nancy's family moves to a new subdivision at the southern edge of the city in a different school district. Peg's family moves to a large white colonial house just on the south side of Governor Street, which is the acknowledged boundary separating Upper-Middle and Upper Class from Working and Middle Class. Living "south of Governor" is a code phrase for well-to-do.

She and Peg and Marilyn attend the same junior high school, but Peg and Marilyn are in another section of seventh grade, so she seldom sees them. Instead of recess, there are sports, which she dislikes and Peg doesn't.

Sometimes, though, she and Shirley Most, the girl next door who used to play all alone in her back yard, walk to and from school together. She's glad to have Shirley's company on that walk because now, for the first time, carloads of teen-aged boys on their way to the high school cruise slowly past, hanging out the car windows and yelling crude suggestions at them. She and Shirley look straight ahead and hurry along, relieved when they come in sight of the junior high school building. It's not just certain carloads of boys who do this. Almost any time there is more than one boy in a car it seems to happen. It's scary, and they start to walk home and to school by out-of-the-way routes, which takes longer, and they have to hurry from the building when school is over and get up earlier in the morning, but it's worth it.

Knacks and Lacks

She wishes she could throw a ball properly. When she tries, she can feel the puny effort in her arm and wrist. She does a little jump to give the throw more power, but the ball travels only a few yards before it plops to the ground. Nick criticizes her method and shows her how it's done when it's done right. When she tries once to imitate him and fails, they leave it at that. Some evenings and weekends her father and brothers spend an hour or more throwing and catching a ball. It never occurs to her to ask her father, or mother—who is athletic—or Nick or even her gym teacher to keep showing her until she gets it right and then follow up with prolonged practice. It doesn't occur to any of them to offer.

She assumes that there are some talents you're born with while there are others that you simply lack and always will. In her head she lists her natural gifts: singing on key and harmonizing, drawing, dancing, spelling, reading, memorizing, understanding and remembering difficult words, speaking articulately; in fact, anything to do with language (except writing well). At only six or seven years old, she could already entertain her family with a French accent and since then has gone on to doing German, Brooklyn, Southern and any other accents she's exposed to.

Things she cannot do: throw a ball properly or do anything athletic, fix mechanical things or understand how they work, construct three-dimensional objects. Oh, yes, and anything related to numbers. As often as she has called Marilyn and Peg and Nancy, the only telephone number she can remember is her own. And no matter how much she tries, she can't keep straight her father's and Marilyn's birthdays because one of them is April 15th and the other is April 17th but which is which?

Yes, numbers are the worst. They turn off her brain. That's why she had to cheat on an arithmetic quiz in third grade. She's heard that victims of accidents and crimes can't remember important details of the events because their brains are too shocked to take in the whole experience. That's how it is for her with numbers. The very sight of them on a page seems to numb her mind. Which must be why they're called *numb*ers. Well, she thinks, at least she can joke about it.

Relief

In Science class she starts to feel a dull ache in her gut and lower back. Always, when she feels unwell, it's an upper respiratory problem or a headache, never anything abdominal. On the one occasion she got a stomach flu she was able to will herself not to throw up; that's what a strong stomach she has. So this unfamiliar pain, which is getting more of her attention as the minutes go by, frightens her. Does she have appendicitis? Should they call an ambulance? Will she have to have surgery, stitches, shots?

After class she hurries to the restroom, thinking if she has a bowel movement maybe she'll feel better. When she pulls down her underwear to sit on the toilet, there it is, the evidence—a dark red stain. She takes a deep breath of relief, pulls her pants up and walks directly to the nurse's office.

"I think I'm having my first period," she says, and describes the blood on her underpants and the ache—"cramps," she remembers her mother calling them.

The nurse raises her eyebrows. "Well I'm impressed," she says.

"You're taking it in stride. Good for you! I'll call your mother to come and get you."

"Why does she need to come and get me?" she says. "It's just a period."

Her mother does come for her and takes her home to fix her up with all the paraphernalia. Before they leave the nurse's office, the nurse says, "I just want to congratulate you on how well you prepared Annie. I've never seen a girl so comfortable with it."

Well of *course* not, she thinks. How could other girls be comfortable with it if they didn't have a mother like hers? Her friends hadn't even heard of periods. She had to tell them all about it.

Outside the nurse's office she and her mother exchange complacent smiles.

Equalizer

It is quite clear to her that her mother will do whatever it takes to prevent sibling rivalry. At no time is this clearer than at Christmas. Christmas, being a secular event in their household, is all to do with the Christmas tree and presents. Mounds of gifts encircle and climb halfway up around the tree. The gifts are not especially big or expensive; there are just so many of them. Months' worth of tweaking for equality in price, number and value to each child is what accounts for this over-abundance of gifts—something like the reverse of what happens when you cut your own hair: trim a little too much on the left side and you have to even it out on the other, but then you cut a little too severely on the right, and you have to trim back the left side again, and so on. But in this case, think *adding* hair. Even at birthdays, her mother always has one present for the non-birthday siblings to be sure no one feels left out.

Now that she's old enough, she is told the reason for her mother's preoccupation with equal treatment. Her mother's father favored her over her sister, who as a result—she is certain—became mentally ill. Furthermore, her mother's father allowed nothing to be celebrated—no holidays, no birthdays, nothing at all. Her mother says that she vowed her own children would celebrate all occasions, significant or minor. So even when they're past the appropriate age, she sends her and her brothers out into the yard to find the colored eggs she has hidden. They carry baskets filled with chocolate rabbits and candy chicks, two of each per grown child.

Grammie

She has never seen much of her maternal grandparents, just a few days a year when they drive over from Evanston, Illinois. They're referred to as Grammie and Lowell, though why Lowell isn't called grandpa or granddad or some such traditional nickname she sometimes wonders but has never bothered to ask. Grammie almost never speaks, and when she does, it's in a shaky voice to match a constant tremor in her hands, which gives her handwriting a distinctively jagged appearance.

Grammie doesn't have Parkinson's Disease, her mother tells her. They're not sure what causes the tremor. Possibly anxiety, she adds, a bitter note in her voice.

Then one day, her mother packs to go to Evanston, telling the family that Grammie has committed suicide, having drowned herself in Lake Michigan a few blocks from their apartment. It's October. The water would have been cold. She was sixty-eight years old. She didn't know how to swim.

Their father drives her mother to Evanston and comes back the same day to look after her and her brothers.

During the few days her mother is away, she takes over her tasks with a great sense of responsibility. She plans meals, cooks, washes up and tidies, even vacuums and dusts, all the while wondering what her mother is feeling and thinking, how she would feel if her mother did something like this, though of course that would never happen.

She thinks about her grandfather Lowell, a stout, somewhat hearty man with a deep voice, who, at Christmas gives her and her brothers ten-dollar dime banks—one hundred dimes tucked into slots in a cardboard booklet. He did all the talking while Grammie sat in a corner or brought up the rear on walks, silent and wearing a mild, self-effacing smile.

Lowell

When her mother returns from the funeral, she thinks she hears her crying in their bedroom. Her father is inside behind the closed door, comforting her mother in a quiet voice.

"Is Mom okay?" she asks when he comes out.

"Yes, Annie, she's just very sad."

Later that day her mother emerges from their room, composed and smiling wanly.

"Thank you for taking charge, Annie," she says. "You really helped your Dad, and me."

She is proud of having stepped up and feels guilty for having been so lazy about helping her mother in the past. From now on, she promises herself, she'll do better.

A few days later, Lowell comes for a visit. Her mother is coldly courteous to him. They don't talk about Grammie or any possibility of his staying longer than the two days he has been invited for. When he leaves, she overhears her mother tell her father, "I can't bear to be in the same room with him."

Committed

It is the following summer. She and her mother scramble up a sand dune and sit at the top gazing at the lake and at Nick and Ted and her father having a swimming race toward a log floating some distance out.

"I wish we lived close to Lake Michigan," she says. "Did you love growing up three blocks from the beach?"

Her mother doesn't answer for a moment. She picks up a stick and draws a line back and forth in the sand with it. "I walked that beach for miles every day after school to avoid going home."

"What do you mean? Why?"

She sighs. "I never knew what kind of mood my father would be in."

"Lowell had bad moods?"

"He had a terrible temper."

She has never seen this in her grandfather. When he visits, he takes out his walking stick and leads the family on tramps in the woods, commenting jovially on the flora and fauna. "That's the female cardinal," he says. "You can tell by its drab color."

"What did he do?"

"Well ... I've repressed a lot about my childhood, but I remember he'd go into rages and shout and swear and slam things down at the dinner table. It was very scary."

"What was he mad about?"

Oh, just anything. You couldn't predict when he'd go off like that or what would set him off. Other times he'd be calm and pleasant."

"Did he hit you and Aunt Dot? Or Grammie?"

"Well ... I'm not sure. I seem to remember something that sounded like hitting behind the closed door of their bedroom. But as I say, my memory of childhood is so hazy. That could just have been my imagination."

She wonders but doesn't ask if this is why Grammie trembled all the time, and why she killed herself.

"When my sister and I were kids—I think I was about ten and Dot would have been around eight—Lowell was put in a kind of mental hospital for a few months."

"A mental hospital!"

"Well, I think it was a fancy sanitarium out in the country. I kind of remember Mom saying he played golf while he was there and lived in a cottage with some other men. It was only much later that she told me it was a mental hospital."

"Did he want to be there?"

"The way I understand it, his parents and my mother arranged to have him committed."

"What happened to make them do that?"

"I don't know. He must have done something very extreme."

"Is that when his law firm fired him?"

"Maybe. I don't think I knew much about it, even then."

Her mother hops up off the sand and says, "Let's get the others and have some lunch."

It's an intriguing mystery. She wants to learn more, but it seems there's nothing more to know since it's a mystery to her mother, too.

They catapult down the dune and land at the bottom, their bare feet burrowing into the sand.

"Guys! Lunch!" her mother calls, and that's the end of the subject.

South of Governor

That fall her parents prepare to sell their home and move into a three-story, four-bedroom, two-and-a-half-bath mock Tudor house a block south of Governor. They can afford the house only because it's in terrible shape and the price is very low for the neighborhood. Her parents have conceded the need for professional contractors to repair the roof and paint the exterior, but they will have to do the interior renovation themselves.

The house had been owned by an eccentric, elderly poet who died, leaving an ancient dismantled roll top desk in the basement and five hundred copies of his self-published poetry chapbook stacked in a corner of the attic. The rest of his belongings have been carted away by relatives. The poet lived out his whole adult life in the decaying house without ever making any improvements. Squirrels—at least it is hoped they are only squirrels—can be heard scurrying inside the attic walls.

For three months, they all spend every weekend laying out drop cloths, climbing ladders to scrape wallpaper, repairing dented and crumbling plaster and sanding the spackle by hand before painting, running a rented sander over the floors and re-varnishing them. When the renovation is finally complete, they have to thoroughly dust and deep clean. She and her brothers are more than sick of it and try to get out of the work with any excuse they can come up with. They are generally thwarted in these attempts.

On a Saturday in early January, movers bring over the large pieces of furniture, and everyone helps pack the smaller household items into their two-wheeled trailer, taking four trips. She will have her own second-floor bedroom with tall windows facing south and east, but she lingers for a few minutes in her old attic sanctuary, which looks small and dingy without her belongings in it. Still, she loved it there. Almost too late, she remembers to remove her diary from the hole in the wallboard.

There's no time to dawdle getting everything into the new house if they are to beat a predicted snow storm. By nine in the evening, all is safe inside and everyone sits exhausted and rather dazed among the boxes and jumbled furniture. Her mother locates paper plates and napkins and hands around potato chips, sour cream dip and apples. It will have to do until tomorrow when they have the energy to unpack the kitchen. At least their beds and bedding have been assembled.

They all go to their separate rooms. It's strange sleeping in this new house. A wind has come up and she lies awake for a while, listening to tree branches brushing against a window pane. But for some reason her usual insomnia in an unfamiliar place doesn't take hold. The wind soothes her. The room is on the back side of the house looking over a forest and ravine, making it very dark. For once, she sleeps through the night.

Welcome

Wakened by brilliant sunlight streaming between the blinds, she jumps out of bed and pulls the blinds up. The sky is an intense cornflower blue. Light pours into the room reflecting off the deep, blinding snow that bows the great oak and maple branches almost to breaking. These trees surround the house and climb down the slope into the ravine and up again on the other side. The ground that, yesterday, was covered with a drab clutter of brown leaves is now a pristine white blanket of diamonds capturing the sun.

She hears the household stirring. Soon they're all racing to find their boots and hats and mittens, forgetting breakfast in their eagerness to get outside.

The snow is knee deep and powdery. They fling themselves into it, frolic in it, push through it, grab the laden bushes and shake the snow onto each other's heads. Ted Dog leaps among the drifts. Into the ravine they all plunge, like puppies let loose. Not just she and her brothers, but her parents, too. Her mother is all in red—red hat, red scarf, red jacket and snow pants—her favorite color. Her father is wearing the watch cap and rough outdoor clothes from the ski trip in Germany he took with his brothers before the War.

Thus are they introduced to their new, old house. Here is a welcome that they had not anticipated.

The Joy of Cooking

Her mother had to teach herself how to cook when she got married because her own mother didn't know how. All the cooking in her household was done by her mother's mother, who banned her daughter and granddaughters from the kitchen.

Hence the mortification of her mother's first Thanksgiving at Opa's when she wanted so much to make a good impression on her glamorous new in-laws. She humiliated herself by putting the turkey in the oven un-thawed. It came out a lovely golden brown on the outside, but on the inside ...

After that horrible episode, her mother turned to the simple, reliable recipes in her *Better Homes and Gardens Cookbook* and *The Joy of Cooking*.

Having heard the story of her mother's mistake, she set out at a young age to acquire the basics. Her mother taught her how to bake potatoes, crack an egg without breaking the yoke, fry crisp bacon. She learned how to measure with teaspoons, tablespoons and measuring cups and how to follow a recipe.

Her motivation is maintained now by her addiction to sweets. Since moving to the new house, she and Teddy sometimes bake a double batch of Toll House chocolate chip cookies and take them up to the attic still warm in a big bowl. There they sprawl on the dilapidated gray sofa and consume all the cookies in one sitting while watching comedies on the ash blond TV console. Her mother dislikes both television programs and the television itself, and has banished the set to the third floor so she doesn't have to look at it. There in the attic, she and Teddy sit with the giant bowl of cookies between them—like the TV set, out of sight, out of mind.

Baby Grand

Their Tudor-style house sits at the highest point of a quiet, dead-end street. Encircled by lofty hundred-year-old trees, it looks almost medieval. Her mother is proud of its leaded casement and bay windows, steep gable, wood shingles, and contrasting dark brown half-timbering against the new bright white paint. So superior to the lowly bungalow of her childhood.

Her mother longs for a grand piano to do justice to their spacious high-ceilinged living room. Her father agrees to splurge on a used baby grand from the local music store. There is not a scratch on its surface or on the matching wooden piano bench. While her mother may let other house cleaning tasks ride, she religiously dusts and polishes her gleaming black piano.

There is almost no time to play, but occasionally in the evening her mother steals a few minutes. The sounds of those halting sonatinas and minuets once again make their way up the staircase as she lies in bed trying to sleep.

The Sylvan

For as long as she can remember, her family has visited The Sylvan Museum of Modern Art, a long, low-slung limestone building set solidly at the highest rise in Sylvan Park. The best part of the museum is the reflecting pool. She and Ted run through the galleries to push the heavy door open onto the courtyard where a larger than life-size bronze sculpture of Pegasus flies at a tilt, its great wings spread and just one hoof touching the support in the middle of the pool. A statue of a naked man, arms outstretched to the sky, appears to have leapt from the horse and is flying upward, barely attached to the horse's wing by one toe.

How the sculptor achieved this balance always baffles her. It looks as if she could wade into the pool and with one finger push the whole thing over. Copper pennies lying at the bottom of the water gleam in the sunshine. She and Ted always throw in pennies of their own and make wishes.

Just south of the art museum there is a maze-like rose garden with a sundial in the middle and little plaques everywhere telling the names of the exotic breeds of roses. She and Ted like to run around the walkways to see who can reach the sundial and touch it first. Past the rose garden, the grassy park proceeds under the shade of huge oak trees down a long slope to a pond at the bottom. They have loved this park for years and now it is practically in their own backyard.

Beyond the park is a wood entered by a secret path. Their favorite game in the woods is Chased by the Killer. They walk carefully and vigilantly, startling at noises and shushing each other with fingers to lips whenever either of them snaps a twig or rustles leaves. The trail meanders for about a mile before it comes out on a bluff overlooking the waterworks and the airport.

When they return and plunge down through the ravine behind their house, they feel almost as elated as if they have really thwarted a killer.

Sickle

She is studying for an exam over the first three chapters in her seventh grade American history textbook, a fat tome of four hundred and some pages. This task bears no resemblance to the little quizzes over vocabulary words or arithmetic problems she took in grade school. This test requires intensive memorizing if she's to answer correctly not only the multiple choice questions but two among four essay questions.

Here her dramatics class experience comes in handy—she had become adept at learning lines—but now she has to concentrate in a different way. With no cues to prompt her, she must create her own mnemonic devices and decide which facts are important.

She is slouched on the wing chair in the den, copying sentences from her textbook into the notebook on her lap and thinking she has written almost as much in the notebook as there is in the text. She'll be at it forever at this rate. How can she pick and choose? How can she summarize? The test is in two days.

And then she begins to notice a glare blotting out a letter or word here or there, similar to the afterimage when she has looked too long at a bright light. She blinks several times trying to focus. The glare jumps around on the page. When she shuts her eyes to let them adjust, she sees what's blocking her vision. Glittering light in the shape of a sickle or scythe has formed behind her eyelids on the right side of her visual field. As she keeps her eyes closed the sickle gets bigger, and when she opens them, the right-hand page of the book is missing.

She moves her eyes around the room. Anything she tries to look at directly, disappears. It's like the scene in *Through the Looking Glass* when Alice finds herself in a shop where "Whenever she looked hard at any shelf, to make out exactly what it had on it, that particular shelf was always quite empty."

Her studying forgotten, she sits with eyes closed and watches the glittering image pulsate. This strange phenomenon doesn't trouble her; she is fascinated and wonders what could be the cause. After about fifteen minutes the glittering image starts to fade. After another five minutes, it's gone. With its departure a headache begins to come on, located at the base of her skull on the left side. Before long the headache has traveled to her temple and from there to the inside corner of her left eye. It is at this point that her parents return from an evening out.

"Mom!" she says. "The strangest thing happened." As she describes the event, her mother sets down her purse and stares.

"The exact same thing used to happen to me when I was a teenager!" she says. "It's a migraine aura. With mine, I also had aphasia. I'd know what I wanted to say, but the words would come out nonsense." Here is yet another installment in her mother's intriguing background story. "As I got older, the migraines tapered off and finally went away. It's nothing to worry about," she adds.

With sleep, the headache is gone by morning. This is by no means, however, the last of her acquaintanceship with the sickle.

Girl's Job 2

Even at twelve, Nick used to earn good money mowing lawns, delivering newspapers, and shoveling snow. At thirteen her only option is babysitting for twenty-five cents an hour.

At her first babysitting job, she is responsible for watching a five-month-old infant while the parents attend a dinner. They are clearly reluctant to leave the baby, but the dinner is important and their regular sitter, an older woman, is unavailable. They've asked her because they are friends of her parents and believe a Lang daughter will be reliable and competent.

She is shown the bottled formula in the fridge and the saucepan for heating it up and how to test the temperature. They point out the diapers, safety pins, powder and wash cloths in the nursery and remind her to keep the baby covered. After they've gone, she huddles by the crib, praying the infant will sleep until they come home.

All is peaceful. She sits in a rocking chair near the crib for a while before tiptoeing out of the room, leaving the door open. That's when the baby starts to cry and then to scream. She runs in. Does he need changing? She's scared to lift him out of the crib for fear of dropping him; her arms are skinny and he's a hefty baby. When she attempts it, he screams louder, red-faced, furious and kicking. She puts him back down.

But if he needs changing, there is no getting around the fact that she is going to have to pick him up and lay him on the changing table, hold him in place with one hand while managing the wash cloths, powder, diapers and pins (and now she can't remember where the dirty diaper is supposed to go).

Just in time before picking him up, she remembers to run to the bathroom first and dampen a wash cloth. When she finally does take him from the crib, still screaming, she discovers that he doesn't need changing after all. So. He must want to be fed.

She lays him down again and hurries to the kitchen to warm the bottle. She takes the formula from the refrigerator, but the stove is an ultra-modern electric one, and she isn't sure how to turn it on or adjust the temperature of the burner.

His screams aren't so piercing now, and she thinks maybe she can calm him down by walking back and forth with him as they do in the movies. She returns to the nursery, lifts him under his armpits and holds him awkwardly, the way an armload of firewood might be carried. She forgets to wrap him in the blanket. His head flops, and she slides a hand under it.

For some time, she walks him around the house this way. He's gone from screaming now to fussing, whimpering and squirming. Her arms are getting tired.

The parents are now due home in twenty minutes. She feels this will be the longest twenty minutes of her life. How, she wonders, do parents do this sort of thing for weeks, months, years on end? In this big, lavish, south-of-Governor house, she feels claustrophobic.

When the front door finally opens, the baby startles and as if on cue begins to scream again. The mother swiftly takes him and heads for the nursery. The father pays the seventy-five cents they owe her, bundles her into the car and drives her home. They don't call for her services again, which is both a humiliation and a relief.

Girl's Job 3

The other memorable babysitting job is for the family across the street—the Bosworthys, who have three boys, seven, eight and ten. The Bosworthy boys are notorious in the neighborhood.

Prior to babysitting them, her most recent experience of these boys is an incident one evening at a neighborhood party. She and two little girls are sitting on a screened porch when they discover a magnificent Luna moth clinging to the ceiling next to a light fixture, its pale green wings spread wide to show four colorful eyespots and two long, trailing tails. Its fat yellow antennae look like ferns. She and the girls gaze up at the moth for some minutes, enraptured. It's like a creature out of a fairy tale.

"I hope it won't fly into that light," says one of the little girls. "Moths like to fly at lights. It might get burned."

"We could turn the light off," she says.

"But then we won't see it," says the other little girl. They sit for a while, gazing ceiling-ward and pondering this moral dilemma.

Just then the three Bosworthy boys push open the door. Immediately they notice the direction of the girls' gaze. They look up, see the moth, and without a moment's hesitation start flinging things at it—a plastic cup, a squirt gun, whatever is handy. Fortunately the ceiling is quite high and their aim isn't very good.

"Don't do that!" she says. "You'll kill it!"

But of course that is the point.

When she shows up at seven-thirty on a Saturday night to babysit, the Bosworthy boys have already been dressed for bed. They're allowed to stay up until nine o'clock since it's a week-end and can have one snack each.

As soon as the parents are out the front door, the older boy—Marvin—leaves by the back door, the younger two close behind. She calls them to come in, but it's too late. They've run into the yard where Marvin picks up some coiled clothesline, wraps it around his brothers' waists, and holds the slack ends. They gallop around the muddy yard in their footie pajamas and pay no attention to her shouted commands.

She remembers the snacks and takes the packages from a top shelf. They are to have one Hostess Twinkie each, plus one for her. At the back door she waves the packages in the air. "Twinkies!" she calls. Marvin drops the reins and the little boys shrug off the ropes. They all run into the kitchen, leaving muddy prints on the linoleum. The bottoms of their footies are filthy. How is she going to explain this?

Rather than eating the snacks, the boys stuff them whole into their mouths and have an unintelligible conversation, spitting out bits of Twinkie at each other and then licking the bits off the counter, imitating dogs.

In the bathroom, instead of washing their sticky hands and faces, they direct sprays of water at each other by taking turns pressing fingers to the faucet opening. At least they are taking turns, that's something.

She finally succeeds in herding them into their room by nine-thirty, but when she looks in, having heard what sounds like the reverb of a bass drum on a car radio, Marvin has put the two little ones under their bed while he jumps on it. When she tells him to stop, he doesn't even look at her. Not only has she no authority with these boys, they completely ignore her as if she's not actually there.

When the Bosworthys return at ten-thirty, they don't seem surprised to find the boys coming out of their room with muddy feet. Mr. Bosworthy gives her a twenty-five cent tip on top of her fee before sending her back across the street to her house. At home she realizes that she can never have children because there would be a fifty-fifty chance of her having boys.

Girl's Job 4

Since she can't bring herself to take on any more babysitting jobs, she tries to think how else she can earn money, and hits on the idea of taking in ironing.

She rather likes ironing. For a couple of years now she has ironed her own clothes and sometimes helped her mother with the family ironing. Each step is easy, soothing, and almost contemplative. The curved handle of the iron with its finger grooves fits her hand perfectly and the iron itself feels heavy and substantial.

She fills the oversized salt shaker with water, sprinkles the garments and rolls them into sausage shapes to dampen them thoroughly, then turns the dial to the cotton setting. She's always impressed at how fast it heats up.

The best part is gliding the iron over the fabric and watching it make a perfectly smooth path through the wrinkles. She starts with the collar and the yoke, then the sleeves, then the right side, back, and left side, and if it's a dress, saves the skirt for last, carefully sliding the point of the iron into the gathers. How satisfying it is to hang up the shirts and blouses and skirts and dresses all crisp and refreshed as if new from the store.

She puts the word out in the neighborhood that she will take in ironing at fifteen cents per garment and right away is asked by Mrs. Milsap down the street to do her husband's shirts. She collects the pile of freshly laundered shirts with a bunch of hangers and a bottle of spray starch. Mrs. Milsap likes her husband's collars stiff. All the shirts are white or pale blue oxford cloth and big, Mr. Milsap being a large man.

It's quite a job. There are ten shirts in all. After shirt number six she takes a break when her wrist and elbow begin to ache a little. She flaps her arm and hand around for a minute or so before returning to the job. On shirt number seven, to save her muscles the exertion, instead of pressing down on the iron, she lets it sit on the collar for a few seconds, and when she lifts it, there is a large triangular scorch right in front.

She stares at it, horrified. She has ruined the expensive shirt. There's no way to undo this mistake. The scorch can't be washed away. It can't be disguised. There it is with its rusty glare, accusing her of carelessness and incompetence. How is she going to face Mrs. Milsap?

And now she has to finish ironing the last three shirts as well as this one. She approaches each shirt with short swipes of the iron, afraid to linger on any one area. It takes her twice as long as before and when she finishes, the ache in her wrist and elbow has spread to her shoulder. She turns off the iron and contemplates the ten shirts hanging from the pole in her closet.

What she ought to do, what she *must* do is bring the shirts back to Mrs. Milsap and confess to having ruined one and offer to pay for it. Her parents would lend her the money and she could repay them a little at a time out of her allowance. But it's not the money that daunts her, it's the shame.

If she carries the shirts pressed together on their hangers, the scorch will be hidden until Mrs. Milsap hangs them in her husband's closet. By then she can be back at home and won't have to see the look on the woman's face when she sees the ugly scorch.

That is what she does. She walks down the street, knocks on the door and hands over the shirts. "Oh thank you, Annie. This saves me a lot of time!" says Mrs. Milsap. She starts to walk away, but Mrs. Milsap says, "Wait a minute," and gets her purse, takes out a dollar fifty and puts it into her hand. "Here you are," she says, "and a little something for a tip."

How can she take the dollar fifty and a tip when she owes eight or nine dollars for the shirt? But if she doesn't take it, she'll have to explain why. She murmurs her thanks and walks back down the street.

For two weeks when the phone rings, she braces herself for the angry, disappointed, disillusioned voice of the woman, calling to chastise her or worse, to tell her mother. The call doesn't come. The best case is that Mrs. Milsap has assumed she didn't notice that she had scorched the shirt, and thought of her as careless rather than dishonest.

She is not asked to iron Mr. Milsap's shirts again, nor does she get any other ironing requests. She imagines the word in the neighborhood has spread that she scorches clothes and doesn't own up to it.

How she envies Nick! It would be so much less harrowing to make money mowing lawns or shoveling snow.

Homemaking

Girls take Homemaking. Boys take Shop. The boys learn how to use electric drills and saws, clamps and wrenches, screw drivers and levels. They learn how to build things. Girls learn how to use a sewing machine to run a straight seam in order to make a gathered hostess apron with pockets. They learn how to bake snickerdoodles and pineapple upside down cake. She doesn't know how many hostess aprons she'll want to make in her lifetime and by seventh grade she has already been taught at home how to pre-heat an oven, follow easy recipes, and bake cookies. Although Homemaking is pretty much a waste of time, at least they get to eat the sweets that their teacher hasn't sent down to the Shop boys.

Privacy

Her parents usually knock on a closed bedroom door, but this time her father, sent to call her to dinner, absent-mindedly opens her door and catches her in the act of passionately kissing the oversized teddy bear she won at Riverside Amusement Park. With a polite "Excuse me," he withdraws and gently closes the door behind him.

Time Out

For his birthday, Nick has, seemingly out of the blue, asked for a drum set. He never asks for much, so even though it's expensive and will up the ante for her and Ted's birthdays, her parents buy it for him, the whole kit—bass and snare drums, tom, cymbal, brushes, sticks, stands, a pedal and a stool. It takes up most of the open space in his room. She and Ted aren't allowed to touch it.

With his allowance he has been collecting jazz record albums—the Bill Evans trio, Dave Brubeck Quartet, Oscar Peterson, Art Tatum—and now he practices for hours, playing along with and imitating Art Blakey and Joe Morello on drums. Outside his closed door, the family hears him becoming more and more adept and then very, very good.

Where did this talent come from? Her mother is fond of classical music and practices when she can, but she remains heavy-handed on the piano, with frequent starts and stops and misplayed notes.

Having picked up her mother's tendency to psychologize, she wonders if Nick's drumming is motivated by anger at the teasing his glasses let him in for throughout his childhood. But as she listens to him outside his bedroom door, it becomes obvious that good drumming requires subtlety and discipline. He's not just banging away.

And now, at sixteen, he looks cool in his horn-rimmed glasses, a little like Dave Brubeck or Paul Desmond on the back cover of *Time Out*.

New Friend

A year after they move to the new house she makes friends with a girl one year younger who lives on her street. Mary-Claire Byrne attends Holy Cross Academy and gets to wear a uniform to school—white blouse, forest green tie, pleated skirt, and a navy blazer with the Academy's insignia on the lapel. She has two of these outfits, so she never has to stand at her closet door unable to make up her mind what to wear to school.

Mary-Claire's accounts of life at the Academy fascinate and amuse her. Sister Mary Joseph hides beef jerky under her apron; Father Aaron falls asleep when he takes confession; practically every girl's first name is Mary; and there are too many Theresas to keep track of.

The Academy girls attend functions with the boys of St. Thomas Aquinas High School, and Mary-Claire has crushes on a number of them. She herself has a crush on Mary-Claire's older brother Clyde Jr., who is Nick's age, handsome and athletic, modest and a bit shy.

After school, Mary-Claire will come over and they'll throw balls or sticks into the ravine for Ted Dog to fetch. Or if the weather is bad, they stay inside and sing along with recordings of Broadway musicals—especially *West Side Story* (her favorite) and *South Pacific* (Mary-Claire's)—to which they have learned every word of every song ("When you're a Jet, you're a Jet all the way, from your first cigarette to your last dying day ..." "I'm gonna wash that man right out of my hair and send him on his way ...").

Under the influence of *South Pacific* and the fact that her father was a Navy captain in World War II, Mary-Claire has made up her mind that after high school she'll get a nursing degree and become a Navy nurse. She imagines herself on the deck of an aircraft carrier—in a crisp form-fitting uniform with a starched cap atop her black wavy hair—keeping her chastity until marriage while a ship full of sailors and pilots lusts after her.

Mary-Claire is a cheerful, fun companion. When she teases, she does it in baby talk. She's taking biology this year and has learned about flagelli and bacilli, words she finds hilarious. "Oh Annie, you big ba-*silly*, you," she lisps.

They don't often hang out at Mary-Claire's house. Her father, Captain Clyde E. Byrne, Sr., US Navy, retired, is in a wheelchair at home, very gradually dying of multiple sclerosis.

Affection

In the Byrne's living room, where Clyde Sr. sits in his wheelchair, it seems the curtain sheers are always drawn shut, letting in only a dim, washed-out light. As she and Mary-Claire pass through on their way to the kitchen, her friend never fails to bend down and give her father a hug, a heartfelt "I love you, Poppy," and loud smootchy kisses. He kisses her back and returns the embrace, to the extent that he can move his arm.

Mary-Claire never finds her mother in the kitchen without saying "I love you, Mommy" and trying to kiss her cheek. Mrs. Byrne invariably presses her lips together and turns her head as if to avoid an overexuberant, face-licking dog. "All right. All right," she says impatiently.

She wonders why Mrs. Byrne withholds the hugs and kisses Mary-Claire craves. If she's bitter about her husband's illness, if she feels cheated, why take it out on her exceptionally loveable daughter? She figures it's a psychological enigma that Mrs. Byrne herself may not have the answer to.

Her own parents are reasonably affectionate with her and her brothers and with each other—a peck on the cheek, arm around a shoulder, pat on the knee, tousling of hair. No one says "I love you," though. They would all consider it embarrassing, unnecessary and forced. Anyway, in her family, isn't the unspoken sentiment obvious? No one turns away. No one says "All right. All right."

Evangeline

Mrs. Hawkins, her eighth grade English teacher, announces that every Friday until the Christmas break she will, for a treat, start class by reading from a beautiful and famous narrative poem by the American poet Henry Wadsworth Longfellow.

She and her classmates take this news with a degree of complacence, for already Mrs. Hawkins has established herself as a kind and trustworthy teacher who would not subject them to anything downright insufferable.

"Now this is a very personal story," says Mrs. Hawkins, "about a girl and boy back in the eighteenth century who love each other deeply but are separated when the British burn their village and force them and their families and neighbors out of the land where they were born. The people were called Acadians, and here is a picture of the land of Acadia." She holds up a print of a painting. "It's called 'The Pastoral State' by the painter Thomas Cole, and it shows the idyllic homeland they had to leave. Please pass it around."

They all take a look at the luminous painting, with its mountain peaks in the background wreathed in clouds, a blue inlet below and a shepherd herding sunlit white sheep while a young couple strolls along a woodland path under huge ancient trees. Mrs. Hawkins says, "You can see what a great loss it must have been to be exiled from this lovely homeland where—".

She raises her hand. She has quickly learned that it's okay to interrupt Mrs. Hawkins with a question.

"Yes, Annie?"

"But why did the British make them leave?" she asks.

The teacher explains that the English and French were at war, and the Acadians, whose ancestors came from France, were living on valuable and strategic land. The lovers, Evangeline and Gabriel, are forced onto different boats headed to different parts of America. For many years they search and search to find each other.

By now, in eighth grade, she and most of her classmates have discovered what it is to long for someone out of reach. They settle in for the first ten-minute installment of *Evangeline*.

The teacher begins.

"'*This is the forest primeval—, but where are the hearts that beneath it,*

Leaped like the roe, when he hears in the woodland the voice of the huntsman?
Where is the thatch-roofed village, the home of Acadian farmers?...
Waste are those pleasant farms, and the farmers forever departed!
Scattered like dust and leaves, when the mighty blasts of October
Seize them, and whirl them aloft, and sprinkle them far o'er the ocean...'"

When she comes to "'*The murmuring pines and hemlocks... stand like harpers hoar, with beards that rest on their bosoms...*,'" there is scattered snickering by some boys, but by the time she reaches "'*... There, in his feathered seraglio... strutted the lordly turkey, and crowed the cock...*'" they snicker no more. No one fidgets or teases or yawns.

Maybe their rapt attention is due to the hypnotic power of the wave-like dactylic hexameter intoned in Mrs. Hawkins' straightforward Midwestern voice, not embarrassingly impassioned but so clearly loving the material. Whatever it is, all the students—girls and boys—lean forward on their elbows, eyes front, ears soaking up the archaic words and images.

For eighteen Fridays they follow Evangeline and Gabriel up and down the bayous, forests, mountains and prairies of America as, unbeknownst to the seeking lovers, they miss each other by days or hours. Mrs. Hawkins prefaces each reading with a few words of explanation. ("Remember last week when Evangeline found Gabriel's father, Basil the blacksmith, and discovered that Gabriel was only a five-days' ride ahead? Well, today we're going to see what happens when Evangeline and Basil ride after him together.")

On the nineteenth and final Friday, Evangeline is now an old woman caring for the mortally ill in an almshouse "'*moistening the feverish lip, and the aching brow....*'" There she recognizes the dying Gabriel—"'*Gabriel! O my beloved*'" she whispers. Vainly he strives to rise and she kisses his lips.

*"Sweet was the light of his eyes; but it suddenly sank into darkness,
As when a lamp is blown out by a gust of wind at a casement."*

Her chin is trembling and she keeps her eyes on the teacher, but from all around the classroom she can hear subdued sobs. With a glance to left and right, she sees tears in the eyes of both boys and girls. Mrs. Hawkins quietly hands out sheets of paper and asks them to write whatever they would like about the poem *Evangeline*.

Blinking the tears out of her eyes, she bends over the task and begins to write.

Medicine

She is, as usual, miserable with an upper respiratory infection—the difficulty swallowing, the racking cough that makes sleep impossible, the fever. Also as usual, she's restless and wakeful in bed. Maybe when she was very young she slept well, but she doesn't remember it. The bed itself is a kind of adversary.

Their pleasant, efficient pediatrician Dr. Pollack makes a house call. He looks in her throat, listens to her chest and her cough. She's afraid he'll give her a shot. Instead he leaves a bottle of cough medicine. It's a bit strong, he says. It contains codeine, and they should be sure she takes it only as prescribed.

Within twenty minutes of taking the medicine, her body and the bed are merging with each other. She is a cloud in a soft summer sky, a cat stretched out on a sun-drenched carpet, a piece of flotsam floating on a placid lake. Remotely, she can feel that her throat still scratches and it aches to swallow, but these are just sensations, interesting but not disturbing, and her cough has subsided.

She lies dreamily sunk into the bed. For several hours her contentment is eternal, though she suspects it will only be temporary. It's a revelation that a drug can lift her out of her burdensome body into a quietly joyful realm like the heaven that Christians are always claiming for themselves. Later, when she is no longer taking the medicine, it's still reassuring to know that a chemical can bring relief if things ever get unbearable.

Slouch

Her mother, always loathe to say anything critical about her physical appearance and just as reluctant to nag, doesn't mention it. If only her mother had made a game of challenging her to walk around the house balancing a book on her head, maybe it would have offset the awful posture she developed in childhood from so much reading.

She walks around unaware until she sees it in photos of herself. In grade school, the nurse once told her, "Annie, you should stand up straight like your mother. She has such beautiful posture. Don't you want to look like her?" Her mother belonged to a dance group during the two years she attended college before marriage. Sometimes when an especially rhythmic tune comes on the radio, her mother snaps her fingers or makes graceful arm and hand gestures, ticking off the beats with her tongue—tch ... tch ... tch.

Yes, who wouldn't want to have beautiful posture like her mother's? But by now, in junior high, her slouch has settled in and made itself permanently at home.

DJ

Although she herself is fourteen, teenagers as a group get on her nerves. She disdains what she thinks of as the teenage accent—the rushed phrases and gushing, exaggerated emphases in the speech of girls in her class like Mary Woods and Cathy Carpenter—difficult to describe but easy to privately mimic.

And she dislikes the music, can't understand how anyone would swoon over these greasy-looking rock and roll stars. Elvis Presley, Frankie Avalon, Ricky Nelson, Paul Anka. She doesn't listen to them on the radio or watch them on television or buy their records. The music seeps in anyway. It's impossible not to know every tune and all the lyrics, which play like advertising jingles in her head. Everyone she knows worships the disc jockeys who play these songs as if they contributed something worthwhile to the world.

At school it's announced that a DJ from a local radio station will come to the Friday afternoon assembly to answer questions. How stupid, she thinks, and then comes up with an inspiration—the perfect question, simple, provocative, and sophisticated. No one else will think to ask it.

The DJ stands on a riser, a microphone in hand. Kids crowd in close, hoping to get an autograph before he leaves. She has made sure to get a place at the front and raises her hand high among the other frantically waving hands. She holds it in the air persistently as the minutes pass and other questions are answered. At last, he turns to her. Her arm is practically in his face. Pointing to her armpit, he says into the microphone in his smooth, bass DJ voice, "Do you use Ban?"

The instant uproarious laughter drowns out her question, which she murmurs automatically, helplessly, and which no one hears: "Do you take payola?"

As he turns to someone else, she eases her way out of the crowd, afraid to catch anyone's eye, her cheeks burning. How will she face her classmates on Monday after this implication that her armpits stink? And why did she imagine they would care about the payola scandal or even have heard of it? All they care about, she thinks bitterly, is the stupid music, whether DJs are bribed to play it or not.

Stash

Everything about her reserved older brother intrigues her and on the rare occasions when the rest of the family is gone from the house for a reliable length of time, she goes into Nick's room and snoops.

When he was twelve, he found a dead bird—a Killdeer—lying in the grass without a blemish as if it had simply lain down and died. It's a beautiful brown and white amber-eyed bird, decorated on the chest with two bright black bands. Never having shown a particular interest in birds, Nick, nevertheless, convinces their parents to have it stuffed and mounted. It stands as if alive and just about to fly off the top of his desk.

He has a microscope, which he has allowed her and Ted to look into under his strict supervision. On one slide, for their edification he has placed a hair from his head. Under the microscope it looks as thick as a wire. On another slide a perfectly round dome of his spit reflects the colors of the rainbow.

Stepping carefully around his drum set now, she peeks through the open door of his closet and is surprised to find a heavy metal tool box on the floor. Nick doesn't fix things or even use tools as far as she knows. That's more Ted's domain. He's the handy one, even at eleven.

The tool box is padlocked, which only increases her curiosity. It takes a minute to find the key in Nick's desk drawer, open the box and discover the magazines. She has glimpsed such magazines at newsstands but always averts her eyes to keep anyone from thinking she is looking. Now she is free to look.

Leafing through one after another, she becomes more and more stimulated. Something about the exposure of the women's bodies, the idea that they exist to be watched by lustful men is tremendously exciting. Though in real life such exposure would terrify and traumatize her, in the fantasy world of the magazines she gets to identify with the women's vulnerability. She can imagine her own body displayed in erotic poses.

Unlike the breasts of these colossally busty women, her own breasts are still budding and small, but they are already exquisitely sensitive to her touch. She takes the magazines to her bedroom, careful to keep them in the order in which she found them, and spends an hour in their company before putting them back and returning the key to the drawer. Every month or so when there's an opportunity, she revisits them.

Gallia est omnis divisa in partes tres

Miss Titus, the Latin teacher, has petit mal seizures. She has not warned her students of this; she doesn't need to because it's common knowledge. Everyone knows that she will go blank now and then. Her pauses in the proceedings become a quite ordinary experience. The students sit quietly and wait them out. Most of her classmates can take Miss Titus or leave her, but she likes the teacher for the simple reason that she likes Latin.

In the first semester they are given a long list of prefixes, suffixes and roots, from which the logic of many English words can be extracted: interruption from *inter* (between) *rup* (break) *tion* (noun form). What fun!

And the grammar. Now the real fun begins: teasing out the case functions of word endings, the gender endings of the various declensions, the verb conjugations, subject-verb and noun-adjective agreement. It's better than Scrabble or crossword puzzles.

Three whole semesters of word games, including the game of translation: *Gallia est omnis divisa in partes tres,* Julius Caesar apparently having written in nice simple sentences suitable for ninth and tenth graders.

In subsequent semesters she takes French, and many years later, Spanish. With her background in Latin, she finds these romance languages a piece of cake. English, too, of course.

Skin Deep

It begins sometime during her twelfth year or maybe before that, but it starts with hair and gains momentum in junior high. In the carefree days of childhood she wore her hair in thin braids ending in sparse, wispy strands and thought nothing of it. Yes, she envied her friend Marilyn's wavy hair and the blonde tendrils that framed her delicate features. But in those days, Marilyn and Peg and Nancy and even Teddy looked on her as a kind of leader, the one who made things happen, the one who thought things up. Her physical appearance didn't enter into it.

Now she hates her thin, straight hair. A pony tail pulls it away from her face, so at least she doesn't have to see it in the mirror. But that only makes her coloring, or lack of it, more prominent. How pale and ghostlike she is! And the circles under her eyes! From a photograph of herself as a baby, she sees that she was born with these circles as well as an extremely high forehead like a man's with a receding hairline ("a *five* head" she describes it bitterly to her father, from whom it has been inherited). She hides it with bangs.

And then there are the emaciated calves (another Lang inheritance). No meat on the bones at all! Yes, she has pretty eyes—deep set, big and bright blue like those of all her relatives on both sides. But that's it. Everything else is unacceptable.

In the summer before seventh grade, Ted sees her in a bathing suit for the first time since the last summer. "What happened to your *butt*?" he says, giggling. Her mother rushes in with typical reassurance. "Annie has a very *nice* butt!" When she's alone at the long bathroom mirror, she holds up a hand mirror to look at her bottom. Since her hips are no longer the skinny, straight hips of a little girl, her bottom has widened, too, and flattened. It's a *terrible* butt. She is appalled by it. She'd had no idea.

This is when the compensatory strategies begin. First, she gets her mother to give her a home permanent and assists it with nightly pin curls. The perm lasts for about a month in her fine straight hair before it goes flat and frizzy. Later she will endure the agony of trying to sleep wearing large plastic rollers, which will involve an elaborate stomach-lying position, re-arrangement of pillows throughout the night, and the trick of propping her forehead with her hands. Not the wisest strategy for an insomniac or for anyone seeking to minimize circles under the eyes. But what choice has she? Good hair is paramount.

She cannot disguise her skeletal calves if she is to wear the skirts mandated for girls by the school authorities (in any case slacks shout, "See how unshapely my bottom is?"). She wears only the daintiest of ballet flats to de-emphasize the skinny calves.

As soon as she's fourteen and her mother allows it, she uses a touch of rouge on her pallid cheeks, and applies eye liner to enhance her one good feature. Her mother's eyelash curler gives the illusion of thickness for the few minutes before her lashes droop. From the first time she sees herself in make-up, she is no longer willing to venture out in public without it. "I'd look like George Washington!" she hyperbolizes.

Her mother's fondest wish is for her to like her body. She never tires of complimenting her long legs, her eyes, the reddish highlights in her hair. With all these reassurances and her mother's contradictory disparagement of her own body, it's not lost on her that a woman's looks are crucial. The point of it is to please men; thus, her mother wears make-up and sexy underwear to bed. And what does the *man* have to do? Lay his crew-cut head comfortably on the pillow and sleep in baggy undershorts (she's seen her father on the way to the bathroom in the morning). She carries out women's beauty edicts laboriously but is profoundly resentful at the double standard.

Drowned Rat

She doesn't see much of Marilyn or Peg anymore, so it's a surprise when Peg invites her to swim at the Arcadia Golf and Country Club pool.

She's heard her parents criticize the Arcadia Club for its unwritten prohibition against membership by Blacks and Jews. Arcadia's racism and anti-Semitism is well-known.

Her parents boycott Arcadia on principle, but they might not have joined anyway because the club's annual fee is exorbitant. Her parents themselves are socially acquainted with only two Black people—the city's first and only Black municipal judge and his wife—but probably half of their close friends and associates are Jews: university faculty and colleagues, members of various boards, the psychiatrists and psychologists her mother has gotten to know from her part-time psychological testing job at the hospital, the parents of Nick's high school friends.

Despite Arcadia's reputation, she accepts Peg's offer because she's pleased to connect with her friend again and she never can resist a swimming pool.

Peg and her parents pick her up and drive to the club. There they have lobster salads for lunch and then sit poolside, where Peg's mother rubs sunscreen into her and Peg's backs and shoulders before sending them into the pool. Peg's father sits under the umbrella and drinks a second martini.

She and Peg swim and chat in the water for half an hour until unexpected clouds cool the air and they come out of the pool, shivering. Clutching towels around their huddled shoulders they pad barefoot back to the table. Peg's father watches them approach, and in a voice completely devoid of affection, says to Peg, "You look like a drowned rat."

Education

She's never paid much attention to the books on the shelf above Nick's desk when she's been snooping, but today she takes a look at the titles: *Night, Man's Search for Meaning, The Long Goodbye, Lord of the Flies, Mrs. Bridge, The Wall, Hiroshima, The Great Gatsby, The*

Pat Hobby Stories. With only these titles to go by, she isn't particularly enlightened as to Nick's enigmatic personality, so she sits down on the bed to peruse the first book at hand—*Night* by Elie Wiesel.

Skipping the Foreword, she leafs through the first pages. When her eyes stop on "All Jews, outside! Hurry!" she realizes what this book is about. She knows about the Holocaust from having read *Anne Frank: The Diary of a Young Girl*. Now, like coming on the scene of an accident and unable to look away, she slows down her reading and starts to take it in.

The cattle car ("Lying down was not an option, nor could we all sit down. We decided to take turns sitting."), the arrival ("In front of us, those flames. In the air, the smell of burning flesh. It must have been around midnight. We had arrived."), the selection ("'Men to the left! Women to the right' ... that was the moment when I left my mother.")

She cannot stop reading. Only when she hears the front door open does she set the book back on the shelf and slip quietly out of the room.

There are other times when she skims surreptitiously through her brother's books: two more about the Holocaust—a novel and another first-hand account—and one that describes the aftermath of America's atomic bomb drop on Japan.

She jots down the titles and obtains all these books from the public library. In her own room, she can take the time to read every horrifying sentence. She takes it all in with a feeling that she must prepare herself. The last book she reads—*Lord of the Flies*—delivers a profoundly grim message: a few abuse power, many others are complicit, the remaining resist fruitlessly or cringe in terror. Remembering the Army-McCarthy hearings her father had been so passionate about, she thinks, these things could easily happen again, here.

On her father's side, she's German. What, she asks herself, would I have done as a Gentile in Germany during the Holocaust? She is quite clear about the answer: she would have privately hated the regime and done nothing except keep her head down and behave as a coward.

When she finally finishes all this reading, she carries inside her a vague sense of guilt, a deep, lasting pessimism, and fear of what the future holds. She is not quite fourteen.

Friends

Friendships ebb and flow. At any one time she counts maybe four or five classmates as friends. They are not necessarily friends with each other, although some are. In grade school she had thought of Marilyn, Peg and Nancy more as a unit than as individuals. Now, in junior high, she is conscious of her new friends' separate personalities, their strengths, their vulnerabilities, what she likes about them and what irritates her. She even notices the character and idiosyncrasies of their parents. At this point in their school life, associations are loose and fluid, depending on the interests and activities that throw people together one semester and scatter them the next.

Her eighth grade friend Sarah White is an impish, sunny girl who smiles with her whole face. Her freckled cheeks rise so high in laughter that her big hazel eyes turn to slits. And yet her background is tragic. Her mother died when she was a baby and her father handed her off to his parents to raise. She rarely sees this father and doesn't seem to care. She loves her grandparents, who are born-again Christians and attend a Baptist church with prohibitions against dancing, playing cards, and a variety of other pastimes that most people consider harmless.

At only fourteen, Sarah has a sixteen-year-old boyfriend, Tyrone, whom her grandparents don't object to because she met him at church and as far as they know spends time with him only there. He has access to his parents' car, so they sneak away whenever possible to secluded places where they sit in the car and make out.

She meets this Tyrone when Sarah invites her to church one time. He's a tall, good-looking polite boy—more a man than a boy actually. She's fascinated by the double life they're leading inside a church that she considers to be as outlandish and extreme as the Episcopal Church her mother had made her attend briefly, though at least her friend's church doesn't have a tortured Jesus hanging from the wall. Sarah doesn't proselytize. In fact, she seems not to be particularly religious but happily goes through the motions to please her beloved grandparents.

Another friend, Rob Ransome, is a sturdy, quiet boy whose black hair is always neatly combed. He wears well-ironed button-down shirts, creased khakis, and loafers like every other boy his age. His voice is soft and subtly effeminate, as are his gestures. She assumes he has what is called "homosexual tendencies." His younger brother is similarly effeminate and she wonders if these tendencies are inherited.

She doesn't remember exactly how she and Rob struck up a friendship. They just seemed to gravitate toward each other, maybe because she is outgoing while he is diffident. Even with her he has the habit of glancing away when he makes eye contact as if he doesn't quite believe he has the right to be seen. Sometimes he comes over and they make popcorn, go up to the attic, sit on the old gray sofa and watch television. Once, to test the waters, she leans against him and puts her head on his shoulder. He stiffens and becomes silent, so she gives up on that. She isn't really attracted to him romantically, but she has an ever more urgent wish these days to be desired.

Like Rob and Sara, her other friends don't fit into any category at school. They don't have extremely wealthy parents and aren't star athletes or beauty queens, nor are they outcasts or "troubled youth." They give off an air of intelligence, creativity, and moderate non-conformity.

Defection

In spite of Carla Glenn's long-ago jealous insinuation that she got the star roles in Dramatics because of her father's University position, she and Carla have remained friends. In fact, she seems to be Carla's only friend, which is puzzling since there is nothing to estrange her from any particular group. She's affable, not homely, relatively intelligent and fashionable enough. She lives south of Governor in a large house and her father is chief accountant in the prestigious firm of Glenn, Cooper and Holt, which means her family has to be well-to-do.

She is astonished when Carla tells her that she isn't going to go to Benjamin Franklin High School—the high school in their district—but is planning to go to City Technical High, a trade school for kids who are unlikely to go on to college. Tech is a working class school, whereas Franklin is synonymous with money, professional parents and high SAT scores.

Why? she wants to know. And she finds Carla's answer to be both simple and, upon reflection, oddly brilliant. Carla doesn't want to be a small fish in a big pond. At Franklin, with its 1,800 plus students and preponderance of rich girls, she can't shine. At Tech she anticipates being a star, good at everything, elected to student offices, a leader in every club, and with its large boy-to-girl ratio, sought after by the opposite sex.

She's amazed that Carla has thought this through so carefully, and that she has actually gotten her parents to go along with it. But this is one thing that she has come to realize about Carla: her friend is headstrong and confident. There is no doubt that she will spend the next three years bathed in glory at City Technical High School.

Mrs. Abendroth

She has heard that Mrs. Abendroth, her ninth grade junior high English teacher, is tough and strict, and indeed, right from the beginning of the semester, Mrs. Abendroth herself boasts about it. Miss Rasmussen back in first and second grade had also been tough and strict (and certainly misguided regarding the pants-wetting incident) but not vicious. Mrs. Abendroth is vicious. She emits particularly nasty little chuckles when students make mistakes at the blackboard and shakes her head in apparent disbelief at their stupidity. She draws an enormous red F on papers that aren't perfect and holds them up for the whole class to see before handing them back.

But the thing for which she can least forgive Mrs. Abendroth is her public humiliation of a boy in the class named Jeffrey, who, judging by the state of his clothes and his lack of a decent coat in cold weather, comes from a poor family. Never a very good student, one day he commits the additional crime of having a dripping nose and sniffling during a quiz.

"Did your mother never teach you to use a *handkerchief*, Jeffrey?" calls Mrs. Abendroth in her stentorian voice from the front of the room. Everyone looks up from the quiz they're taking, a little startled. Jeffrey isn't quite sure what she's getting at. His sniffling has probably been unconscious. In his thin, short-sleeved shirt, his pale skin is almost blue with cold.

The teacher takes a clean white handkerchief from her purse and strides down the aisle between the desks. She holds the handkerchief out for him at arm's length. Jeffrey stares at it for a moment before the light dawns and a flush spreads up his skinny neck. He sits there, his jaw working.

Mrs. Abendroth lets the handkerchief go and everyone watches it flutter down onto his quiz paper. His eyes dart toward the door as if he is willing himself to be elsewhere. The teacher waits, her arms crossed over her large but un-maternal bosom. Finally he grabs the handkerchief up and swipes his nose with it. Mrs. Abendroth ambles to the front, removes a ruler from her desk drawer, and strolls back to Jeffrey. Wrinkling her nose as if at an unpleasant smell, she uses the ruler to scoop up the handkerchief. Holding it again at arm's length, she returns to the front of the room where she conspicuously drops handkerchief and ruler into the wastebasket.

She longs to stand up and denounce Mrs. Abendroth then and there in front of the whole class. You're a terrible teacher and a terrible person, she would like to say. I'm going to tell the Principal what you've done. I'll get you fired.

But even though her stellar work, her straight As on every assignment, gives her some standing with Mrs. Abendroth, it won't protect her from being crushed under the weight of her mockery. Worse yet, she knows that if she starts to speak out, the depth of her emotion will cause her to immediately burst into humiliating tears. She is too much of a coward. Jeffrey must go undefended.

Parents

Occasionally she thinks about Peg's father and his brutal comment: "You look like a drowned rat." As with Mary-Claire Byrne's withholding mother and dying father, she is thinking more and more about how different her friends' parents are from her own and how fraught their relationships must be with hostilities and disappointments and hurt. Her own father would not in a million years have told her she looked like a drowned rat, not jokingly or any other way. Her parents' role has always been to shelter her and her brothers not only from hardship and danger but cruelty. Lately her friends have begun to say "I wish I could trade parents with you, you're so lucky." Television comedies are full of teenagers who roll their eyes at their mothers or fathers and beg them not to do something embarrassing. She can't imagine her parents doing anything to embarrass her. In fact, she likes to show them off to her friends. She's proud of them. They're reasonable people. She *is* lucky and she knows it.

The Mother Weeps

She and her father walk into the kitchen after breakfast and find her mother in tears at the sink.

She stops in her tracks. "Oh Mom, what's wrong?"

Her father hurries over and puts an arm around her shoulders.

She has never seen her mother cry except when she tears up at sad movies, and then they both laugh at themselves over their shared sentimentality.

"It's nothing," her mother says without looking up from the dish water. "I'm sorry. I'm just feeling a little overwhelmed. I'm just so busy."

She is stricken with guilt. She never helps her mother. Nobody in the family helps. They all expect her to do everything. She picks up a cup and saucer from the kitchen table and sets it down by the sink. "Let me do the dishes," she says.

"No, that's all right." Her mother sets them in the soapy water. "I'm fine." She gives a weepy little laugh.

She leaves her mother and father together in the kitchen, runs upstairs and starts cleaning her parents' bathroom. When she finishes it, she cleans the other bathroom and the half bath downstairs.

Later, when her mother leaves to study at the University library, her father gathers her and her brothers into the living room for a talk.

"Your mother could really use some help around here. She's going to school, trying to keep up with her coursework, working part-time. With cooking and doing housework it's just too much. We've all got to pull our weight."

Yes, she thinks, and her mother chauffeurs Ted to Little League and Nick to drum lessons and me to friends' houses, and she has to go to PTA meetings and reciprocate the dinners and cocktail parties given by her father's colleagues and attend University functions, which she hates. And she never has time to play her beautiful baby grand piano.

Nick and Ted run around emptying wastebaskets and hauling the bags to the trash can in the driveway. They all pick up any of their stuff that's scattered about the house. She vacuums the carpet and sweeps and dusts the screen porch.

When her mother returns, she smiles sheepishly as if she is ashamed of herself. "Well, the house looks lovely. But don't you worry about me. Everything's fine."

They're more inclined to help after this, sharing among themselves the tasks of setting and clearing the table, washing and drying the dishes. Occasionally she cooks when her mother is going to be late getting home. But her mother doesn't ask them to do any of it, and they could do much, much more.

Sometimes she wishes her mother didn't take it all on herself. Her friends have chores, and their mothers enforce them sternly. She is glad she doesn't have a stern mother, but it gives her pause to think that someday if she gets married she'll have all that work on her own shoulders.

Circulation Desk

For three summers, starting after her sophomore year, she has a job at *The Leader and Gazette* circulation office. *The Leader and Gazette* is a statewide newspaper with a morning and evening edition. From six a.m. to noon, she answers calls from customers whose paper boy has failed to deliver the paper or who has thrown it into a puddle or on a roof or in the neighbor's yard. She is completely unprepared for the fury, to say nothing of the obscenities these irate customers level at her personally.

"Listen, bitch, if you don't fire that lazy little asshole, I'll come down there and fire him myself, and get you fired while I'm at it!" "What do you do, just ball up my fucking complaints and throw them into the fucking wastebasket?!" "This is the third time I've called this week, you cunt! What does it take to get you off your fat ass and do something about it?!" And so on. It seems there is a pattern of incompetence in certain carriers (they are, after all, twelve-year-old boys) and of peoples' expectations that they are entitled to a perfect world at six o'clock every morning.

She is used to her father muttering the occasional Damn it! or Jesus

Christ! or even That bastard! when another driver cuts him off or runs a red light. But to start the morning with this level of customer abuse makes her tremble as soon as the first call comes through her headset.

She sits with three others around a horseshoe-shaped table presided over by Marian, the jaded middle-aged, cigarette-voiced Head of Circulation Inquiries. The customers' rampages bounce right off Marian personally, but now and then she'll put a caller in his place (it's always a he). "Listen, Bub, that's no way to talk to someone who's just trying to do her job. I'm hanging up now. Don't call again until you can control your temper." The Circulation Department Head always backs her up. She's been in her position for thirty years. They can't afford to lose her.

Her second day on the job, she and the others at the desk are taken by Marian to a downtown diner for lunch. As they sit at a table, she begins to feel cold and clammy. The room is getting dark, and Marian, sitting across from her, appears to be far away as if she's at the end of a tunnel. Her boss takes one look at her and without leaving her seat says, "Annie. Put your head down between your knees." She does so just in time and after a couple of minutes, when she raises her head, the diner has brightened again and Marian has returned from the end of the tunnel. "Girl, your face was white as a piece of paper." Marian picks up the menu. "Okay, what are we ordering?"

Cartoon

Ted is giggling over a *New Yorker* cartoon.

"What's so funny?" she asks.

He presses the magazine to his chest, still giggling. "I can't show you."

"What? Let me see."

She reaches for the magazine and he relinquishes it with suppressed laughter, hunching his shoulders and covering his mouth.

The cartoon shows two bare-chested men standing behind bushes that cover their nether parts. A sign indicates they're at a nudist camp. One man says to the other, "I know you're not *supposed* to get one, but what if you *do*?" She reads it aloud. Ted shrieks. "I don't get it," she says. "What's the joke?"

He shakes his head vehemently. "I can't tell you! I can't tell you!"

She studies the cartoon but gives up. "I'll ask Dad," she says. Ted follows close behind to her parents' room, snickering all the way.

Her father is standing by the bureau, taking a handkerchief out of a drawer. She holds out the magazine. "Dad, why is this cartoon funny?"

He looks at it for a few moments and puts down the handkerchief. "Well, Annie," he says placidly, "have you ever heard of an erection?"

"Oohhh," she says. Of course she's heard of an erection. She's fifteen. Ted breaks into a renewed fit of giggles, which she and her father both ignore.

Prank

She and her friend Rob have a mutual friend, Mike Walenta, whose father is president of a local insurance company that will not issue auto insurance to anyone who drinks alcohol.

Neither she nor Rob is in the habit of playing practical jokes. In her own family, no one has ever tried to scare or embarrass or make someone look like a fool. Yet for some reason, she and Rob decide it would be hilarious to put empty liquor bottles in the back seat of Mike's father's car. She pulls a few empties from the trash, puts them in a paper bag and rides with Rob to Mike's house late in the evening. They plant the bottles on the floor of the back seat in the Walenta's unlocked car and speed away.

The next evening at dinner she regales her family with an account of this exploit. They're sitting at the picnic table on the screen porch enjoying the summer air and watching fireflies begin to turn on and off in the dusk.

Her father compresses his lips, levels her with a look as if she is someone he doesn't recognize, and shakes his head slowly and deliberately.

"That was a very foolish and thoughtless thing to do, Anne," he says without one iota of humor or "Oh, you kids!" tone to his voice. She has never heard him so stern, and furthermore, he never calls her Anne. "You could have gotten Mike in a great deal of trouble with his father. And more to the point, you could have ruined his father's reputation if someone had found those bottles. In fact, how do you know if damage hasn't already been done?"

In rapid fire, profound embarrassment hits her in the face, which flushes instantaneously, followed by a shot to her heart of guilt, which, transformed into defensive outrage, ricochets off her chest, and fires full force back at her father. She stands up abruptly.

"I never get to do *anything* fun!" she shouts. "You expect me to be Miss Goody Good, Miss Perfect all the time, twenty-four hours a day. I do one small thing and you jump down my throat—"

"Lower your voice, please," he says with a deadly calm.

"Oh, you're so worried about what the *neighbors* will hear?" she accuses, still shouting. It does occur to her that the neighbors might be hearing enough of her rant to question what kind of man her father really is. And now she's run out of accusations, all of which she knows to be pathetic, false, and unfair, so she storms from the porch, runs up to her room and slams the door.

Mike Walenta phones her that night. He has discovered and removed the liquor bottles before his father has seen them and has somehow figured out that she and Rob had put them there. Or … could her father have called to tell him?

She apologizes. "I'm sorry, Mike. We only meant it as a prank. I'm really sorry. Rob and I just weren't thinking."

"No," he says, "you weren't." And that is the last time he speaks to either one of them.

She knows she should apologize to her father, too, but she is too mortified to bring the subject up again. He has had his say and probably judged the depth of her regret by the shrillness of her tirade and doesn't mention it again.

This is the one and only time she ever plays a practical joke on anyone.

Fill 'Em Up On Soup

Professor Stan Dobre is a bombastic and self-centered professor of Classics at the University. He is also the father of eight children, the latest one an infant. His wife Helen, a modest, reserved, intelligent woman, is a cellist with the City Symphony Orchestra.

Her father once asked Dobre how he was able to feed eight children on a professor's salary. Stan replied, with one of his explosive guffaws, "Fill 'em up on soup!"

Her mother has a special fondness for the quiet, unassuming Helen and respect for her musical talent. Whenever Dobre's name is mentioned, she curls her lip and sneers, "'Fill 'em up on soup!'"

Recently Helen Dobre has had to quit the orchestra. Stan thinks it's taking up too much of her time. He himself is never willing to look after the children during those evenings when she has rehearsals.

At the dinner table, hearing that Dobre has made Helen give up her chair in the orchestra, her mother's eyes narrow and, as if she has forgotten her family can hear her, she exclaims, "Someone should *castrate* that man!"

The Meaning of a Nose

On the first day of her junior year, she sees her old grade school friend Peg in the hall, except that it isn't exactly Peg. Over the summer she has had her nose "fixed." This is astonishing and shocking. For one thing, she's never known anyone who has had plastic surgery, much less a girl of sixteen, but more importantly, it is as if the distance between herself and the Peg of her childhood has suddenly and finally become permanent. They say "hi" in passing, neither of them commenting on the change.

There's nothing wrong with the new nose. It's just that in straightening the slight bend in the old one, the surgeon has removed a certain distinction to Peg's face, an aristocratic or even exotic quality which had made Peg *Peg*.

Why did she feel she had to change the shape of her nose? She wonders if Peg's father had something to do with it, the father who told his thirteen-year-old daughter, "You look like a drowned rat." Had he criticized or mocked her nose? If so, he probably mocked Peg's mother's nose, too, because that's who she got hers from.

Or maybe it's just that all female movie stars are virtually required to have straight or upturned noses: Sandra Dee (*Gidget Goes Hawaiian*), Debbie Reynolds (*Tammy and the Bachelor*), Natalie Wood, Marilyn Monroe, Annette Funicello, Connie Francis. Whatever the reason, she will always feel a little sad when she sees her old friend and wonder if Peg regrets, or will someday regret, the loss of that lovely little bend in her nose.

Hairdo

In the girls' restrooms between classes, they're lined up at the mirrors re-teasing the giant football helmets that constitute their hairdos. Rat-tailed combs are wielded mercilessly. The acrid reek of hairspray fills the air. Even those like herself with thin, straight hair that can only maintain the "bouffant" shape by hourly reconstruction, even they have succumbed to it.

Halfway through the semester, Mrs. Grossman, the Girls' Vice Principal, calls her into her office. She doesn't mince words.

"Annie, your hair is too big. A hairdo that big is unsightly."

She could take this statement at face value and feel humiliated, or she could bristle with indignation and stalk out of the office. She does neither. Mrs. Grossman's opinion is irrelevant. *Too* big? *Really*?! She works at it all day long to keep it this big. If anything, Mrs. Grossman's assertion is a compliment.

"Okay," she says.

"All right then. Just a word to the wise."

"Thank you."

Mrs. Grossman walks her to the door. She hurries to her locker and glances at her hair in the mirror. The hair could do with a touch-up, but now there's no time before class. In the hall, big hairdos are bobbing before, behind and beside her. She wonders why Mrs. Grossman has singled her out. It doesn't occur to her that the Vice Principal may have been calling in all the girls, one at a time, and that eventually the woman will realize these little conferences are pointless.

Wrong Number

The boy on the line asks for Terry, and she tells him there's no Terry at this number.

"Sorry," he says. "What number did I call?" She tells him. "Oh. Off by one. Sorry," he apologizes again. Then, flirtatiously, he says "But *you* sound nice. I wouldn't mind talking to *you*."

She laughs. "You never know, I might be horrible."

"That's true. But I'm a pretty good judge of voices."

"Oh really? How often do you have to do that?"

"At least once. Like now. Are you in high school or are you an old lady?"

"Very funny." He sounds like a high school boy himself. "I'll guess you're in high school, too," she says.

"So what school do you go to?"

"Franklin," she tells him, and waits for the usual reaction.

"Uh oh. Does that mean you have your nose in the air?"

"All the time." Where has she come up with this flirty banter? She has never flirted with anyone in her life, hasn't really known how. It must be the anonymity of the telephone. "What school do *you* go to? And is *your* nose in the air?"

"St. Thomas Aquinas," he says.

"Oh! A good Catholic boy."

"Yeah, but we don't lord it over anyone."

"So, Mr. St. Thomas Aquinas, it was nice talking to you."

"Jim. I'm Jim. What's your name?"

"Annie."

"Well, Miss Annie, it was nice talking to you, too, and I'd like to talk some more, but my girlfriend wouldn't like it."

"So you're a faithful kind of guy. That's good."

"But I've got a buddy who's unattached. I'll bet you and him would hit it off. How about if I give him your number?"

"Another good Catholic boy?"

"Yup. His name's Murray."

"Murray what?"

"Murray Tierney."

"How old is this Murray Tierney?"

"Seventeen. How old are you?"

"Sixteen."

"So can I give him your number?"

"Why not?"

They say good-bye. She feels sophisticated and smug.

Murray Tierney

Murray calls her the next day and asks if he, Jim and Jim's girlfriend can drop over on the weekend when he has his father's car. She gives him her address.

From the dining room windows she watches the three troop up the walk and ring the bell. She comes out and sits on the front steps with them. Murray is soft around the edges—not pudgy exactly, but nowhere like the lean, lanky boys she prefers. Jim is the tall, skinny one. Still, Murray has a bashful expression, which she does like. Jim's girlfriend, Melanie, is short and squat and homely. She says almost nothing, but smiles amiably. It seems she's just along for the ride. Apparently, getting Murray a girlfriend is a team effort.

She has told her parents about the wrong number and what has followed. When the entourage arrives her parents make sure to come out of the house to be introduced. Murray and Jim shake hands with her father and introduce themselves with polite formality. Her mother asks about school and what classes they're taking. Murray offers the information that he works in his father's print shop after school and on Saturday mornings and that he and Jim have been friends since grade school.

Her parents, satisfied that these are just kids, harmless teenagers, withdraw and leave them to it. The unstated purpose of the visit is for her and Murray to check each other out and launch a romance. The launch goes according to plan, and within a few days the foursome is double dating.

On that first meeting she has noted the subtle signs of class distinction. Murray wears polyester shirts instead of cotton broadcloth, jeans instead of khakis. He and Jim and the girlfriend start a sentence with "Him and me" instead of "He and I." There is an inordinate amount of talk about automobiles. Murray and Jim are rebuilding a Corvette engine though they don't as yet have the rest of the car to put it in.

In the evenings, they "scoop the loop" along with droves of other teenagers at the wheels of their parents' cars. Cruising the eight-block square of central downtown, these boys periodically squeal around turns, rev their engines at stoplights and burn rubber when the lights change. Murray is chagrined that his father's Pontiac has an automatic transmission. Even with her and Jim and Melanie in the car, Murray apparently feels no shame in faking the motion of shifting gears. He holds his elbow just high enough to be seen by other drivers as he guns the motor and lurches forward. Maybe they're all doing this.

They go to vintage auto shows. Some nights they stop for pizzas or take in a drive-in movie when the boys can afford it. Other times they park by the airport and make out, Jim and Melanie in the back and she and Murray in front. It's all very silent except for the occasional rustle of clothing and a giggle from Melanie. The making out is the main reason she's dating Murray, since they have no other interests in common. That, and the fact that no boy from Franklin has indicated an attraction to her.

Driver Education

In eleventh grade she takes Driver Education. The teacher is patient and calm. He has an extra set of brakes, but he almost never uses them. She practices in the high school parking lot for a while before venturing out onto nearby residential streets. In a week she is able to turn onto busy Governor Street and manage its stoplights downtown and after a few weeks goes even farther afield, entering the freeway and exiting a mile later. Back at the parking lot, she becomes unaccountably good at parallel parking. At the end of the semester, she gets her credits for completing the course and should be ready to apply for her license.

The problem is that the cars used in Driver Education are automatics, and her family's car has a stick shift, so she has to start all over again, mastering the foot- and hand-work of a manual transmission, and to do this, her father has to teach her. Not surprisingly, this is a nerve-wracking experience for both of them. He is a man who, in the best of circumstances tends to see accidents waiting to happen. Now, every time she causes the car to stall, jerk, lurch forward, or grind its gears, her father jams on imaginary brakes and blurts out uncensored oaths, mostly "Jesus, no, not like that!"

After a week of this, she decides she doesn't need a driver's license yet. She can walk most places, and she has a boyfriend with access to a car. Her father, she thinks, is relieved to have the lessons end. She could probably learn to drive if her mother taught her. She is a calmer, and if truth be told, a better driver than her father. He gets irritated in traffic and is also in the habit of coming up to stop signs too fast so you're not sure until the last moment if he is actually going to stop.

She considers asking her mother for driving lessons, but instinctively understands that it would put her mother in an awkward position and decides it will be better to go without a driver's license than to risk slighting her father's male ego. Although her mother drives all over town on her own, if her father is with her, he is always at the wheel. The image of a woman driving while her husband sits in the passenger seat is almost unimaginable.

Just Call Me Ginny Wallace

Coaches are generally assigned to teach the history classes at Franklin. She has World History with Mr. Gryer, the head football coach, who enjoys all the glory associated with that sport at such a large high school. He can often be heard spouting clichés on local radio and television interviews.

His teaching strategy is to assign the reading of a chapter from the textbook and then get students to orally summarize the chapter. He doesn't need to do anything except sit on his desk and field the occasional joke question: "So was Queen Elizabeth really a virgin?" Har har.

On Monday mornings, as students file into class, he banters with the boys who sit in the first row, recounting his and his team's weekend shenanigans on the road, what they did to put one over on a hapless player, coach, or fan from the other team or regaling them with some excess of male prowess. Today it's the latter.

"My boys had an eating contest before we came home. Went to a steakhouse to replenish the old proteins after the game. These guys have big appetites." He winks at the boys in front. "But guess who won?" He's sitting on his desk, his muscular thighs stretching the fabric of his khakis. He points to his own chest. "Twelve-ounce, two-inch-thick T-bone."

"He scarfed the sucker down in five minutes and thirty-two seconds," says a boy sitting front and center.

"Bullshit!" someone shouts from the back row.

"Language, boys," says Mr. Gryer jovially.

"He did! My brother told me." His brother is the star quarterback on the team.

"Just call me Ginny Wallace," says Mr. Gryer, and the class breaks out laughing.

No. Can he really have said that? *Just call me Ginny Wallace*? Yes, of course he can. He can say anything he likes.

She doesn't take any classes with Ginny Wallace, but whenever she passes her in the halls she feels almost sick with sympathy. Ginny has a glandular disorder which has made her not just fat but circus sideshow obese. In addition, she's tall, maybe 5'8" or 5'9", so there's no way to make herself inconspicuous except by keeping her mouth shut. Does anyone ever hear Ginny speak?

Mr. Gryer is a forty-year-old man, not some thirteen-year-old. How can he be so juvenile as to make fun of a teen-aged girl with a handicap she can't help? And in front of a whole classroom of her peers even if she, hopefully, will never hear about it.

Just call me Ginny Wallace.

Oh, there are names I'd like to call you all right, you sleazy, self-centered, infantile jerk, she thinks, and "Ginny Wallace" isn't one of them.

Here it is, another Mrs. Abendroth moment. Another chance to stand up against mindless cruelty by a teacher. And she's older now. She has no excuse to stay quiet.

She's having a good hair day after a night of curler torture, her make-up is fresh, and she's wearing an outfit that accentuates her small waist. She's the opposite of Ginny Wallace. What could he use to mock her with?

If only, if *only* she had the confidence to get up and let him have it right now, right to his face. But once again she doesn't trust her chin not to tremble, her eyes not to well up, her voice not to come out shaky. She doesn't trust herself not to break down in this sneery, smug atmosphere of male superiority, a world where an obese girl is fair game. Where all girls are fair game. Once again she can't do it.

Torpor

Except for Children's Theatre back in grade school, she resists committing to activities which require showing up punctually at a certain place for a certain length of time and doing things she's not naturally good at.

The piano lessons had been a bust, except that she had at least learned how to read music. She tried tennis lessons one time at her mother's urging ("How I longed to take tennis when I was a teenager!") and thought the ninety-degree heat reflecting off the asphalt would melt her, but she puts her foot down when her mother suggests summer camp: "Oh Annie, I think you'd enjoy meeting people and being out in nature, sitting around the campfire singing songs in the evening." Her mother's grandmother had paid for camp one summer back in the 1930s, and it was her fondest childhood memory.

No! She absolutely refuses to go to camp, a place where she will have to dive off diving boards and swim across lakes, bunk with a bunch of strangers (precluding any chance of sleep for the duration), and get into row boats crawling with daddy-long-legs. At the lake by Aunt Trudi's house, two of these hideous insects had once been found scrambling to hide under the row boat's oars and she has never forgotten it.

Her always pallid face gets paler from so much inactivity, and through an open window she overhears her father comment to her mother while raking leaves outside, "She needs to be out here getting some exercise. She looks like a ghost." This makes her drop her book and bound out of the house to pick up a rake. Still, within days she sinks back into her usual torpor.

She wants only to be free to loll around the house reading and talking on the phone with friends or with Murray (despite their having almost nothing to talk about), and of course to have evenings free for riding around in his car followed by the only activity she engages in that might qualify as exertion as it takes her heart some minutes to slow down afterwards.

Self-Control

Murray is not a very hairy guy. She's not even sure he has to shave. But he has reddish fuzz on his forearms, and she knows boys like to have their masculinity admired, so she caresses the fuzz at least once during the evening and tells him he's a grizzly bear.

Soon enough Jim and Melanie drop out of the foursome, leaving her and Murray to their own devices. Nothing much changes. They continue to make out in the front seat of the Pontiac. Only the venue is different. Now they routinely head for Sylvan Park, just the other side of the ravine behind her house, where they get in an hour of mutual arousal before ten p.m. closing time when the police cruise by to tap on steamed-up car windows and shoo the couples out of the park.

For the first few months they stick to endless kissing and mashing their bodies against each other. No tongues, though. That particular practice is called "French Kissing" and has an unsavory reputation. She is repulsed by the very thought of it.

Good Catholic boy that he is, he never pushes her beyond what she herself wants and allows. To the embracing and humping is gradually added hands under clothes, unfastening and unzipping, the exposure of more and more bare skin; i.e., everything but .... Sometimes his hands on her breasts is all it takes for the release to come rolling over her.

He maintains a hard-on during these sessions and stays that way after she has silently finished with a little frisson of private embarrassment and says it's time to go home. Even then she doesn't have a moment's concern that he will force her, and he doesn't. It's probable that he has no idea what has occurred inside her and assumes she's just had enough for the night, which she has. Murray's self-restraint may be due to the cautionary lesson of Jim and his girlfriend. Jim has gotten Melanie pregnant, so they now have to get married; that's a given. They've even set a date.

She needs no cautionary tale. The last thing on the planet she wants is to be a teen-aged mother, or a mother of any kind. In theory, at some day in the dim future, she supposes she'll have children, but she has no interest in them, maybe because of those two claustrophobic babysitting experiences, one with the helpless infant and the other with the ungovernable boys. In any case, she is content to go on and on, night after night, month after month grinding and groping, exploring and exposing without any need to go all the way.

Nick

Throughout high school, Nick has hung out with a group of boys, a foursome like hers in elementary school. Two of the boys are handsome and friendly, and she has crushes on both of them. The third is a misfit who wears oversized glasses that maximize his eyes and minimize his nose. He has acne and a sardonic sense of humor. Nick seems to get a kick out of him even more than the others. Occasionally she has a chance to eavesdrop on their conversations and is struck by how lighthearted Nick is around his friends. They tease each other and laugh. He never laughs around the family. Sometimes with his friends he laughs until he's doubled over. His whole face comes to life, abandoning the removed, neutral expression that makes him look like a movie spy hiding his real identity.

In September, Nick leaves his microscope, his stuffed Killdeer, his tool box full of girlie magazines, his Holocaust books and goes two hours away to the state university, taking only his records, stereo, and drum set. All he really wants to do is play drums and develop a jazz career, but he manages to stay in school, playing at club gigs on weekends. The family seldom sees him and when they do, whatever gaiety he might be enjoying in his life is hidden as he steps once more into his movie spy persona.

Physics

Every girl knows to keep her blouse buttoned up to the neck when she enters Mr. Houk's physics class. At the beginning of the semester, just to see for themselves if it's true, they test the rumor by leaving their top two buttons open. Indeed Mr. Houk comes and bends over their shoulders from behind, sometimes putting a hand on their backs. To the boys, he speaks seated at his desk. This is all she learns from physics.

Fiction

In eleventh grade English she is required to write a short story. Searching her brain for a plot, she draws a blank for several days until she finally hits on a two-character, first person stream of consciousness story about two old maids—Edna and Agatha—competing for the attention of their unmarried pastor. The reader is privy to the thoughts of each woman as she snidely cuts her rival down in her mind.

She is given an A for the story, with the comment "quite humorous." Gratified, she reads it over to herself again and realizes at once that she has put together a hackneyed story line and characters taken from countless films and television shows that pit women against each other and ridicule them for being unmarried past the age of thirty.

Once again, as before when she gave up her childhood ambition to write, she is ashamed of her lack of originality. But she's forgotten Mark Twain's Miss Watson "a tolerable slim old maid, with goggles" who threatens Huck Finn with Hell if he doesn't take his book learning seriously. If she could remember this, she might at least forgive herself for rehashing a nasty stereotype. She is, after all, in good company.

Den

A small, cozy den with a fireplace adjoins the living room, an old-fashioned pocket door dividing the floor-to-ceiling bookcases in two. On the bottom shelves the family photo albums and over-sized *New Yorker* cartoon books are kept. Churchill's fat histories of World War II—*The Gathering Storm, Their Finest Hour, The Grand Alliance, The Hinge of Fate, Closing the Ring, Triumph and Tragedy*—fill a top shelf. Since she was a little girl those titles have accumulated one by one on the bookshelves in the old house and now the new. She has never seen anyone read them, but they represent for her the history that preceded her birth and her parents' somber memory of it.

The rest of the shelves are filled with fiction, biographies and autobiographies. Her parents have bought books authored by the literary stars of the twentieth, nineteenth and eighteenth centuries and a few from the classical past. These she dips into on a regular basis, whiling away a winter afternoon in one of the wing chairs by the glowing fire.

To her father—maybe reminiscent of a summer he spent as a youth camping in the Sierra Nevadas—the act of carrying in a load of firewood and kindling, tumbling them into the wood box, and bringing a fire to life appears to be a sacred ritual. He pokes his head into the den occasionally. "How's that fire going, Annie? Shall I put another log on for you?" He places the log carefully, sending up a crackling of sparks, and kneels to stir up the flames with an ancient leather bellows kept by the wood box.

Today she has just finished James Agee's *A Death in the Family*, a novel so simple, poignant, and perfect that it reaffirms her conviction that she will never be able to write.

Boy Scout

By the end of her junior year, the charms of groping in Murray's father's Pontiac have begun to pall, and the relationship dies a natural death. This is due in part to a mutual attraction between her and another boy scout—in this case a literal one. Bill Phelps is an Eagle Scout, (BSA, Order of the Arrow).

They are in an English class together, and she's had her eye on him for some time. Bill plays trumpet in the school orchestra as well as the marching, concert, and pep bands. He belongs to the Math-Science club, was on the football team his sophomore year but let that drop and won a Science Fair Award instead. He is intelligent, unassuming, still wears a crewcut, and has an aquiline nose. She sets about flirting and he responds.

Bill's mother is a widow who struggles to raise him and his two younger sisters alone. The last thing his mother needs is a troublesome son, so Bill is always on his honor to do his duty to God and his country, to be trustworthy, loyal, helpful, and so on.

He doesn't often have access to the car, so they don't see much of each other outside of school and he has little cash with which to take her out. She is content for them to meet at her or his house occasionally, where they hold hands a lot and kiss a little. She attends the statewide Scout Jamboree with his family and watches badges and patches get added to his uniform and ceremonial sash. His sisters sit on either side of her, entranced that their big brother has a girlfriend.

Every summer, Bill earns a salary working at a Boy Scout camp as a camp counselor. In the middle of the summer there is a week-end during which one group of scouts vacates and most of the counselors go home for a day. Bill has to stay at camp to prepare for the next group's arrival on Monday. Her parents agree to drive her the thirty miles there so she can spend the day with Bill before he takes up his duties again. They will come back and pick her up in the evening.

Bill comes out looking handsome in his army green uniform with his official-looking STAFF patch sewn on the pocket. He greets her parents politely and makes a little small talk about the camp before they take off. It's a mild summer day, the woods are quiet, the air soft. He takes her around the camp and down to the lake, shows her the canoes, the bull's eyes for bow and arrow practice, the big fire pit. Hand in hand they make their way to the counselors' large tent pitched on a wooden platform. They climb the steps and enter into the pale green light. All his bunkmates have gone home. She and Bill have the tent to themselves.

There is a record player on the bedside table and a small pile of 45s—"Stranger in Paradise," "When I Fall in Love," "Misty," "Moon River"—two of which she has given him for his birthday and for Christmas. They sit on his bunk while he takes the records out of their paper sheaths and stacks them on the spindle. These are slow-dance songs, the songs that cause chaperones to tap couples on the shoulders and separate them by several inches.

She and Bill get up and sway to the music, her arms around his neck, his around her waist. When "Moon River" drops onto the turntable, they sway their way back toward the bunk and without speaking lie down together.

At first they lie facing each other on the narrow bed. She likes the sensation of her softness melting into his sturdy and firm chest. As they kiss, he slowly rolls her, or maybe she rolls herself, until she is lying on top of him. Their legs entwine. Her hands cup his face, stroke his hair. Her weight presses him into the mattress. The music on the record player ends. His kisses are tender and passionate, gentle and breathless. With her groin pressed to his, she feels the hardness straining against his pants. They hold each other closer, uttering inarticulate sounds.

And then the action suddenly stops. Their heavy breathing is now the only sound in the quiet tent. She feels herself being taken by the shoulders and shifted away from his body. He lies still beside her, his breath becoming quieter.

He has stopped them before they go too far. He has taken it on himself to be the chaperone. What *she* knows, and he doesn't, is that she has had no intention of going too far. Whether or not they get naked, whether they touch each other in forbidden places, whether he reaches the point of no return and comes, he has nothing to worry about—she is not going to urge him or allow him to come inside *her*.

Slowly they sit up and straighten their clothes. They don't speak of their feelings. He says, we'd better go down to the main lodge and have something to eat before your parents come for you. She says okay.

For the rest of their time together as the sun sets, leaving behind a slash of gold and crimson on the horizon across the lake, she feels put down, subtly reprimanded. The girl is the one who is supposed to set the limits, and he has not trusted her to set them. Trustworthy, Brave, Clean, Reverent, and Morally Straight, he must think less of her now. A Temptress. Weak.

Their relationship continues for a couple of months after the summer ends. They hold hands again and kiss a little and exchange love notes. But then, without an overt declaration, he slowly and subtly withdraws. Perhaps he has thought it more gentlemanly to break up with her a little at a time instead of all at once.

Despite a vague sense of humiliation, she misses him and nurses the memory of that intense sexual excitement they both felt before he took the responsibility away from her to shut it down.

Grief on the Gray Sofa

The news comes on a Friday afternoon while she is in fifth period English class. Through tears, the teacher tells them the President has been shot and killed. It seems unbelievable, but when the Principal comes on the loudspeaker to confirm the news and tells everyone to go home, she understands that it's real.

Her parents have idolized this president and his cultured, softspoken wife, and because they were supporters, she has been too, but not with equal enthusiasm. For some time she has disapproved of charming men, and there have been rumors about the President.

She doesn't feel bereft. She's simply fascinated. It's all so dramatic: the footage of the actual shooting, Jacqueline, climbing out the back of the car in her pink suit. And then on Sunday, Oswald the assassin being shot on live television. She and Ted and her parents squeeze together on the old gray sofa in the attic and scarcely leave it from Friday to Monday, when the funeral procession is televised.

On Saturday, the flag-draped casket is brought to the White House. On Sunday it's taken to the Capitol Building rotunda where for twenty-one hours a hundred thousand mourners line up eight abreast for forty blocks to view it. The people look stunned. They hold handkerchiefs to their faces or cry openly. This collective grieving starts to bring home to her that it's not just about one man being killed; it's about the country being deeply wounded.

On Monday, they watch the procession of dignitaries and marching soldiers and sailors; the riderless, skittish horse; Jackie, black-veiled and numb walking hand in hand with her little children; two-year-old John Jr.'s poignant salute. But you wouldn't even have to see these things to be affected. The sounds are enough. For moments at a time she closes her eyes and just listens to the slow, endless drum beats; the clop of the horse's hoofs and rattle of the caisson's wheels; the marching feet; then, at noon the sudden quiet as the procession halts and across the country all traffic stops and planes are held up on runways for five minutes out of respect. And then the bagpipes' dirges re-commence, and military bands play the funeral march and the hymn "Eternal Father, Strong to Save," and at Arlington the fighter jets roar across the sky, and the cannon and twenty-one guns fire their salutes. Finally, the lone bugler plays "Taps."

Her throat swells, and when she opens her eyes, she sees that, for the first time in her experience, tears are streaming down her father's cheeks.

Glad to Have Been of Help

Her mother has smoked cigarettes ever since she can remember. Not whole packs a day like some people, but a cigarette or two after dinner and at cocktail parties or while sitting on a deck chair in the back yard watching her and her brothers play. It's natural to see her mother delicately holding a cigarette between her fingers and tilting her head to avoid exhaling smoke in anyone's face. She's so used to it that she doesn't notice the smell of cigarettes on her mother's breath or the smell of it saturating the curtains or upholstery.

Almost everybody smokes—not only her mother but her parents' friends and people in the movies and on television. Edward R. Murrow smokes while reporting the news. After cocktail parties, cigarette butts—many with lipstick marks—fill the ashtrays. Her mother goes around the next morning emptying them.

Her father is an exception. He doesn't smoke except for a rare cigar after dinner on special occasions. Her mother has told her, "Erich doesn't like me to smoke, so I've been trying to quit." She tries many times but always relapses.

It is unfathomable that her mother—so self-disciplined and reasonable, and also so concerned about pleasing her husband that she never lets him see her without makeup and tolerates his insistence on driving even when he's almost falling asleep at the wheel on vacation trips—that she wouldn't quit smoking at his request. Clearly, it's not a case of wouldn't but of can't.

If her own mother is that addicted to cigarettes, how seductive must they be—as seductive as heroin! In high school a few kids smoke behind their parents' backs, but with her mother as an example, she wouldn't touch a cigarette with a ten-foot-pole. She imagines that one puff would hook her for life.

Then, on January 11th of her senior year the report comes out. Headlines are plastered on front pages across the country: SURGEON GENERAL: SMOKING CAUSES LUNG CANCER, HEART DISEASE. Her mother quits smoking the very next day and never picks it up again. She has always enjoyed extremely good health and intends to keep it that way.

"Mom," she tells her, "Your smoking saved me from lung cancer."

"It did? How?"

"If you hadn't smoked, you wouldn't have had so much trouble quitting, and if you hadn't had so much trouble quitting, I wouldn't have seen how addictive it was and been scared away from it."

"Oh. Well, that's good. I never thought of that," she replies, and adds, "Glad to have been of help."

White Face

Her extracurricular high school activities are few and far between and though she dislikes joining things, she doesn't relish having just two or three lines by her picture in the yearbook when she graduates, so she joins the Mime Group, sponsored by Mr. Trent, the Drama teacher. Mime is something she might be good at, given her background in Children's Theatre.

It's a group of only seven students. Mr. Trent shows them some techniques to practice. They learn how to apply white makeup and how to create the illusions of opening and closing imaginary doors, appearing to be trapped inside small rooms with invisible walls, walking and running in place, projecting sadness, happiness, fear and anger. That's about it. They don't actually perform for anyone.

A member of the group is Harriet Jessup, one of only eleven Black students at Franklin. She's the daughter of Irma Jessup, a well-known civil rights leader in the city. After mime class one day, Harriet mentions that she'll be touring churches with a CORE group. "Congress of Racial Equality" she explains. This opening leads her to tell Harriet how much she admires the courage of civil rights protestors in the South, how brave they are to risk their lives. She admits to being a coward herself and feels bad that she has done nothing to further the cause.

This may be why at the next mime class, Harriet asks if she would like to come along on the CORE group's church tour the following Sunday. Harriet's mother and a group of Black ministers and other activists will visit primarily White rural churches and talk from the pulpit about civil rights. It is Mrs. Jessup's idea that Harriet and her mime class friend do a brief pantomime performance at the end to show their skills and provide a bit of entertainment. She's flattered to be asked and immediately agrees. Her parents readily consent.

On Sunday, she is dropped off at the Jessup's house where a small caravan of cars is about to head into the countryside. She and Harriet are the only teenagers in the group, and she is the only White person. She feels special, singled out for her enlightened views, possibly admired and even the object of gratitude. Mrs. Jessup greets her matter-of-factly, introduces her to the others and moves on to a brief discussion of logistics. She feels a little strange in her thick white mime makeup while everyone else is dressed formally for church. But Harriet is in the same boat, so she guesses it's all right.

At the first church, they file in and are seated in the front row of reserved pews, from which the local minister introduces them. The speakers eloquently describe the struggles and violence endured by Black students at Central High School in Little Rock; the cruelties and humiliations meted out to Black people for trying to eat at a lunch counter; the vicious beatings suffered by the Freedom Riders. The speakers talk about Christian values.

After the speeches, she and Harriet come up on the platform and are introduced as classmates in a mime class, where they're learning acting skills. They proceed to open and close imaginary doors, press their hands against invisible walls, walk and run in place, and project sadness, happiness, fear and anger, to scattered applause.

She wonders if the congregation is as confused by this performance as she is. Somehow it had made sense before, but now she's struck with its strangeness. What do their mime illusions have to do with the subject at hand? Is it her sole White presence that Mrs. Jessup thought would make some sort of point? Or maybe it has nothing to do with race. Maybe her mother just wanted to give Harriet a role to play, a chance to show her skills, with a friend for support.

The CORE group does a lunch program at the next church and an evening program at a third. By then her thick white mime makeup is dry and cracking and falling into her eyes. Walking just behind Harriet as they all file out after the last service, she hears a man in the congregation turn to another man and say, in an unnecessarily loud voice, "I'll bet that Black girl likes putting on that white face." She doesn't know if Harriet hears this. It makes her wonder if there is ever such a thing as changing people's minds.

The Problem We All Live With

In her senior year she is asked again to write a piece of fiction. This time she chooses an omniscient narrator observing the thoughts of a Black child and the child's mother on the opening day of first grade at an all-White school. She draws her inspiration from the Norman Rockwell *Look* magazine illustration: "The Problem We All Live With," which depicts a six-year-old Black girl in a white dress, her pigtails tied with white ribbons as she walks to school accompanied before and behind by federal marshals. On the wall in the background are the stains of a thrown tomato and part of the word "Nigger" in capital letters.

The child in her story is happily imagining herself starting first grade. The mother is agonizing over the fact that for fear of losing her job she can't walk her child to school on that momentous and fraught day.

This time the teacher gives her an A+ for her story. "Very moving" is the comment. She re-reads her A+ story on her way home from school and once again feels that prick of shame. She has chosen "Addie Mae" for the name of the little girl because it sounds like the kind of name a Southern Black girl would have. But how can she presume? What does she know about this subject? Of the almost 600 students in her class—the senior class of 1964—two are Black. Of the 1,800-some students in her high school, eleven are Black. All the teachers but one are White. This is what it means to live south of Governor.

Dramatics Again

Passing a sign announcing "Auditions!" at the door of the high school auditorium, she goes in on a whim and in short order finds herself cast in *Arsenic and Old Lace* as one of the two old women who enjoy poisoning men. Maybe because it's a comedy, or because she has a friendly and unassuming co-star, or simply because she wasn't invested in getting the part in the first place, the stage-fright and self-criticism she suffered toward the end of her Children's Theater days with Miss Desmond doesn't return. She has a good time.

After this performance she is asked by the drama teacher to co-write, direct, and co-host The Senior Frolics, a student variety show featuring any individual or group of seniors with some sort of talent to perform. She must write segues tying these disparate acts together. The title and theme she's chosen with her co-host, Merilee Ayres, is "The Lisa Languish Story" in which the two of them portray rich drama queens rehashing the imaginary Lisa's ups and downs of her life in the theatre. They get to wear evening gowns.

When her parents come backstage afterwards to congratulate her, she grumbles about the cast's flubs, poor timing, and amateur efforts, which she feels reflect badly on herself. Her mother, having choreographed dance troupe performances in college, casually mentions that once the show is over, a director's role is to graciously praise everyone's performance and thank them very much. Fortunately, her mother makes this suggestion before she has allowed anyone else to overhear her disgruntlement.

Good School

Although she could attend her father's university without cost, her parents are willing to pay the relatively high tuition to send her to a "good" school. She applies to several and is accepted at one, Carroll College, two hours from home and far enough away to permit the illusion of independence but near enough for convenience.

Carroll College meets all her criteria: high admission standards; small size (only 1,200 students); a prohibition against sororities and fraternities; a progressive reputation; indifference to collegiate athletics; a pretty, historic campus; and no math requirement. The college has a certain regional caché and is referred to by some as the Harvard of the Midwest. She is proud to have gotten in.

Last Walk

On a Sunday afternoon in late August, she and Ted Boy and Ted Dog take a final long walk through the woods before she goes off to college. They clamber down the steep ravine and up the other side to emerge in the park, where they meander through the rose gardens, checking out the sundial on their way down to the outdoor natural amphitheater. They take turns projecting their voices from the sylvan stage, he singing O Sole Mio, she reciting the bits she's memorized from Shakespeare: "To be or not to be ..." "Romeo, Romeo, wherefore art thou Romeo ..." "How sharper than a serpent's tooth it is to have a thankless child."

From the park they follow the trail past the swimming pool and into the woods. They're too old to pretend to be running from some malign criminal as they used to. Now they casually pick their way through the grasses and weeds that overlap the path. They cross over the creek, balancing on an old log, and carry on until they come to the cliff overlooking the waterworks and the airport in the distance. Here they stop and sit on a fallen tree to eat sandwiches and chocolate chip cookies she has made for the occasion and watch Ted Dog catch in midair the crusts they toss for him.

Ted Boy talks about the girlfriend he brought along on their family vacation to Michigan that summer and how the trip had tolled the death knell on their relationship. Although they had snuggled and held hands, the truth was they didn't have much to talk about and she seemed bored with the lake and the beach. He's not sure how to officially end it.

Ted's story reminds her of the months-long saga of Murray Tierney and the Adventures in His Father's Pontiac. She tells Ted an expurgated version of it, and they have a good laugh. It's delightful to find that she and her brother are on a grownup footing now, and that he looks to her as a pal and a mentor.

III

Carroll College

She had visited the campus last spring and thought it pretty, and now that she belongs here and is free to wander through the gothic-, classical- and tudor-style buildings, climb their creaking stairs, listen to her echoing footsteps in the hallways or just stand in the middle of central campus and absorb it all, she feels she has stepped into an English novel set in Oxford or Cambridge.

The women's and men's dormitories, built around World War I, are lined up as far from each other as possible along the northwest and southeast edges of campus. All the dorms are entered by way of loggias, enclosed on the women's side and open on the men's. A crenellated gothic tower stands halfway along the men's loggia, while on the women's side the loggia ends in a great hall with massive cathedral-like stained glass windows and a formal dining room paneled in dark, carved wood.

As she walks about the campus, it strikes her that she and the new freshmen passing her on the sidewalks, in their khakis and crew sweaters and straight skirts and turtle necks look like tourists visiting a stage set for a period film. They fit in better with the only two modern buildings which slash the central campus, aggressively out of place: a low-slung glass and limestone library and a student center called The Hub.

Rash

The male students at Carroll College, looking for prospective dates among the incoming freshmen, have been studying the photos in this year's "herd book." Upon learning of the existence of this book, she's dismayed at the impression her picture must be making. In her photo her hair is three sizes too big for her face. (Since it was taken, she has adopted a simple page-boy hairdo, never imagining that her high school photo would come back to haunt her just as she's trying to project a new image.)

Worse still, in person she looks like a ghoul, with half her face covered in poison ivy blisters oozing through a plastering of pink calamine lotion. That last walk in the woods with Ted Boy and Ted Dog turns out to have been a big mistake. And on top of all that, she's walking around with balled up Kleenexes and a raw, dripping nose because she has come down with one of her typical head colds. She's only grateful that she doesn't have a migraine.

Hours

It is New Student Orientation Week, and the other first-year students assigned to her dorm meet that evening to become acquainted with the housemother, the Resident Adviser and Council, and the sophomores, juniors and seniors who will live alongside them. The dorm she has drawn is Manning House. Her roommate's name is Marcia Rusk. She and Marcia met that afternoon as they unpacked and negotiated who would take which bed, which closet, which desk. Marcia has large spaniel eyes and a tentative manner.

To avoid exposing Marcia to her cold germs, she sits a little apart from her on one of the sofas in the spacious lounge. After the welcoming speeches and introductions, the RA gets right to the house rules.

"Okay," she says, "Hours. So freshman women have to be in the dorm by 11:00 p.m. Sunday through Thursday and 12:30 a.m. Friday and Saturday nights. The doors to the loggia will be locked at 10:30. If you get back between 10:30 and curfew, come in through the main door of Carroll Hall at the other end of the loggia and sign in. But if it's past curfew, those doors will be locked and you could be suspended if there's a bed check and they catch you out."

"Who is 'they'?" someone asks.

"Well," the RA tilts her head with a rueful smile, "*they* is actually *we*." She indicates herself, the housemother, and the Resident Council members. "We have to do random bed checks every so often."

Since junior year in high school she hasn't had a curfew of any kind. She doesn't remember there ever being even a discussion of a curfew. She sometimes came home as late as one a.m. on the weekend. During the week, she managed her own bedtime, insomniac that she is, always concerned about getting enough sleep. She hasn't anticipated these enforced "Hours." She and Marcia raise eyebrows at each other.

"What about the med's hours?" she asks through her stuffy nose.

"Med's?"

"Men's," Marcia interprets.

The RA shrugs. "Well, the men don't have hours. I mean they *do*, but they really aren't enforced. Their loggia isn't enclosed, so it can't be locked. There's nothing to keep them in."

"The doors to their houses aren't locked at night?"

"And what about bed checks?" someone else says.

Again the resigned smile and shrug from the RA. "Yeah, the men's houses are locked. But the guys can just climb out the windows on the first floor of their dorms. And it's pretty much impossible to get the men's RAs to do bed checks."

There is some grumbling from the first-years and jaded muttering by the others about how, if anyone, it's the *boys* who need to be locked in. But the objections don't rise to the level of a rebellion and the RA is allowed to finish the rest of the rules: skirts or dresses to be worn to class, to sit-down dinners, chapel services and concerts; slacks only if the temperature is below fifteen degrees. Permission needed for out-of-town trips. No smoking or drinking. No men in your room except during Sunday afternoon visiting hours, and the door must remain open. No ownership of cars except for seniors.

Apart from her father constantly warning her of trip hazards and poison ivy patches, she has never had so many rules laid out so explicitly; in fact, she didn't grow up with *any* rules laid out. But since she hasn't had anything to rebel against, she has not learned to be a rebel. If these are the rules, she guesses there is no choice but to follow them like everyone else. She doesn't drink or smoke anyway, doesn't have a driver's license and will probably get a lot more studying done if she isn't making out with someone every night. As far as freezing legs are concerned, Franklin High had the same stupid rule and her legs are used to it.

Still, why *don't* the boys have to be locked in? And why do the men get to have warm legs? Even here at progressive Carroll, the double standard reigns.

BCWCB

At the end of Orientation Week, after the dance and the picnics and the House parties have sufficiently thrust everyone into each other's company, the unattached males have girded themselves for rejection and are starting to call women up for dates. On every floor of the women's dorms a phone sits on a recessed counter in the hallway next to a tablet with a pencil on a string. Messages are in a well-established code: "Nancy—BCWCB" ("Boy called, will call back"), "Chris, MCPCB" ("Man called, please call back"—undoubtedly

Chris's father), "Angela call Sally ASAP." On Sunday evening after dinner, there is a message for her: "Annie, BCWCB." Who is this boy and when will he call back?

Whoever he is, he doesn't call back that evening. She and Marcia make small talk before she settles in to write letters and Marcia heads for the communal bathroom to take a shower and wash her hair. She and Marcia so far haven't clicked. There's no animosity, just a distance between them. They don't have much in common and she finds Marcia a little too shrinking or bashful, a quality she rather likes in a boy but doesn't know what to do with in a girl.

She listens for the hall phone to ring, which it does several times, but the calls are not for her. Marcia returns from her shower and by mutual consent they turn out the lights and go to bed. Marcia falls asleep quickly. Her breathing—not quite a snore—can be heard from across the room. How strange it is to share a bedroom with another person. The last time was with Teddy when he was eight and she was eleven. By then she was no more conscious of his presence than if he had been a piece of furniture. Now she keeps herself awake worrying that the rustling of her blankets or the creak of her bedsprings or even her own breathing will bother Marcia. Around eleven she finally falls asleep but wakens in the middle of the night needing to go to the bathroom. Afraid of disturbing her roommate, she holds it uncomfortably until morning.

Boy Calls Back

The boy does call back. His name is David Kirschner. He mentions having met her at the college picnic on Sunday and wonders if she would like to go over to The Hub that evening for coffee. She doesn't remember meeting him but says yes, sure, that sounds like fun.

"Oh. Well, thank you," he says, rather humbly, and she thinks, better humble than arrogant. After she hangs up, she runs to her room to look up his picture in the herd book. He wears black glasses and has a thick shock of wavy black hair, warm brown eyes and a self-deprecating grin. He's a junior, with a double major in physics and math. If he's a junior, he must be twenty, but on the phone she has detected the slight hoarseness of a boy whose voice hasn't completely changed.

When she comes downstairs that night, he jumps up from a sofa in the lounge, a tall, gangly boy. The sleeves of his white Dacron shirt and the legs of his polyester pants have not kept up with his wrists and ankles. He is wearing white socks and hush puppy shoes on long feet that splay slightly when he walks. The brown eyes are as warm as they were in the photo, the grin less self-deprecating, happier.

"I'm David," he says. "Pretty nice digs, huh?" He looks around at the wing chairs, the sofas, chandelier and fireplace. "You got lucky when you drew Manning."

"What dorm are you in?"

"McCollum." There's a pause. He looks around again. "I haven't been in Manning lounge before. McCollum's is a lot smaller. And kind of dark."

Having exhausted the topic of lounges, they stand smiling at each other for a few moments before he says, "Okay. Shall we head over to The Hub?"

"Let's." The single word sounds flirtatious in her own ears. He's gawky and a late bloomer, but she likes his eyes.

David

Despite her prejudice against modern buildings, she has to admit The Hub has been designed by someone who understands students. David shows her around. The South Lounge is studded with red ottomans that glide on wheels over the purple carpet. Already students have configured the ottomans into small corral-like enclosures to give couples an illusion of privacy, or larger ones that three or four people can sit on or sprawl inside on the floor. On the lower level there are rooms for pool, ping pong, bridge games, meetings, student government offices. Large colorful banners hang in entryways and on landings. Floor-to-ceiling, wall-to-wall windows let in the amber and ruby twilight just now filling the sky. It's both a playful and elegant place to congregate.

"It just opened this year," David tells her. "It's got about everything you'd want." They've taken a table at the Grill. He orders a coffee, she a milk shake.

To manage their initial shyness they ask each other about their families. She tells him the essentials—two brothers, father in university administration, mother getting a degree in clinical psychology. "My parents are very liberal, politically. And also personally. We've never had many rules to follow. We don't go to any church." That seems to cover it. There isn't much to tell.

What he has to say about his family amazes her.

He has an older and a younger sister. Before the three of them were born, his parents came to the United States from Vienna with nothing except their lives. An old family friend, now a famous symphony conductor, had come to the United States well before Hitler rose to power. He sponsored their flight from the Nazis.

His parents barely slipped through the Austrian door before it slammed shut. If the conductor had not sponsored them along with David's paternal grandparents, aunt and maternal grandmother (the grandfather having died young), they all would have succumbed to the camps. His mother's beloved younger brother chose to stay in Austria, where he was caught up in the Holocaust, survived the war years in a concentration camp and then emigrated to Israel, only to die five months later in a boating accident.

David's parents, with little English and virtually no money, at first toiled as orderlies in a mental hospital until his father could establish his academic credentials from before the war and obtain a position as

Assistant Professor of History and Political Science at a small liberal arts college. His mother, once an aspiring athlete at university, is a good Austrian hausfrau who managed to feed, clothe and shelter three children, her mother and three in-laws, her husband, herself and a family dog in a three bedroom house and on an assistant professor's salary.

They're secular Jews, devoted not to religion but to culture. David loves classical music and plays it in his dorm room to study by. With some excitement he mentions that his mother gave him as a going away present a record of the Bach Goldberg Variations played by Glenn Gould. He says this as though she would certainly have heard of it. "We could listen to it sometime in the Music Room here."

"I'd love to." she says.

Gracie

Classes start on Monday. She's taking Inorganic Chemistry, Intermediate French, Classical Antiquity, and General Psychology. The first class of the day is Classical Antiquity, required for freshmen and taught by a lean, unsmiling young man named Mr. Smits. She's learned that Carroll teachers who are not full professors are addressed as Mr. instead of Dr., even though they have PhDs, perhaps in the same egalitarian spirit that motivates Carroll's prohibition of sororities and fraternities.

Their textbooks are three volumes of Greek plays and an annotated copy of *The Iliad and The Odyssey*. Mr. Smits goes over the syllabus in great detail and assigns them to read seventy-five pages from *The Odyssey* and come up with five discussion points by Wednesday. "Any questions," he asks with a downward inflection that suggests he doesn't want any. He lets them out three minutes late.

It's in this class that she meets Gracie Miller. They're moving side by side toward the door, behind students who are pushing forward to get to their next class on time.

"There they go," Gracie says, "like a herd of turtles. Or is it a turd of hurtles?"

They walk across campus together.

"I'm Gracie Miller. And who might you be?"

She introduces herself. "So what do you think of Classical Antiquity?"

"Jesus! Seventy-five pages by Wednesday. Is he kidding?"

"And that's just one class."

Both are carrying heavy stacks of required books that they purchased that morning. They continue up the sidewalk approaching The Hub.

Gracie says, "Hey, you want to get coffee or something? The coffee here doesn't stink too bad. I don't have a class 'til ten."

At the Grill, they unload their books on a table and go up to the counter to order. She doesn't really like coffee, but gets it anyway. Loaded up with cream and sugar, it tastes okay, and it might keep her awake through today's classes following her typical night of disturbed sleep.

Gracie boasts of being the local bad girl in the small farming town where she's from. Her nickname in high school was "Garbage Mouth Gracie." This she asserts with some glee. She is the middle child between an older sister and younger brother. Her mother is an elementary school teacher and her father is a mail carrier. She has come to Carroll on a partial scholarship and will make up the rest of her fees with a campus job. She'll be serving at sit-down dinners in the men's dining hall.

"It'll be a swell way to meet the fellas," she says in a Mae West voice.

Gracie wants to major in economics, because she plans to go to law school. She can picture Gracie, brash and sarcastic, cross-examining crooked Wall Street brokers.

"So what are *you* going to be when you grow up?"

"I'm thinking about majoring in psychology and probably go into clinical psychology."

Reasonable People

"Wonderful. Then you can shrink my head. I could use a personal head shrinker to figure out what in the hell is wrong with me."

They make a plan to get together on Tuesday night and write the *Odyssey* discussion points together.

"Áu reservoir," says Gracie blithely when they part and head off to their ten o'clock classes.

French

She has Intermediate French next. The textbook, in addition to a fat unabridged Larousse dictionary and a slim grammar book, is an obscure novel that has never been translated into English. Monsieur Durand is working on a translation himself as part of a postdoctoral research project. They are to translate the first ten pages for Wednesday.

"I'm assigning you to translate this book in particular because it's a small masterpiece that has been sadly overlooked, and therefore you won't be able to plagiarize your translations."

A smart-aleck in the front row raises his hand. "But how do we know *you* won't plagiarize *our* translations?" The class laughs.

Monsieur Durand shakes his head. In a tone that suggests their translations will be beyond pathetic, he says, "Trust me, that won't happen."

"So you don't trust us but you want us to trust you?"

"*Exactement*."

Tuesday

She has Inorganic Chemistry and General Psychology on Tuesday. The chemistry text is a seven hundred-page hardback tome riddled with symbols and formulas, which does not bode well. For Thursday they're to read the first chapter and solve the problems at the end. If she runs into trouble, though, she might ask David for help.

The general psychology text is an overview of the field and could be interesting. Some of it she's already familiar with from quizzing her mother over her course notes all those years when she was getting her bachelor's degree.

The psych professor, Dr. Steiner, is a tall, stooped, middle-aged man who paces slowly from one side of the classroom to the other, studying the floor as he talks. When he does look up in response to a question, he nods several times, frowning contemplatively before answering.

Maybe the best part of taking a psychology course is the psychology building itself. Built in 1885, Mustin Hall is the oldest building on campus. It's a gothic hulk of an edifice made of roughly hewn sandstone blocks the color of dead roses. Dr. Steiner has his office in the squat round tower at the top where you might expect to encounter a confined mad woman. It's reached by a narrow, creaking staircase. Worn to bare wood by the continuous tread of students ascending and descending for seven decades, it's treacherously smooth. The low-ceilinged psychology classroom, with its wrap around blackboards and miasma of chalk, looks like it should be sepia colored, and almost is.

Blue Canal Water

On Tuesday night she and Gracie meet in Manning House lounge to work on the discussion points for The Ancient World class.

"Let's write ten points. You can take five and I'll take five," says Gracie.

"But what does Smits mean by discussion *points*? Discussion *questions*? Statements? Controversial statements?"

"How about this for a discussion point: Does Smits's ass suck blue canal water? Why or why not?"

She falls over on the sofa laughing. "Oh my God! Where did you get that expression?"

"Isn't it common knowledge?"

"It makes no sense. Canal water isn't blue."

"It is if the canal flows by a dye factory."

"And asses don't suck. They do the opposite."

"Unless the ass is a freak of nature."

It takes them until eleven o'clock to finish their lists.

Bach

On Wednesday, she and David have a study date in the south lounge of The Hub. They hang out on the floor, surrounded by ottomans, she reading her *Odyssey*, he working out problems in his math book. He has brought his Glenn Gould album, and after an hour they take a break and climb the three steps to the glassed-in Music Room overlooking the lounge. He puts the record on the stereo and sits on an ottoman in an attitude of rapt attention, bent a little forward, his hands clasped between his knees. She sprawls on the carpet, hands behind her head, eyes closed. For the last half hour she's felt a headache coming on and she hopes to stave it off while listening.

It's an awful lot of Bach piano to take in for forty minutes. She opens her eyes occasionally to show that she hasn't fallen asleep. Each time, she finds him in the same attentive position, with eyes half closed, head bobbing to the rhythm.

"Wow!" she exclaims after the scratching needle assures her that the last quiet notes really mean the record has ended.

"Isn't it great?"

"Very ... soothing," she says, restraining herself from pressing a finger to the knife in her eye socket. "Yeah, I can see why you like to play it while you're studying. The pianist is so skilled! Thanks for introducing me to it." She wouldn't dream of revealing her obtuseness, or that the record has failed to prevent the headache. He seems satisfied, and while the music hasn't stirred her, his delight in it has.

Critique

Mr. Smits assigns their first paper for the Classical Antiquity course, an analysis to be titled "Effectiveness of the First Book of *The Odyssey*." With characteristic diligence, she spends several days on it, unlike Gracie, who pulls an all-nighter. Today Mr. Smits hands back their essays. If they have any questions, he invites them to make an appointment after class to see him during his office hours.

Flipping through the paper, she skims past the scattered one-word comments without reading them and quickly turns to the back page to find out her grade. There, at least half an inch tall, flying like the flag of a despotic government, is a conspicuous blue F. She suppresses an audible gasp, shoves the paper into her book bag and hurries out the door before Gracie can catch up and ask the inevitable question, What did you get?

She sleepwalks across central campus and over the railroad tracks (fortunately the morning train has already passed), her thoughts stuck on the mortifying pride she had felt about this paper when she finished it and read it aloud to herself. How clever it had sounded. She's so glad that she didn't read it to anyone else before handing it in. In twelve years of schooling, she has never received an F on anything. Not even in algebra or gym.

Thank God her roommate is in class. At least she'll be alone when she steels herself to face Mr. Smits's criticism.

She opens the paper to the back page, lays it on her desk and sits down. Mr. Smits has written a page of critique underneath the towering F, separating his points into paragraphs, the lines evenly spaced. Has he been this meticulous with everyone's paper or only with hers? And are there so many things wrong with it that the corrections had to take up a whole page?

She takes a breath and reads:

> You have the ability to be a superb prose stylist. You

combine humor, clarity, force, efficiency and sophistication. In addition, you avoid the pretention and self-conscious overuse of metaphor which is so common among good young writers.

She is stunned. She's not a terrible writer after all. She's unpretentious, she's sophisticated, humorous, clear! Then what's wrong with the paper?

This talent puts a greater burden on you to be perceptive and analytic. Unfortunately, you have not written a critical paper at all. Up until your last paragraph you have merely summarized. Each event, each scene should have been examined to determine its significance and the values for the poem as a whole.

So. Her only failing is that she didn't do what was assigned.

She turns the paper over and reads the short comments in the margins. The first one refers to her introduction as "Very clever." She lingers on these two words, savoring them. Next there is a question about word use and in her third paragraph he points out two "who" clauses that are "a bit too similar." Yes, she sees that. She had overlooked them when she proofread.

Still, the problem is she didn't write a critical paper. She failed to analyze the text for its significance. What does he mean, though, by "significance?" What is he talking about? She thought she had done that, and if she had the chance to re-write the paper, she still wouldn't know how to go about it. He must expect her to figure it out by herself; otherwise, in such a scrupulous evaluation, he would have provided an example of what he was looking for, which means there's no point in intruding on his office hour.

Mighty Oaks

The lawn between the railroad tracks and the women's loggia is a conveniently timbered area of campus. The thick trunks of the giant oaks stabilize lovers expressing their passionate goodbyes (of necessity in a standing position) just before curfew. There is usually at least one available trunk per couple, and often several to spare.

She and David have been going out for several weeks, skirting decorously around the girls pressed against boys whose backs are dug into the craggy bark. But tonight, after an evening at the library together, by unspoken agreement they stop at an untenanted tree. It's a chilly evening. They slip their hands inside each other's open coats, and when she lays her head on his chest she feels his heart do a little lurch and speed up.

Tenderly, she puts a hand on his cheek. He takes her hand and kisses the palm. Then he leans down shyly, kisses her lips, and kisses her again—and again, and for so long that they almost fail to notice the sound of locks clicking up and down the loggia and the girls around them drifting regretfully back to their dorms.

"Oops!" she says. "Gotta go." She gives him one quick kiss and runs for the nearest door.

In her room, she lies down, closes her eyes, and relives the last fifteen minutes—the feel of her breasts against David's lanky chest, his arms around her waist, his eager lips (even if these lips protruded a bit fishily), most of all the hectic thrum of his heart. She wonders what he's feeling now. Is he the kind of guy who will go back to the dorm and make sly, suggestive remarks about his date? No. She doubts it.

Coveted Property

The couch in the alcove off the Manning House lounge is coveted property, a semi-private hideaway (first come, first served) for making out. Occasionally she and David manage to get there ahead of everyone else after the house mother has gone to bed and before curfew. For a week or so, it's four feet on the floor, according to the rule. Then, bending the rule a bit, two feet. Finally, they're stretched out body to body with no attention to feet at all. The RA usually turns a blind eye since she and her boyfriend can frequently be seen to occupy the couch in just such a position. Everyone who does this stays dressed, of course. The place is not *that* private. And there's no fiddling underneath clothing. But it's definitely better than pressing up against a tree.

It is on this couch, their legs entangled and her cheek snugged into the hollow between his collarbone and chest, that he tells her she is the first girl he has ever kissed, in fact she is his very first girlfriend. This news is extremely gratifying. It explains why he is as enthusiastic as a frolicking colt, why he's all smiles when they're together. It also explains why his fish-lipped kissing could use a little work (though she isn't going to spoil his newfound delight by even a suggestion of criticism).

Lion Imagery

Inorganic Chemistry isn't as hard as she expected; in fact it's kind of interesting and possibly useful for understanding how the physical world functions. David is there to explain things if she gets stuck. So far, she's getting B and B- on her lab work and quizzes. It could definitely be worse.

She expected to get As on her Intermediate French translations and is surprised at all the Bs, but a lot of other students are getting Bs, too. Maybe at this brainy college, only the most exalted prodigies are given As on principle. While she thought she did A work in high school, it must translate as B work at Carroll.

However, her General Psychology teacher, Dr. Steiner, is apparently not one of those professors who abides by the prodigy principle. In any case, she's happy with her A on the first essay exam in his class. Thank you, Mom, she thinks. All those evenings of quizzing her mother on her 3x5 cards has paid off.

With trepidation she receives, folded for privacy, the graded second essay of the semester in Classical Antiquity. She has worked hard on "The Function of Lion Imagery in *The Iliad*," conscious all the while of Smits's high opinion of her prose style, and hoping—even optimistic—that this time the paper has delivered the goods as assigned.

If anything, while Mr. Smits's critique is shorter, the letter grade on the paper is even taller and more conspicuous than the earlier F. He's given her a D+ and half a page of primarily negative comments. Her prose merits one sentence of perfunctory praise: "This paper is well written and shows an excellent perception of one of the major functions of lion imagery." But—"You should have made it clear that this is only one function among several ... analysis of individual images and how they work could have formed excellent evidence for your more general contentions" etc. etc. The marginal comments are no better: "Why?" "I hope this does not indicate that you are going to be prescriptive" "You are getting pretty far away from the text" and now he is taking her to task on her prose too, crossing out phrases and whole sentences as redundant, and complaining about an "artificial transition."

She slumps in her chair as the other students file out. Gracie flops down beside her.

"How'd you do?"

Listlessly, she hands Gracie the paper. She is too discouraged for shame.

"Well, that sucks," Gracie says, philosophically. "I've heard that to get a B, you'd have to squeeze it out of Smits's ass. And probably squeeze an A out of his dick." Smits has given Gracie a respectable C.

The United States of America

David has a collection of classical albums he studies by. *The Goldberg Variations* is just his current favorite. He is primarily a Beethoven fan. But his all-time favorite record, which he doesn't study by, is the comedy album *Stan Freberg presents the United States of America*. He can quote all the lines by heart and tosses them out whenever the occasion arises.

"What did you think of it?" he asks after playing her the album the first time.

"Now I see where you get all those quips," she says. "You're like those theatre majors who stick in lines from every play they've been in."

"Jeez, I ask a simple question, I get a pageant," he quotes.

His imitations are actually quite good. She's impressed with his ability to capture the snide and ironic intonations, even the narrator's artificially basso voice quavering with patriotic fervor. And the album is, indeed, very funny.

In fact, they have the same sense humor. Both are great fans of the comedy album *Mike Nichols and Elaine May Examine Doctors*. Her favorite part is the Albert Schweitzer sketch in which Schweitzer endures an abrasive American tourist who's visiting his clinic in Gabon. After asking about his "reverence for life" philosophy, she begs him to wait while she gets her husband for a snapshot with the great man. "Well, I am very busy, Madame," says Schweitzer, mildly. "Oh it won't take a minute," she brays. "He's just down the road taking pictures of lions." After she leaves, Schweitzer turns to his assistant and says, in his thick German accent, "Wamba, if zat woman comes back, kill her." She and David use this line on any number of occasions.

Beds

They're in McCollum lounge, where they've been studying, when David off-handedly reveals that the men have their beds made for them by the housekeepers on Thursdays.

"What?!" She's astounded.

"Well, you know, when they bring the clean sheets?" he says, tentatively.

"They don't just set them on your mattress? Folded? In a pile?"

He raises his eyebrows. "They don't make the beds for the women?"

"No, they do not."

"Hm. That ... doesn't seem very fair."

"No kidding." Now she's suspicious. "So on Thursday mornings, you strip your beds and put the sheets outside your doors, right?"

"Jeez. That's how it works over there?"

"Yes. That's how it works over there. What happens on *this* side of campus?"

He glances over her shoulder as if looking for someone to come into the lounge and interrupt them.

"Um ... the housekeepers strip the beds," he murmurs.

She jumps to her feet.

"You don't even strip your own beds? And on top of that, they make your bed for you? I don't believe this."

"I guess maybe they think a lot of men don't know how to make a bed?"

"Do *you* know how to make a bed?"

"Oh, yeah. My mother taught me."

"And how hard was it? Do you think these guys might be able to figure it out *all by themselves*? Maybe by *un*making their beds and working backwards?"

He laughs nervously.

"What is the idea, anyway?" she continues. "Is their masculinity so precarious it'll suffer permanent damage at the image of themselves making their own beds? Oh, no wait! Correct me if I'm wrong, but isn't bed making the first thing they teach men in *boot camp*? Sheets so tight they can bounce quarters off them? Those hospital corners they're so proud of?"

He has no answer. Fortunately for him, his roommate Jae-sung and his girlfriend poke their heads into the lounge. "You guys coming to dinner?"

It's almost 5:30 and if they don't head down to the dining hall now, they'll miss the sit-down service. She's hungry, and it's fried chicken with gravy and mashed potatoes night. In any case, the discussion has pretty much run its course.

Green-eyed Monster

It may have been creeping up behind her for some time before it pounces, but the onset is sudden and fierce.

She becomes violently jealous of the two reigning Carroll College beauty queens in her class. One of them, Roz Cohen, lives in her dorm. Since the beginning of the semester they have crossed paths before or after showering or while brushing teeth in the communal bathroom. For those first weeks, she feels only envy. Envy and *awe* but not jealousy.

When Roz towels off her dark, luxuriant hair, it springs into soft waves that frame her perfect face. No curlers, no hair dryer. She doesn't even have to *brush* her hair. And her features! Those heavily lashed green eyes, luminous olive skin without a touch of make-up. To say nothing of her figure! The slender waist, perfectly proportioned limbs, graceful dancer's body. In fact, she is a dancer, a member of Terpsichore, the college dance troupe.

Roz even smells good. She always leaves behind a subtle scent like something delicious to eat, something with vanilla in it, maybe freshly baked cookies. When she asks her, Roz says the scent is called Shalimar. She writes her mother asking for a bottle, but the cologne smells over-sweet on her own skin, more like the incompatible mix of scents at a perfume counter.

On top of all this, Roz is quiet, thoughtful, smart and modest. Still, until now she has only been envious of Roz, not painfully jealous.

The other campus queen is Lily Roberts. She's a completely different breed of beauty, more like a model out of *Vogue*. Like Roz, though, she has a well-proportioned body according to the current notion of proportion in women—slim hips, "shapely" legs, flat stomach. Her large hazel eyes are emphasized by her auburn hair, worn in a thick page-boy. Unlike Roz, Lily has turned cosmetics and hair styling into an art form. As if a make-up artist has prepared her for a photo shoot, her artificially blushing cheeks, spectacularly lined and shadowed eyes, and smooth, curved hair and bangs (surely the product of rollers and a hair dryer) turn heads as she walks across campus.

Lily has adopted the turtle neck style. Seeing how well it looks on Lily, she buys two turtlenecks for herself from a dress shop downtown.

Why, she asks herself, has she gone from being simply envious of these two to becoming so desperately jealous?

She traces it to the night she and David attend a Terpsichore dance concert.

They're watching the performance together, and she has already been feeling uneasy having to witness Roz's lithe body spotlighted gracefully floating around the stage in her pale lavender leotard. Then she is stricken by the words of two boys sitting just behind them.

"Whoa!" says one. "Roz Cohen!"

"Yeah," says the other. "No kidding!"

Her first thought is, did David hear that? Now she imagines David's attention to be riveted on Roz. Who could ignore her? Surely he, too, is thinking "Whoa! Roz Cohen!"

By the end of the concert, she has worked herself into such a private state of jealousy that when she parts from David at the loggia, she assumes an attitude of cold indifference to his goodbye kiss and slips in the door before the kiss can be repeated. She is certain he has no idea why she is acting so stand-offish or that she has been overcome by an irresistible impulse to punish him. For what? For possibly harboring fantasies about Roz Cohen? Yes.

Within a week of this incident, she sees a photo of Lily Roberts in the college newspaper. The photo isn't accompanied by an article. It's just there because the student photographer—a male—thinks she's beautiful. Instantly she is jealous of Lily, too.

Why now? she wonders. Is it because she and David have entered into the making-out-in-the-alcove phase of their relationship, cementing the idea that they are officially a couple, and as her official boyfriend, he can't be attracted to anyone but herself and only herself? Yes, somehow that feels like it. That *is* it. But my god, how unrealistic. How unreasonable. And how is she going to live with these feelings?

Never Enough

She wonders sometimes about a beauty queen of the Lily Roberts type. She looks like a *Vogue* model, but does she ever let anyone see her without cosmetic enhancement? Possibly, like Roz, she would be just as stunning. But how does *Lily* think she looks without it? She and her mask seem inseparable.

Lily's roommate Mary is an extraordinarily homely girl with bone structure as unlucky as you can get. The two are tight. Mary is like Lily's courtier. Maybe Mary is the only one privileged to see Lily in her raw state. It reminds her of how her mother never goes to bed without her makeup on. And doesn't she herself avoid going off for her morning class before putting in the usual hour drying her hair in curlers under a plastic bonnet and applying those little touches to her eyes and cheeks? If she has this look on, she thinks she's pretty enough. Well, not *enough*. That's the kicker. It's never enough. There's always someone with a better look, more easily attained.

Once she told her mother how her friends at school always talked about what a beautiful mother she has. Her mother replied dismissively, "Oh, I've just found a look that works for me." Is that what Lily has done? Searched for the look, found it, worked at it and refined it?

Maybe 99.9% of beautiful women have found the look with varying degrees of labor while the .1%, like Roz Cohen, are truly born with it. And where do the standards for beauty come from? Don't they vary from culture to culture and era to era? So why call it beauty, as if it is something inherent, universal and eternal? She prefers the term glamour as more truthful.

She doesn't dislike or blame the glamorous women for being glamorous. It's the men she judges harshly. It's because of the men that she spends that hour every morning. If there were no men, she would shave her head, wash her face clean and never have a reason to look in a mirror again. It would be heaven.

Male Solidarity

Two guys in David's dorm see her in the entryway about to come up to his room at the top of the stairs. As they pass by his open door, one says to the other as if finishing a conversation, "Women. They're so screwed up." And then to David, who's writing at his desk, "Isn't that right, Kirschner?"

"Yeah," David mumbles absently without looking up from his work. "So screwed up."

The guys grin as she halts with one foot on the first step and does an about-face. She's halfway along the men's loggia when David catches up with her. Apparently the guys have told him of their prank.

She knows his comment was made without conviction. She knows he really doesn't feel that way about women. His reply was just a meaningless parroting when his brains were otherwise occupied. And she's mad at herself for giving these stupid goons the satisfaction of getting him in hot water and, at least to themselves, proving their point. But what is "screwed up" about a woman objecting to her sex being ridiculed? If she were Black, and the remark had been racist, what would they think of her objection then, these supposedly *so* liberal boys at supposedly *so* liberal Carroll College? How is it that women are fair game even here?

She says all this to David as they walk back across campus. He apologizes, he agrees, he doesn't try to excuse himself, he quotes Stan Freberg, "Yeah, you give us an inch and we take over." She laughs. His Freberg imitation gets her every time.

My Brother Esau

David has his Stan Frebergisms and now, after a British satirical improv group Beyond the Fringe performs at Carroll, she too has lines to quote. Or *one* line, to be exact: "... 'but my brother Esau is an hairy man, but I am a smooth man.'" It's a parody of a pinch-mouthed upper class British vicar giving a meandering, pointless sermon with the utmost gravity. The actor goes on to repeat the momentous phrase: "... But my brother Esau is an hairy man but *I* ... but *I* ... am a smooth man. Perhaps," he continues, after a significant pause, "I can paraphrase that, saying the same thing but in a different way ..." and proceeds to quote at length a series of population statistics from *Genesis*.

Whenever she recalls the sketch, it makes her laugh. For one thing, it takes a swipe at the absurdities of religion, and for another it sends up those preachers, lecturers, political leaders and pompous professors (like Professor Dobre whom her mother wanted to separate from his private parts) who orate instead of speak like normal people. On that account alone Abraham Lincoln would have won her approval hands down in his debate with Stephen Douglas.

Now, when she strokes David's darkly hairy arms, she intones, "My boyfriend David is an hairy man, but *I* ... but *I* am a smooth woman." He chuckles agreeably.

Operant Conditioning

She would like to comfort herself by finding personality flaws in the two women she's so jealous of. Roz Cohen, though, is a thoroughly fine human being, so there's nothing she can cling to there. Lily Roberts is of a different ilk. She doesn't see much of Lily but has noticed in her what can best be described by the two adjectives haughty and sneering.

Lily and the guy she's currently dating are sitting with her entourage of homely girls at the next table during Sunday brunch. Lily's voice rings clear and, as always, subtly derisive above the laughter of her hangers on. She is entertaining the group with the story of a prank she organized to play on Mr. Fraser, teacher of the other Intro to Psych section (not her own respected Dr. Steiner, whom she would stand up for even against the likes of Lily Roberts). Since finishing the textbook chapter on operant conditioning, Lily and her cohorts have trained Fraser to address the left or right side of the class by smiling attentively at him from one side or the other.

What could poor Mr. Fraser have done to be made such a fool of? She wouldn't pull something like that even on Smits, regardless of how she and Gracie mock him in private. She recalls the shameful liquor bottle trick she and her pal Rob played on Mike Walenta in high school. Her father's reprimand still makes her shudder: "That was a very foolish and thoughtless thing to do."

She's tempted to tell David about Lily's prank, but reporting her meanness would just make herself sound mean, *and* jealous, and furthermore, she doesn't want Lily's glamorous face and figure to appear in David's thoughts regardless of the circumstances.

Knife in the Eye

It always starts with tension in the neck at the base of the skull, usually on the right side. She can press and press on the spot, knead it, stretch her neck to the right, to the left, drop her head toward her chest, let it fall back, but once the pain starts there is no stopping it. It spreads up into her temple, and from there it jumps to the inside corner of her eye into the notch of bone just under her eyebrow. Now it's at its worst, and it won't let go until it's good and ready, after she's spent a fitful night trying to sleep through it and finally succeeds. Or maybe it's there the next day, too. She presses and presses with a thumb, a forefinger, the heel of her hand, an ice pack. None of it helps. Aspirin doesn't touch it. She calls it the knife in the eye.

Two or three times a year the head-ache is preceded by the sparkling sickle that blots out a piece of her vision on one side. Ten or fifteen minutes later the aura recedes and the head-ache starts, always on the side opposite. Every six weeks or so it comes on without an accompanying aura. She has no idea why. The first time she had it, in seventh grade, it was while she was studying intensely for a test. But since then it comes at any time for no discernible reason. She might be in the middle of eating dinner or taking a book back to the library.

With her immersion in the field of psychology and the unavoidable, if unwanted, influence of Freud, she has come to believe it's psychosomatic. This makes her feel she's at fault somehow and if anything, that makes it worse. What would be her motivation? To get attention? Sympathy? The last thing she wants is to interact with people, to talk, or to move when the headache is upon her.

She endures it as she endures her frequent head colds, as she endures her chronic insomnia, her jealousy, her pessimism. Sometimes she thinks, I am not a happy person.

Up and Down the Ladder

With each subsequent paper in Classical Antiquity (and she has to crank one out every two weeks) she hauls herself, rung by rung, up the ladder of Mr. Smits's approval. "The Analysis of Book Twenty-Four as a Conclusion to *The Iliad*" gets her a C for a "valid and well made" main point but a lack of other central themes. Her paper on *Agamemnon* delivers a lofty B+ but with no accompanying comments except for a scattering of negatives: "Not true." "Not wholly accurate." "No." She slips up and down the rungs with alternating Bs and B+s. Finally, on the last essay of the semester, "Socrates' Use of Analogy," it's down once more to B. On this one "... the tone is often a bit too chummy for a critical paper."

In the end, she isn't sure what she's learned, if anything, about classical antiquity or the purpose of analyzing its literature or even how to analyze it. And once again she wonders if the grading system isn't simply arbitrary, or possibly a way to humble first-year students who arrive at Carroll thinking they're hot stuff. She could be wrong, but she'll never know because she just can't see herself sitting down in Mr. Smits's office and asking for help.

Meeting the Folks

During the winter break, David drives the family car three hours to her house and brings her back to his home town for an overnight stay. He wants her to meet his family. He met hers when they came up to Carroll for a visit in November. They all liked each other. His cheerfulness and amiability charmed them, and of course they're impressed with how smart he is.

She's not as sure that his parents will take to her. The family is now reduced to David's mother and father and twelve-year-old sister Rachel. His older sister has married and moved to the East Coast, and so has his aunt. The grandparents died some years ago.

On the drive there she recalls how her mother got her feelings hurt when Leah Kaplan, a close friend and highly educated and cultured psychologist, said she would be inconsolable if her daughter Miriam married a non-Jew. At the time, Miriam and Nick were in the same high school class, not that they were seeing each other or that there had been any interest on either side, but her mother took it as an insult to her son, especially since Leah wasn't even religious.

But she herself can understand Leah Kaplan's feelings on the subject. If she were Jewish, she's pretty sure she'd feel the same way; she had read those first-hand Holocaust accounts on Nick's bookshelf back when she was fourteen. They'd made a deep impression. Of course her mother, too, must know of the horrific things that happened, but she may never have read about them in their terrible, stark details, and her mother's Jewish friends, she assumes, don't discuss it.

David's mother greets her with a hug and a wide smile. His little sister is equally friendly.

"You know, you are David's first girlfriend!" Sarah Kirschner exclaims in her Austrian accent, pleasantly reminiscent of Opa's German one. She is all rosy-cheeked with happiness.

David raises a sardonic eyebrow at his mother. "Good thing for you that Annie does know this already."

Rachel takes her by the hand and shows her the room they will be sharing that night. "We'll be roommates!" She's tall for her age, a little gangly like David, and has his deep brown eyes and her mother's pink cheeks and porcelain skin.

Later she meets Professor Kirschner. He comes home from his office in the Political Science Department promptly at six o'clock. Dinner is ready for him. David's father is quite a homely man—pallid, with large protruding ears and an oversized head that's virtually bald. He stands and walks with a stoop as if this head is almost too heavy to carry around.

Daniel Kirschner greets her politely, but doesn't seem much interested and says very little as he eats. She wonders if he disapproves of her. Still, no one seems nervous about his silence, so maybe it's just his way. At the end of the meal he mentions some research he's doing which brings up the subject of Israel. Mrs. Kirschner shakes her head. "I never liked the idea of Zionism," she says. "Even when I was young, just in college. I always thought it would only lead to more war, and you see I was right."

So Sarah Kirschner is no Leah Kaplan. Apparently the first girl—Jew or Gentile—to fully appreciate the value of her son David is all right by his mother.

Middle Ages to the French Revolution

Spring semester the two required courses for freshmen cover the Middle Ages to the French Revolution. One course involves the political actors and events of the period; the other examines its literature. She has drawn Smits again, for the literature course, and starts out stronger than last semester with a B for her paper, "The First Canto of *The Divine Comedy* as an Introduction," but then, for the papers "Analysis of Sonnet 130," "Lear's Realization of a Greater Self Knowledge," and "Analysis of 'The Schoolboy'" it's C plus, C minus and C. Her prose style is "effective," but she "overstates," "speculates," and "fails to support with evidence." Her last paper has no comments at all as if Smits has finally exhausted himself trying to explain her faults. Despite all her efforts, she seems never to have been able to give him what he wants.

Maybe it's this sense of pessimism that prompts her to throw caution to the winds with her first paper in Mr. Frederickson's history class and write a parody about Martin Luther's toilet training called "Inside Martin Luther." Four pages of evidence support the notion that Luther had an anal retentive personality.

She has fun with this paper, especially since she has come to despise Freud, and this effort doubles as a send-up of the famous psychoanalyst.

Mr. Frederickson doesn't get the joke. He writes,

"This is clear, written with wit, but ultimately it's shallow and even foolish. The plausible sounding reduction of Luther's, or any man's, ideas and views to a psychological a priori has a fatal weakness you should have seen."

And yet, instead of failing her on the paper, Frederickson writes, "As Essay: A, As Historical Essay: C minus." Considering that he didn't realize the whole thing was just a spoof, that's pretty generous.

His comments on the rest of her papers are thoughtful, often helpful, and she even manages an A minus on one, but the grades are all over the place and her final paper gets a D. By the end of spring '65 she is convinced that she doesn't and never will understand how to write an academic essay.

Occasional Student

At the end of her freshman year she has officially declared her major in psychology, and is assigned Dr. Steiner as her advisor. She and Gracie get the idea of spending their junior year abroad. Others do it. Why not they? Dr. Steiner approves the idea and recommends University College London's highly respected psychology department. She'll be able to take courses in Learning and Memory, Emotion and Motivation, Perception, Abnormal and Clinical Psychology and others, plus non-psychology electives.

The best part is that she will be what is called in England an "Occasional Student," which means she will not have to take exams. She'll just show up for classes, take notes, hand in papers that won't be evaluated. When she returns to Carroll in the fall, all she has to do is submit a summary of her academic experiences. She will get thirty credits for the year and no grade. And something that will make her parents ecstatic—tuition for an Occasional Student is thirty dollars a semester. It seems unbelievable, but when she gives her father this figure, he corresponds with the University College London administrative office, and confirms that it is indeed true.

She and Dr. Steiner work out the program of courses she'll take at Carroll her sophomore and senior years to meet her major requirements, and he signs off on the plan. He sends a letter to London, supporting her application. What a guy! She is so lucky to have snagged him for an advisor.

Gracie, too, gets right to work applying to universities in England, and soon they find out that another Carroll student, Beth Laurenson, is making similar plans. The three of them decide to go to England together, and of all their ideas the one that thrills them most is how they're going to get there. Ocean liner.

It turns out that the five-day trip across the Atlantic on the S.S. France is not exorbitantly more expensive than taking a plane, and considering how much they'll be saving on tuition, it's an easy sell to all three sets of parents. Beth will finance her trip with her diligently saved earnings from summer jobs. Now they have to wait. It's almost a year and a half away.

Mimsy

The jealousy keeps cropping up. At campus events, it pounces when either of its two objects are present. Why is this plaguing emotion harassing her?

In *Alice's Adventures Through the Looking Glass*, Humpty Dumpty, when asked the meaning of a word from the poem "Jabberwocky" replies, "When I use a word it means just what I choose it to mean—neither more nor less. ... 'Mimsy' is 'flimsy' and 'miserable'. There are two meanings packed up into one word." Just so, her jealousy carries far more than one emotion. It's a sickening agglutination of insufferable feelings all obsessively rolled together. She could certainly add "mimsy" to the packing list—"flimsy" and "miserable."

Thought Police

She's not jealous of other women's accomplishments, intelligence, belongings, wealth, families, or boyfriends. To these she's either indifferent or happy for them. Her jealousy is completely focused on physical appearance. Is she the only girl on campus to suffer from this? She'll never know because she would never admit to having such an obsession.

Not even to Gracie does she confide these feelings. Oddly, she isn't jealous of Gracie. Why not? She's quite pretty in all the conventional ways—face, figure, hair—and is sometimes around when she and David are together. She's fun. She's amusing. She's certainly feminine, but she's not at all flirtatious or seductive, and there's something about her flippant, wise-ass personality that makes her non-threatening. Gracie has told her that in high school she was considered one of the guys—"Garbage Mouth Gracie." Not a girl that gets put on a pedestal. Too rowdy to be a beauty queen.

Why can't she be more like Gracie, who seems oblivious or indifferent to the shade cast on the rest of them by the luminescent Roz and Lily?

And what is it that she fears from these two? Certainly not that David will leave her. In the first place, neither of these women would give him a passing thought. As superb a human being as he is, David is a quintessential nerd, and these girls only date the Big Men on Campus. No, it's just that he might entertain fantasies about them, and that when they are around, his attraction might be stirred and that, hypothetically, if somehow one of them *did* pay attention to him, he would heed the siren song and let himself be lured away, or at least want to.

Imagining his having such ideas is so annihilating, so crushing that it sometimes seems preferable to end the relationship entirely just to escape her own thoughts. Her fear isn't of being alone. Being alone would be a relief, from the jealousy itself and from the guilt she feels for messing with the mind of this guileless, kind-hearted guy by playing hard to get, feigning aloofness, and casually mentioning other boys whenever she feels threatened.

Social Work

In May, determined to avoid a fourth summer stint at *The Leader and Gazette* complaints desk, she applies for and gets a job as a social work aide, making home visits to recipients of welfare checks, primarily single mothers and grandmothers caring for young children. Ostensibly the purpose of these visits is to see how the clients are getting along and whether they're aware of available services but also to be sure their circumstances are what they say they are. She has to appear at their doors without a prior appointment.

Nothing in her own life or the two-days of training prepares her for this role.

"May I come in?" she asks the client, who often stands blocking the doorway, her arms folded across her chest and a veiled look of suspicion and resentment on her face.

She does these home visits on foot. The social worker drops her off in the neighborhood with the understanding that she'll pick her up at a designated time and place and bring her back to the office to finish the paperwork.

At the end of the first week she is no more comfortable than on the first day but hopes eventually to feel less intimidated. Maybe at some point it will become routine.

On that Friday afternoon she's walking through the neighborhood on her way to a bus stop on a main street where the social worker will collect her. The neighborhood she's in today consists of one-story houses and here and there a run-down two-story apartment building. No one is around, the street is quiet and empty. And then a car pulls up. She glances over and sees two men, the driver, and another man in the passenger seat. Not boys. Men. The car has slowed almost to a stop and is creeping alongside her as she walks. The driver hangs his elbow out the window and stares at her while the passenger leans forward to get a look. They say nothing, only gaze at her with appraising and mocking half smiles.

She looks straight ahead and walks faster but is afraid to run, imagining how running could set them off, like dogs after a zig zagging rabbit. They are only a few feet away from her and could jump out and snatch her at any time. There would be no one around to see or hear or, perhaps, care.

In one block, this quiet street will meet a busy thoroughfare. Up ahead, as if they are on a small screen at the end of a tunnel, cars and people are passing. She walks a little faster. The car with the men speeds up to match her pace. Although she doesn't look, she can hear the driver chuckling. With every step closer to the intersection, she expects to hear the car roll to a stop, the doors open, and feel hands grabbing her arms.

Now she can't help herself, she runs to the main street. The car speeds up, but then passes her, and at the intersection turns the corner and drives away. She can see the profiles of the men's faces as they turn to each other and laugh.

Her legs feel weak. She's trembling when she walks into the first business she comes to—a dry cleaning establishment—and startles the man behind the counter by bursting into tears and asking to use the phone.

When the social worker comes to pick her up, she hands over her paperwork, resigns, and asks to be driven home. For the rest of the summer until the August family vacation, she endures the familiar six a.m. abuse at *The Leader and Gazette* complaints desk.

Apart

David's internship at a national laboratory on Long Island and her dismal job at the complaints desk keep them apart most of that summer. They write almost every day.

He occupies his leisure hours reading anything and everything. After reading Sartre's *Existentialism & Human Emotions* he writes that he wishes his conscious and subconscious could accept the burden of self-responsibility and living a life not so "fraught with 2nd thoughts & 2nd guessing." She didn't realize his life *was* fraught with second thoughts and second guessing.

He recommends a book called *The Feminine Mystique*. "You should take heart in it," he says. She has been complaining about double standards—women judged on their looks, men on their accomplishments. She hasn't read the book. Maybe she'll give it a try, but she already knows about the feminine "mystique" and isn't sure she wants to subject herself to more of it.

In letters she and David delve into their relationship and insecurities. She is shocked at his admission that he came out to Long Island to date and find out what other girls were like because she was the only one he'd ever known. A thousand miles away she turns cold and thinks of ways to punish him, even though he adds that he doesn't care to date anymore. "It's you I love," he says and lists all the things about her that attract him. She could mention going on dates herself, though she hasn't had any dates and there's no one around to choose from. She considers letting a week go by before writing again, to make him think she's cooling on him.

"We've both been pretty bad this year," he writes, "you with your petty maliciousness at times, and me with my masochistic feeling sorry for myself but both are manifestations of insecurity which we will help each other overcome." *Her petty maliciousness*! He has her number. Almost. He doesn't really know what causes it. Gritting her teeth, she sends a warm and loving reply the next day.

Her parents pay for her to fly out to see him over an extended July 4th weekend.

The visit comes off well. They attend a clever and funny Mike Nichols play on Broadway, *Luv*, the lines of which become stock phrases in their vocabulary. They spend a great deal of time on the bed in David's cramped little room.

After she leaves, he writes, "I love every one of the 187.65 sq inches of surface area & what's inside (you thought I was asleep Mon. from 9:30 to 10:30. Actually I was 'sizing you up' with my ruler)."

Sophomore

Her sophomore year and his senior year, she and David take up where they left off. He is awarded a fellowship for graduate study at Harvard next year and is elected to Phi Beta Kappa. The guys in McCollum House make him their dorm president because, although he's still pretty nerdy and wears pants a little too short revealing his white socks, he's brilliant, unpretentious and a sweetheart.

No longer subject to the maddening judgments of Mr. Smits, she gets As and Bs for the papers she writes on the works of Nietzsche, Adam Smith, Freud and others in her required history course covering the French Revolution to the present.

She writes to her parents that "Biology is very hard, but the professor is the best I've had" and that her Intro to Philosophy class is fun. "The course and subject are ridiculous and pointless," she asserts without irony, "but the prof is so funny and weird that I enjoy it anyway."

Projection

She's taking Psychology of Personality first semester sophomore year. Among others, they're studying Carl Jung, the Behaviorists Skinner and Pavlov, the Humanists Maslow and Rogers, and of course Freud.

The more she reads about psychoanalytic theory, the more she disapproves of it. The idea of unconscious motivation is sound, of course, but she doubts it's even original with Freud. The so-called Freudian slip has been recognized since antiquity from the first time someone cried out the wrong name while having sex.

All that convoluted Oedipal stuff—boys, fearing castration by their fathers, transferring lust for their mothers to lust for every other woman that catches their eye, and girls' so-called penis envy (Freud's assumption: who *wouldn't* want the dangly appendage?) transferred to a lust for their fathers or a handy father-substitute. Really? And the id, the ego, the superego, all that sublimation—useful constructs in their own way, but Rogers does it more sensibly with the internalized Child, Adult, and Parent.

However, one Freudian concept rings true and hits home, she can't deny it: projection—what you condemn in others is what you unconsciously condemn in yourself. How she dislikes "show-offs"! And yet how often in her life has she tried to call attention to herself! Her Sugar Plum Fairy performance in Opa's parlor comes to mind and her thwarted plan in junior high to stand out as the kid who publicly shames a disc jockey. There have been many, many more examples, disguised from her peers, she hopes, by her bogus modesty.

But Freud can't claim to have originated the idea of projection either. "Methinks the lady doth protest too much." Wasn't that Shakespeare's take on projection four hundred years before Freud? Probably the ancients were discussing it in Socrates' time, too. Now, though, having it shoved in her face by Freud, she can never again disdain a show-off without having to look within.

In White America

In November she and David attend a documentary play on campus called *In White America*. Three Black and three White performers mix monologues and dialogues taken from authentic sources—speeches, letters, newspaper articles, court records, diaries—starting with the importation of slaves and ending with the present-day civil rights movement.

By now, of course, she knows some of this history. Still, hearing it in such hideous detail, she sits in the dark theatre and guiltily presses her fingers to her ears to block out the most brutal words. She should look the history full in the face, but she doesn't want to be haunted by it. Once heard, it can't be unheard. This she has known since reading the Holocaust stories. Her brain was forever altered.

Muddy

In spring of '66 she is required to come up with a simulated study in Developmental Psychology, written in the manner of a journal submission. For this paper she produces twenty-six pages (including an eight-page review of the literature and a bibliography of twenty-two sources). "The Effects of Four Educational Variables on Psychological and Intellectual Development" tests the influence on children's achievement and personality of 1) pacing, 2) enrichment of the curriculum, 3) segregation into ability groups, and 4) early vs. late establishment of the programs. Its scope is reminiscent of her elementary school papers on weather, birds and fur.

The investigation, if implemented, would be so complicated and have so many uncontrollable variables (to say nothing of requiring a massive budget), that even she has trouble maintaining an overview of it despite her numerous tables, summaries and charts. Yet her professor gives the paper an A. Has he read it? She wonders if, riffling through all those pages, he decided that instead of judging the paper on its merits, it would be easier to reward her just for making such a monumental effort.

Poker Face

Dr. Steiner has arranged for a group of psych majors to visit mentally ill patients at the County Home once a week. He encourages her to volunteer this semester since she'll be in England her junior year and may be too busy her senior year. The County Home, or Poor Farm as it used to be called when the inhabitants worked the farm in exchange for room and board, is a mental institution for indigent people. Many are senile elderly or burned out alcoholics or people with psychoses or severe mood disorders.

A few miles outside of town, The Home is a non-descript two-story brick building with wings on either end and rows of blank-looking windows. It sits on a fallow plot of farm land with nothing around but flat fields.

They arrive in a college van and are met by Dr. Donahue, a psychologist who comes from the Barstow Clinic thirty miles away to consult with the staff every week. He ushers her and the other Carroll students into a recreation room where a desultory group of rather shabbily dressed adults of various ages sit on molded plastic chairs.

She's nervous. How do you break the ice? "Hi Chum. I'm Annie Lang, your friendly little college girl. Would you like to play ping pong?" And what will they talk about if she's paired with a middle-aged psychotic ex-farmer? Dr. Donahue and a nurse break the ice for them. Introductions are made and small groups are formed of two sets of partners each. Her partner is indeed a middle-aged ex-farmer. His name is Eugene. Only later does she learn he's also psychotic. He shakes her hand enthusiastically and comments on her size.

"Well, you're a little bit of a thing, ain't you?" She admits she is, though he's not any bigger—about 5'6" and skinny with wiry arms. He's wearing a T-shirt and a stained Pioneer Seed cap.

They join the other pair at a card table and play poker, betting with baby Tootsie Rolls from a glass jar. Eugene seems to be having fun, at least he breaks out in a wide grin from time to time. He wins consistently and she asks him how he got so good at the game. "I learned a trick or two in the service," he says. She asks him about his time in the service. "They kicked me out. Don't tell nobody." He doesn't elaborate but grins at his cards, turns them over and calls. Once again he rakes in all the candy on the table.

It turns out this isn't as difficult as she imagined. After an hour they get up and say their good-byes. She shakes Eugene's hand and says, "See you next week."

"Oh yeah," he replies, and winks at her. "I'll put that on my appointment calendar."

The next week they play hearts, and the rest of the semester they go automatically to the card table as soon as she arrives.

In the middle of May, they visit the County Home for the last time. "I really felt sad to see old Eugene go," she writes her parents. "The week after, we (the group) had dinner with Dr. Donahue. He told me why Eugene would suddenly break out in a grin. It's because he was hearing amusing voices. I don't know why that hadn't occurred to me. I wonder if his voices amused him at my expense. Whatever the reason, I'm glad he was enjoying himself."

Everything But

She never clicked with her roommate Marcia, who found someone else more compatible to room with. Gracie's roommate has transferred out of Carroll, so she and Gracie share one of the rare two-room doubles on campus. "We get along well," she writes to her parents. "We have good talks."

On Sunday afternoons from 3:00 to 5:00 women and men can be in each other's rooms as long as the door is open. Having a two-room double means that during open dorm hours there is complete privacy—she and David in her little bedroom and Gracie and her boyfriend Ethan in hers. The door to the hall is open a crack with a scarf tied to the handle (the significance of which is understood by everyone), and the bedroom doors are quite definitely closed.

From the beginning, it's all play and silliness, a complete lack of modesty or inhibition. Sexual intercourse is out, though. He's willing, but only if she is, and she's not; in the fall of 1965 female virginity is almost as imperative as it was in Victorian times, and she's leery of committing to anything that can't be undone. So they do Everything But. It's vastly better than the silent rubbing and humping in Murray Tierney's father's Pontiac.

She wears her low-cut Bali bras and teases David when he fumbles the clasp. He plays with her bare breasts and calls them her "boobie woobies." They laugh to see his ejaculate arc over the bed and land on the floor. When she's downtown shopping for presents at Christmas, she goes into an X-rated shop where semi-transparent bikini pants and bras are displayed in the window. She buys two sets, pink-tinged and blue-tinged. Translucent! And so sexy she's turned on just looking at herself in the mirror. David is going to love them. He does.

Goldfinger

She and David go to the James Bond movie, *Goldfinger*. It's the only movie playing in town and he suggests it. Why not? she thinks. They've gone to a number of movies that *she* wanted to see.

She's never been to a James Bond movie but assumes they're all about an over-glamorized, over-masculine spy who kills a lot of bad guys and charms women. She hasn't quite realized what she's in for.

Afterwards, when they come out of the theatre into the subzero February night and trudge along the snow-packed sidewalks toward campus, she hardly feels the cold, she is so hot with anger.

Throughout the movie the Bond character is covered up to his jawbone in tuxedo and bowtie, or silk robe, or expensive business suit, while the dozens of half-naked young women are clad only in bikinis or soap bubbles or towels held provocatively to their chests, or are wearing pointed bras under tight sweaters revealing overinflated breasts and deep décolletage. The hero slaps one of the women on the bottom to send her away when he wants to have "man talk." The female lead is called "Pussy Galore."

She is furious.

David says, "Well, it's just fantasy."

"*Whose* fantasy?" she retorts bitterly. "Not mine."

"Geez, yeah," he says. "I can see your point."

She slips her hand out of his and walks a little ahead all the way back to the dorm.

A Mother's Advice

David is graduating this year and will be off to his summer internship at another national laboratory, this one near Chicago. After that, he will be starting grad school and she'll be in England. Their erotic sessions on Sunday afternoons have brought them ever closer to the point where sexual intercourse is a great temptation and logical next step. He never pressures her, but he definitely wouldn't say no.

Although their sexual romps continue to give her orgasms, she is starting to notice that there are little things about him that turn her off. The way he kisses, for example—still puckery and fish-lipped. And outside of the bedroom there are other habits that grate on her—his talking with his mouth full, his inattention to dental hygiene, the way he walks with slightly splayed feet.

Annoyance over such mannerisms probably happens frequently in marriages. There must be a period of adjustment when a couple weighs up the admirable against the trivial and learns to put up with the trivial. He certainly has plenty of admirable qualities. She wonders if finally adding sexual intercourse to their romps might revive her zest for him.

Why not? In the old days, pregnancy was the issue, but there are reliable birth control methods now. Really, is virginity such a big deal?

She decides to ask her mother for advice. Gracie is astounded. "You're going to ask your *mother*? So you *want* to give your mother a heart attack?" She assures Gracie that she can talk to her mother about anything and can expect a thoughtful, rational answer.

She puts the question to her in a Sunday evening phone call after 10:00 p.m. when the rates are low.

Her mother lets her lay out all her arguments without interruption. When she's finished, she says, "Well, Annie, I can understand both of you having very intense urges. That's natural. But I'm inclined to say I think it would be a mistake. Once it's done, it can't be undone, and I think sexual intercourse is a unique and special act that should be saved for marriage. But ... I'd like some time to think it over. Can you give me a couple of days to put my thoughts together about this, and get back to you with a more considered response?"

Two days later her mother's four-page letter comes in the mail. No words crossed out, no marginal addenda. This has got to be a second or even third draft.

The answer is still no, but prodigiously supported. The gist of page one is that "the decision is yours to make" and "I won't deny that it pleases me very much that you ask my opinion. Not only because I think it has value but because I think you're wise to get counsel before making an important decision of any kind."

Pages two and three wax sociological and anthropological. Virginity preserved until marriage is "a symbol for the total commitment which the married state demands if it is to be a creative, constructive relationship." Giving it in marriage shows "acceptance of adult responsibility for the consequences of the commitments and of the ultimate in pleasure which male and female take in each other."

The ultimate in pleasure. Well, her mother certainly doesn't claim that intercourse isn't all it's cracked up to be. She could have left out "the ultimate in pleasure" if she was trying to discourage her, but her mother always tries to be truthful.

"No one has come up with a better plan than monogamous marriage for meeting the human need for love, affection, security, and parental care for the young" and "all available resources should be mustered to strengthen the institution."

Page three gets down to the personal. "There is a different feeling than there is when petting (regardless of how far the latter has gone)." Ah. She's always suspected her mother spent her fair share of hours before marriage in someone's father's Pontiac. She knows whereof she speaks.

"Girls who go all the way before marriage feel particularly vulnerable, more dependent, less protected, more possessive—" *More possessive*! This has her attention. How would it be possible for her to feel any *more* possessive than she does now in her virginal state? She wouldn't want to find out.

Page four ends with the reassurance that "I have complete respect for both of you regardless of what you decide. Love and kisses, from your old-fashioned Mom."

Only after starting to re-read the letter does she notice that although the envelope is addressed to Annie Lang, the letter itself begins "Dear Anne." Not "Dear Annie" or "Annie Dear," her mother's customary greetings in all their correspondence; in fact, she can't remember her mother ever calling her Anne even aloud. Was this "Dear Anne" salutation a deliberate appeal to maturity, to making the adult decision, as well as to show the import of her advice, the seriousness of the situation?

The Dear Anne letter has its effect. She and David part from each other in June, both still in the virginal state.

Line

Her friend Carmen, who convinced her rich parents to send her to lowly Tech instead of the prestigious Franklin High, married her boyfriend Larry right out of high school. Larry enlisted in the military as soon as he was of age and is now training in Army counter intelligence. Both of them had to have security clearances. It's another world.

Larry is on leave and Carmen suggests when she gets home from college they fix her up with Brent, a high school friend of Larry's. David is on Long Island, and she has nothing else going on. It will be a long summer. The four of them go out for pizza.

Brent is a tall beefy guy with the soft belly of a beer drinker. He looks like he could have played football in high school if he'd had the discipline. He was able to graduate by taking a preponderance of courses in auto mechanics.

The talk is mostly about the army—what little information Larry's allowed to reveal—and comparisons of motorcycle engines. Carmen seems content to sit back and let the boys talk. It's unclear whether Larry will end up in Vietnam, but she isn't going to put Carmen's back up by giving her two cents about the war.

Brent asks her out the next week and she accepts, figuring why not? It's something to do in the evening.

She learns that Brent managed to get into the state's ag and engineering university after high school but didn't manage to stay in. He and some buddies rented an apartment and spent most of the semester building a bar in their basement. Last year he worked on an assembly line and this summer got a job in construction. He hates both types of work and worries about getting drafted if he's not in college. Unlike Larry, he has no love for the military but even less for school. "I guess I've decided to wait for the draft," he says. "Sam should be getting me about March."

They have nothing in common, though she is impressed with his mechanical abilities. He takes her to look at a motorcycle he has stripped down and rebuilt. It's the kind of thing her brother Ted would be able to do if he were interested in vehicles. She respects this spatial aptitude, of which she has none.

In the car, he turns to her and says, "Did anyone ever tell you that you have beautiful blue eyes?"

She looks at him blandly and says, "Good line. How often do you use it?"

He grins ruefully. "Well, you can't blame a guy for giving it a shot."

And somehow, even though she knows her eyes are pretty, she feels a little jab of hurt that it was, actually, just a line.

Petty

This summer her correspondence with David is less fraught with introspection and angst than last summer. She has a job doing intake interviews at the county hospital where her mother works. He hangs out with pals from Carroll who live within driving distance of the labs where he is interning. He plays a lot of tennis, some golf and baseball and goes to movies and museums in Chicago.

In every one of his letters he tells her how horny he is and how much he fantasizes about her body, remembering their sessions in her dorm room on Sunday afternoons. "I enjoyed your orgasms almost as much as my own," he writes, without bashfulness, and wonders how he'll stand their being apart for a year while she's in England.

There is nothing in his letters about dating. Maybe he's figured out that it bothered her last summer. Or maybe he has enough of a social life with his friends. At any rate, it's a relief not to be on high alert or wrestling with an urge to punish him. She comes out by train to visit him every few weeks. Their sex life carries on as before—Everything But.

At the beginning of September, they drive out East for a two-week vacation before he begins his first semester at Harvard and she sails away to England. Her parents plan to show up at the dock for the send-off and then take a vacation in Nantucket.

David takes her to a beach on Long Island. It is there and then, while they're horsing around in the surf and he chases her from the water to their blanket on the sand, laughing and playfully threatening to grab her breasts, that she realizes her physical attraction to him is over. It has been fading since last spring, and she is now just going through the motions.

But why?

It's down to those little habits that have bothered her more and more. The puckery kissing, the open-mouthed eating, the unbrushed teeth, the splayed feet. Only these small things.

Even though she always found these habits annoying, she never, over all this time, came right out and told him so. The splayed feet—well there's nothing he could do about that and why should it bother her, anyway? It should be endearing. But the others she could easily have mentioned: "David, this is how I like to be kissed." After all, he had never kissed anyone else. She could have shown him seductively. "Like this." He would have enjoyed being shown. And as regards eating, she could have teased him with "David, close your mouth when you eat! I can see all the way down to your tonsils." He wouldn't have been offended. He would have said, "Yeah, yeah, yeah. My little sister is always on me about that." The same with the teeth brushing. He would have risen to the occasion. He's not a defensive guy.

They've never been shy about bodily functions—he knows when she's on her period, she knows his chronic prostatitis makes him have to pee almost hourly. To say nothing of their familiarity with each other's intimate fluids. Then why was she never able to just speak up about these little things that were bothering her? Can she really have allowed these petty irritations to turn her off permanently? Is that truly what it's about? But what else could it be? There's nothing else wrong with him.

Reasonable People · 185

They're about to leave each other for a year. It would be horribly insensitive to end it from long distance. This would be the time to tell him that it's over. But how can she?

IV

The France

On the pier, her parents and David are miniaturized as the ship backs out of New York Harbor. Soon they are indistinguishable in the bank of little hands fluttering along the dock like leaves in a blustery wind. Once the ship is out of sight, David will get back in the car and drive to Boston to begin his studies at Harvard. Her parents will head for their vacation on Nantucket Island. She, and they, are all gliding far away from each other, the intervening space expanding and expanding. It reminds her of a recurring dream she used to have, of walking alone and almost weightless on a road through wide-open countryside. There is no sound, no disturbing weather, no people, only a deep peace. The air is soft on her skin. She walks in absolute freedom, without fatigue or anxiety, toward some unknown destination miles and miles away.

She and Gracie and Beth stand together on deck, waving for a long time and then as the ship turns, they watch the well-wishers disappear from view.

The backward progress of the giant ship is so smooth and steady that she thinks, I didn't have to worry about seasickness after all, not on a ship this size.

Shortly, the liner emerges from the harbor and plies its way into the Atlantic, vast and empty to the horizon. A breeze picks up. The wind whips their headscarves. She becomes aware of an up and down heave under her feet, a sinking and rising sensation as if she were on a malfunctioning elevator. Making their way along the deck and down a flight of stairs to their small stateroom, she and Gracie hang onto the railings. Beth blithely saunters ahead.

The heave of the ship feels worse in the maze of narrow corridors below deck, and when they reach their room, she and Gracie head for the beds and lie flat on their backs. Being lifted and dropped is less sickening from a prone position. Beth obligingly unpacks for them.

"I think I'll explore," Beth says. "Anyone want to come?"

They look at her greenly.

"Okay then. I'll see you after a while." She opens the door and turns back. "Can I get you anything before I go?"

She asks Beth to search her purse for the Dramamine she brought along just in case. Beth pulls out pills for both of them and hands her and Gracie the complimentary water bottles the ship has provided. They lift their heads just high enough to swallow the pills, then sink back and drift into a hazy drug-induced sleep.

Luxury

By the following day, having ventured on deck and been refreshed by the bracing sea breeze, she and Gracie begin to recover. At lunch in the grand dining room (Salle à Manger Versailles) they notice that for every unattached male, there must be four females, most of them glamorous. In spite of these odds, Beth has already attracted two men, one of whom—a tall American Fulbright scholar who speaks fluent French—sits at their table. This conquest doesn't surprise her. She's envious but not jealous since she doesn't have to monitor a boyfriend's assumed lust for Beth, with her voluminous hair and bedroom eyes.

Anyway, Beth is, as Gracie would say, a good old kid, upbeat, easygoing, and delighted with everything.

There's a swimming pool on the ship. How much more luxurious can you get than a pool floating on an ocean!? They put on bathing suits and make their way there. Beth and Gracie dive right in. She's a little more timid, not so sure about taking the plunge without dipping a toe in to test the temperature. Her hesitation saves her from the harrowing experience of her companions. Beth and Gracie are immediately tossed and buffeted by powerful waves in the pool that slam them back and forth against the sides. They've become fragile vessels on a turbulent indoor sea.

She isn't a strong swimmer and doesn't know what to do for them. There's not a steward in sight. She stands uselessly for some moments, watching their struggles and listening to their shouts. But before she can run for help, they manage to grab onto the pool ladders and hoist themselves out, dripping, pale, bruised, and in Gracie's case, ready to puke.

Passing the MISE EN GARDE/VERSICHT/CAUTION signs, which they had all failed to notice in their initial awe over the luxuriousness of a pool on a ship, they head back to their room to change into warm clothes before emerging on the promenade deck and collapsing into deck chair recliners. A solicitous steward, as if he knew of their ordeal, tucks blankets around their legs and takes their orders for hot tea, which arrives swiftly, along with buttered croissants.

There are too many luxuries to count: a two-story dining room entered by way of a grand staircase, a ballroom, theatre, lounges, smoking room, library, after-hours club for dancing to a live band. But the pièce de resistance is the cuisine. This is, after all, a French liner. She regrets the queasiness that keeps her from enjoying meals for the first day and a half, but thankfully, has recovered by Sunday's gala dinner consisting of ten courses, presented with matchless attention to color and composition, starting with *Le Médaillon de Foie Gras en Gelée au*

Porto, moving on to *Le Consommé de Volaille Madrilène*; two main courses (*Le Suprême de Saumon Rose Victoria* and *Le Caneton Rôti à la Bigarade d'Orange*) each followed by a vegetable dish (*Le Bouquet d'Asperges Sauce Argenteuil* and *Les Pommes Dauphine Dorées*), then a salad (*La Salade Turquoise*); two desserts (*La Pêche Givrée Melba* and *Les Gaufrettes en Eventails*) and an extravagantly decorated basket of exotic fruits. To say nothing of the wines. And this is in Tourist Class. What must the First Class passengers be eating?

There is an endless variety of activities during the day—dancing lessons, deck sports, card games, movies; and far into the night drinking, dancing and listening to live music. Beth is in her element.

In contrast, she and Gracie, the slugs, are usually content to lounge on deck, catered to by the gallant and chivalrous waiters and stewards whom they suspect of mocking them in French. Her French isn't good enough to be sure. In any case, what she doesn't know can't hurt her.

Spend a Penny

The night before arrival, they stay awake until 3 a.m., partly from excitement and partly from gut trouble. She and Gracie have diarrhea (or as Gracie calls it, "dire rear") and Beth is constipated. They wake bleary eyed at seven a.m., bowels churning, and stagger to breakfast. They force themselves to eat a little something.

As the ship nears Southampton, the first thing she sees clearly is a massive medieval castle surrounded by rolling hills and groves of trees. It is unbearably exciting. She is about to step into an eighteenth century English novel. But soon she and Beth and Gracie are rattled by the fiasco of disembarkation, figuring out where to go to buy tickets for the train, change money, search for their suitcases and trunks, pass through customs, get their baggage onto the train and find seats.

When they arrive at London's Waterloo Station, Waterloo Station becomes their Waterloo. They all three have to go to the bathroom, she worst of all. But first they must fight through the mob to locate their luggage and get a porter. The porter leaves her heavy trunk on the floor instead of on a trolley, so they have to stand around for another half an hour waiting for a trolley to be free.

It takes another fifteen minutes to locate a restroom (time wasted because of her failure to ask for the "loo") only to rattle the door of an unoccupied stall, her bladder bursting, and find she has to put a penny in the slot in order to get in. She can't bring herself to beg a penny from any of the English people passing by. Doubtful that she'll make it, she dashes back to get a penny from Gracie (Gracie: "Hurry the hell up, I gotta piss like a racehorse."). She returns to the "loo," and after squirming and dancing as she clumsily inserts the penny, she gets the door open and drops onto the toilet just in time. Then it's back to watch the bags while Gracie and Beth take their turn.

A kindly English woman helps them figure out how to use a phone to call their hotel and where to get a cab. Finally, at eight p.m. they are in their hotel room, exhausted and ravenous, not having eaten since breakfast. They trudge out again and eventually find a restaurant, where the canned baked beans, overcooked tomatoes and sausage links are barely edible. Maybe, she thinks, five days' worth of French cuisine is not the best way to prepare oneself for English cooking.

Innocents Abroad

By the next morning, they've recovered and venture out to see the sights. A group of boys tags after them for blocks even though she and Gracie and Beth ignore them and are in no way provocatively dressed.

"Jesus," says Gracie, "these English girls all wear skirts up to their asses and chorus girl stockings. Why don't these jerks go after *them*?"

Buckingham Palace is one of the sights on the agenda. They can hardly take in the enormity of the place and the fact that it's basically a family home. In a letter to her parents, she describes how afterwards, passing the Queen's Life Guard headquarters, they ask how to get to the Underground station and a Guard, just getting off duty, takes them there, shooing away the harassing boys. "He's young, like eighteen," she writes her parents, "and comes from the country—real quiet, with this shy grin and *adorable* accent. He told us about the ceremonial duties of the Horse Guard and took us eight blocks to the Underground. And then, at the station entrance, this large drunk man starts bothering us, and the Horse Guard guy escorts us down to the train, gets on, and accompanies us all the way to our hotel for fear we'd never make it back by ourselves. How about that for a welcome to England?!"

Bedsitter

After two days of sightseeing in London, Beth and Gracie leave for The University of Manchester, where they were accepted as students. Now she's on her own. She can't pay the expense of the hotel much longer, but how do you go about finding an apartment? She's never had to do it before, much less in a foreign country, even if it is an English-speaking one. She walks to the University and is given a listing of available student "flats" and "bedsits" at the housing office. She also picks up several London newspapers and peruses the "To Let" ads.

Her father has put together a budget which amounts to about ninety dollars a month. At $2.80 per English pound, her maximum allocation for rent is five pounds—fourteen dollars a week.

During the first two mornings she goes out to a nearby red call box and uses up most of her change contacting landladies. Having bought maps of the Underground (the "Tube") and bus routes and a "London A-Z" at a news stand, she spends the afternoons on the double decker buses or the Tube anxiously watching for and missing stops, often having to retrace her route, trudging block after block, shyly knocking on doors. It seems that all the flats are dirty or located on noisy streets or far from public transport or more expensive than advertised.

Then she develops a mysterious pain in her right knee whenever she bends it, making it difficult to walk. In addition to looking for apartments, she has had to tramp all over campus trying to register for classes. She holes up in her hotel room that third day, resting the knee. By the fourth day, with her money dwindling, she has no choice but to limp from one discouraging place to another until late in the afternoon she climbs painfully up the front steps of #27 Cromwell Avenue. It's on a quiet, shady street of semi-detached late Victorian row houses in Highgate, only a couple of blocks from the Archway Tube station.

She is greeted at the door by smiling, apple-cheeked Mrs. Glynis Lambert, a woman in her early thirties whose equally apple-cheeked three-year-old stands next to her. "This is Hugo," she says. Hugo is wearing a child-sized policeman's helmet and soberly inspects her with his round blue eyes.

The Lamberts' bedroom is on the second floor facing the street. Hugo sleeps in a converted dressing room adjoining. The rooms for rent—a reasonably spacious bed-sitting room and a kitchen—are at the back. Mrs. Lambert has taken pains to make them attractive and cozy, furnishing the bedsitter with an antique armoire and bureau, cane chairs, throw rugs, and bed stand with lamp. In the kitchen a bright white vinyl cloth, decorated with pictures of fruit, covers the table, and a flowered tea pot with matching cups and plates sits on a shelf. The toilet is down the hall in a "water closet," separate from the bathroom. These are to be shared with the family along with their refrigerator downstairs. The weekly rent is four pounds five shillings.

She moves in the next day. Her knee pain has mysteriously disappeared during the night.

When she arrives at #27, the red-headed three-year-old, Hugo, sees her at the bottom of the stairs surrounded by her luggage, and asks, in what sounds to her American ears like the received pronunciation of the Queen of England, "Are you going on holiday?"

Burning Feet

She doesn't know how to make friends here. At first, it doesn't matter. After classes and on the weekends she is happy to explore London by herself. Cromwell Avenue is close to Hampstead Heath, a sprawling, hilly park where people walk their dogs, parents wheel babies in "prams," and children sail boats on the ponds. You can inexpensively buy tea, scones and meat pasties from tea carts and sit on a bench to enjoy the panoramic view of London from Parliament Hill. Also nearby is Highgate Cemetery, where Karl Marx lies beneath a solid block of marble holding up a sculpture of the man's great bearded head.

University College is within walking distance of London's most famous landmarks: the British Museum, St. Paul's Cathedral, Westminster Abbey, Houses of Parliament, Hyde Park, and on and on. For a while, these keep her too busy to notice her loneliness.

But after three weeks of wandering around in awe, she longs for someone to share it with. Whereas her classmates take their courses in their particular fields and come to know each other well, she has signed up for all sorts of classes—Psychological Testing, Psychology of the Abnormal Child, British Government from 1832, The Second World War, Social Anthropology, Restoration and Eighteenth-Century Prose, English Literature from 1880—so she doesn't see the same people all day throughout the week. She can't bring herself to intrude on any of them in their tight little groups, and none of them approaches her. It doesn't help that she's an American. From articles in *The Guardian* and *The Times* and snatches of conversation that reach her ears (deliberately?) she gathers that the Vietnam War has made the United States a pariah, especially among students.

In spite of being a pariah by proxy, she is careful not to pick up a British accent, something she could easily do since she's always had a talent for imitating speech of any kind. She has a horror of returning home speaking like those 1930s American movie actors who gesture with long cigarette holders and affect a so-called "Mid-Atlantic" accent in order to appear upper class. The last thing she wants is to come back to Carroll College sounding insufferably pretentious.

However, she's determined not to seek solace from other Americans—it's the full English experience she has come for—so she joins the college choir with rehearsals once a week but is never asked to come along with the groups heading for a pub afterward. She participates in the badminton club even though her opponents rather disdainfully drive the shuttlecock past her three out of four times.

On Monday nights she attends the free jazz sessions in the Union, standing for two, sometimes three hours in the back, swaying with the beat and fixing a deliberately rapt expression on her face to give the impression that she is simply entranced by jazz instead of waiting for some boy to come over and start a conversation. She stands there until the soles of her feet burn and she has to give up and make her solitary way home on the Tube.

Correspondence

The need for human connection drives her to fire off letters to anyone and everyone with whom she's had even a distant acquaintanceship. Of course she's been writing her parents and David all along, but now she corresponds with old high school classmates, her boss at *The Daily Leader and Gazette*, her freshman roommate at Carroll, a grade school teacher she liked. In the past she has seldom written to her brothers, but now she sends them chatty letters describing her solo adventures and asking about their lives. She even writes a letter to Brent, the guy of the "beautiful blue eyes" pickup line. In only a week's turn-around time, she receives his reply.

Surprisingly, and despite his atrocious spelling, his writing is amusing, the prose and content lively if self-deprecating: "How are you? I am fine. How's that for a swave beginning? Letter writing isn't my forte so your have to bear with me" he begins, and ends with "I want to here more about your trip over on the boat and all about school. It's not often that I make with the guilt, so I would like to hear from you."

He encloses a photo of his 1961 Harley Davidson. "Abot my bike. That black streak of lightning, unholy terror of the East side, was on the concrete byways again. But as fate would have it, the black one was soon to be destened for garagedom! How's that for some giberish?" His personality comes out on paper as it never did in speaking.

He says he's going to start work in a fertilizer plant. She finds his aimlessness a little poignant and wonders if his teachers just red-penciled all his spelling mistakes and never praised him for his writing. Where might it have led if just one teacher had told him he had some talent in that direction?

So, she does it herself. "Dear Brent, I enjoyed your letter. In spite of the fact that, like my brothers, you are a crappy speller, you really have a knack for expressing yourself in writing. I recommend that you write an essay in praise of the Harley and send it to the Tech High newspaper as an alum. I'm not kidding. You really are a good writer. I read your letter twice and got a kick out of it both times." She waits a couple of weeks to send this because she doesn't want to encourage too steady a correspondence.

Miles

At last, on the fourth Monday, her stoicism at the jazz club pays off. A boy approaches her. Somehow he knows she's American, but her Americanism is an attribute in his eyes because he has just returned from an enjoyable five-month sojourn in the United States. He's eager to show her a good time in England.

"His name—are you ready?" she writes her parents, "—is Miles Littlewood. No, he is not a supercilious vicar from a Jane Austen novel. He's a 'fresher' (first year student) at the College. A year and a half younger than me, which, at my tender age, is quite a big difference. Also he's an inch shorter."

But Miles is a nice enough guy, not particularly intellectual or stimulating or good-looking, but he seems to have unlimited access to his parents' car. That weekend he drives her up to Cambridge via winding country roads passing through quaint villages of thatched houses, pubs, and old churches. They visit the ancient college buildings entered by way of sweeping, manicured lawns and elaborate gates. Swans share the nearby River Cam, down which boys punt in flat boats. Miles had had his heart set on going to Cambridge, but they turned him down.

On their next trip, he takes her to Stonehenge. They leave London at 4:30 a.m. It has been cloudy and stormy, but as they come near the place, the sky clears and a few morning stars glimmer. The monoliths, in the middle of a large green field, are eerie, looming up out of the flat countryside.

There is no one else around. They climb over the fence and walk across the field, damp with dew. She puts a hand against one of the great stones, touching it where other hands were placed five thousand years ago. She can hardly grasp the ingenuity of the supposedly primitive people who hewed the rocks and hauled them from miles away and erected the giant slabs, placing them just so, in the formation of a cosmic clock that has lasted five millennia.

But when the sun comes up her perspective changes. Now the leaning stones seem worn down and tired in their old age all alone in the middle of nowhere. It doesn't enhance their grandeur that some idiot has spray painted a peace symbol on one of them.

She and Miles go back to sit in the car and drink tea from a thermos and eat little cakes and feel very carefree.

Inevitably, after a few dates, there is a bit of mutual groping in the car or on her bed at #27. Mrs. Lambert had made clear when she stated the terms of the rental agreement that she would be free to come and go independently and entertain in her rooms whomever she pleased.

She suspects Miles of boasting to his friends how he's "shagging" an older American "bird." They aren't shagging, only making out and petting a little, but it doesn't matter—she doesn't know his friends and is unlikely to meet them, so who cares?

The Home Folks

Her mother will get her clinical psychology MA in June. She writes that group therapy is fascinating, that she's having trouble getting all her studying done and is postponing work on her thesis.

She replies with anecdotes about her classes at UCL. "We're about to give tests to each other in Psych Testing. The lecturers are a riotous pair of ladies—Mrs. Dworsky and Dr. Briggs—who kibbitz with each other and puff away furiously on cigarettes."

Much of the correspondence with her father is about money. The man at Midland Bank had recommended writing larger checks to avoid so many handling charges. She writes, "He said somewhat sarcastically, 'Though what's ten dollars more or less?' I'm afraid he thought I was a rich, spoiled American girl, whose father thinks nothing of contributing great wads of dough for the improvement of her mind abroad. Hmm. Now that he mentions it …"

Her father questions her budget for meals (ninety cents a day), which doesn't seem enough and he urges her not to go short on food.

He tells her that the basic budget for the trip over and back, tuition, books, room, board and miscellaneous is about a thousand dollars below the Carroll year and suggests they split this amount, her five hundred going for weekend trips and travel at vacation times. "This is a valuable year and should be fun, so you don't want to spend it in your room. If you find you can't take advantage of as much as you'd like for lack of funds <u>we should change your miscellaneous budget</u>."

She is indeed a spoiled American girl, if not exactly rich. Her parents are making financial sacrifices for her, and for her brothers, so she regales them with her cultural experiences, knowing how happy it will make them.

"I visited #10 Downing St. where 'Harold' lives" and also went to watch the changing of the Queen's Life Guard. The horse took a crap as it was being ceremoniously inspected." She gets a free ticket to a jazz concert being taped by BBC1. "It was the Albert Ayler Quintet—the most avant of the avant garde. A violinist sawed away so hard that there were strings hanging from his bow. The best part was listening to the Nichols and May-like comments during the intermission; e.g. 'But they have such intense control over their instruments.'"

Miles takes her to a formal dinner for members of the U.N. Association given in the House of Commons dining room. "Afterwards we walked to his car and there, towering above us, was Big Ben lit by floodlights."

Her parents keep her up to date on the family doings. Nick is in San Francisco playing in clubs and teaching drumming. "Yes," he has told them, "there is rioting." (She has read in the English papers that a Black teenager was fatally shot in the back by a police officer when the boy ran away from him.)

Ted has had a date with a new girl. The girl's father is divorced from his second wife and is elaborately tattooed, her father reports. She replies, "Glad to hear my horny little brother is making time with the ladies."

Biscuits

Mr. Lambert—Adrian—is a mild, quiet man with sandy "ginger" hair; probably in his youth it was as red as his son's. He goes to work every morning to an office in the city while Glynis stays home with Hugo.

She wants to do something special for the Lamberts to return their unobtrusive kindnesses, and thinks of chocolate chip cookies. Of course. So American. So delicious. She doubts if they've ever tasted this delicacy before.

She finds chocolate "bits" at Sainsbury's, but nowhere can she find a cookie sheet. After inquiring at several shops, she describes to the clerk what it is she wants to bake.

"Oh," says the clerk. "You want a biscuit tin."

This must be what they call something like a muffin pan here. "No, not for biscuits. I want to make cookies." They do have cookies in England, she knows. They're often served with tea.

The clerk brings out the biscuit tin. "I'm sorry, but this is all we have."

Every day she learns more of this new vocabulary. Cookies are biscuits. A car hood is a bonnet, the trunk is the boot, trucks are lorries. So far she can't find anything equivalent to masking tape, which she needs for putting up a poster without damaging the Lambert's wall.

Her chocolate chip cookies go over excellently. She's made the family a double batch and given Glynis the recipe. Now it is a staple in the Lambert household. She is deeply gratified.

Dear Sweetie

David writes regularly. "Dear Sweetie" he begins, and ends "I love you, Annie. Why are you so far away? Many kisses, etc." He says he was so eager to read her letter that he tore it open the wrong way and had to hold the two sides together while he read.

Her responses, while not as effusive, give the impression that their relationship is going on just as it always has. She writes of wishing he were there so she could show him all the places that fascinate her in London. He replies that he doesn't imagine showing her around all the places in Cambridge. If she were there he imagines just making love all day.

Why is it so particularly repellent to be expected (or expect oneself) to get physical with someone who leaves you cold? Making love with him all day is the last thing she would want to do. In a letter she apologizes for having sometimes treated him badly at Carroll and been unresponsive. She has hinted vaguely that one cause was a "sex problem" between them, letting him believe it has something to do with not having sexual intercourse, though that wasn't it at all.

He wonders what other causes there were for her unresponsiveness. "Do I bite my fingernails too much or what?" The irony is not lost on her. No, David, you didn't bite your fingernails too much. Nothing so trivial. She was unresponsive because he chewed with his mouth open. How can she possibly let him know that she's that shallow?

She treated him badly because she was jealous. How can she admit to being that selfish? And if she hadn't been jealous, would the trivial things have bothered her?

They hadn't said anything about being entirely exclusive during this year of separation. She is spending every weekend touring the countryside with Miles and making out with him in her bed. When she writes of visiting Stonehenge with a friend, David replies, generously, "You needn't feel constrained about revealing the identity of the 'friend.' I enjoyed your enthusiastic description of the countryside." So she reveals the friend's name and assures him that she is not interested in him romantically and says she feels a bit guilty for being opportunistic. Miles has access to a car and takes her places.

"I don't think you're being opportunistic," David writes back. "I'm sure (I know from experience) your company is enjoyable whether you're in love with the guy or not."

But when David mentions going to New York with a buddy who fixed them up with dates, and reassures her that the girl was nice enough but not very stimulating or interesting, she doesn't write him for a week.

He has been looking for a clinical psych grad school somewhere near Harvard, and says, "If I find none we should establish one." She doesn't correct this implication that they will be together permanently. She has no interest in marrying him, yet she can't let go of wanting him to want her. What kind of person treats someone this way?

Brrr

The days get colder. Lack of central heating is not something she has thought much about. Now in November the temperatures are in the forties, sometimes even thirties. There's no heat at all in her bedsitting room. The electric fire in the kitchen runs on shillings she feeds into a meter.

At bedtime, huddling close to the hot coils, she takes her clothes off in stages, replacing them with a flannel nightgown, terry cloth robe, long johns, and woolen bed socks. Then she fills a hot water bottle and runs to the bedroom to climb into bed with it under six layers of blankets and a coat. In the morning she tosses out the cold hot water bottle and scurries, shivering, to put a shilling in the meter so she can divest herself of these layers and put on a turtle neck, blouse, wool sweater and wool slacks over thick tights. She does all this before going to the water closet. There, she shudders as her bottom hits the frigid toilet seat.

In her hooded faux suede coat with faux fur lining and mittens, she grabs an umbrella and heads for the Tube station. None of the English people she sees along the way seems even remotely encumbered by so much clothing. Girls are in micro mini-skirts, boys in sweaters with a school scarf tied loosely around their necks. No one hunches against the cold.

Glynis and Adrian Lambert go out in lightweight overcoats, she wearing a headscarf, he a cap. Hugo's cheeks are always red, so it's hard to know if he's affected by the cold or is just English. What must they think of her with all her blankets and layers of clothing?

Typical soft, coddled American whose country never had to suffer through the Blitz.

Reporting In

Her Psychology of the Abnormal Child professor, Dr. Schatz, is a Jungian therapist who sees patients of all ages in private practice and at a hospital. "The professor is fabulous!" she writes her parents, knowing her mother will get vicarious pleasure from her enthusiasm, and her father will consider their money well spent. And she is sincere. "Dr. Schatz is incredibly self-assured. The class represents all a college education should be."

She's also taking a two-hour lecture in Psychological Measurement, which covers intelligence testing. "We're about to give more tests to each other. Thinking of *you*, Mom. I'm well experienced in being a guinea pig—excuse me, a test subject."

She's not impressed with her social anthropology professor, who gives high school-level assignments. "One girl did a long report on a chapter from a well-known classic in anthro. It dawned on me that she had plagiarized the entire report. The prof commended her on a good essay."

But her history courses, "British Government from 1832" and "The Second World War" are enlightening, and she especially loves her English courses, Restoration and Eighteenth-Century Prose and English Literature from 1880.

"I get to read all these English classics I've never read before," she writes. "Pamela—good old Pamela out maneuvers the slimy rapist; Tom Jones—he's charming, sure, but too much of a rake for my taste; Middlemarch—a superior quality soap opera. The Return of the Native—I deeply dislike Eustachia Vye for using the affections of a good and humble man—wait, though. Could I be projecting?"

Of course she had read Jane Austen and The Brontës and Dickens, but never Jonathan Swift. Gulliver's Travels is a *political* satire." (She'd had no idea.) "Ditto Frankenstein by Mary Shelley. Elizabeth Gaskell's North and South is social commentary in depth, and yet so romantic! And, Oh! Anthony Trollope!" When she finishes *Barchester Towers*, there are the rest of his *Chronicles* and then the *Pallisers*, and numerous other novels to read. A treasure trove.

"Yes, even though the air reeks of petrol fumes here, and whenever I blow my nose, black snot appears on my Kleenex, and the skies are gray, the air cold and damp, the plumbing primitive, there are so many fabulous things that compensate. I'm getting such an education, not just at the College but while walking, looking, and listening. I saw Stonehenge at dawn. Imagine! I've only been in England a few weeks, but it seems like I've lived here all my life. Sometimes I stop and catch my breath at the realization that I really am in London, being a student, renting a bedsitter, going to the shops and riding the Tube every day to school. Aren't I a woman of the world?"

Thumbs Out

She sends her parents the itinerary for the European trip she and Beth and Gracie will go on during the month-long Christmas break. "We'll take a discounted student flight to Oslo on December 15th, work our way through the Scandinavian countries, Germany, Austria and the Netherlands and return January 17th."

Her father encourages the Scandinavian countries but cautions, "Above all, do not fly over or near Russian-controlled zones. Stay out of Berlin."

He asks if she has enough money for the trip. She assures him they will be staying in youth hostels and spending altogether only about four dollars a day. They intend to be extremely frugal, she says. This is all to disguise the fact that they plan to hitchhike everywhere.

Hitchhiking through the northern countries in December seems foolhardy, but even in southern Europe it will be cold this time of year, and if they plan to go south at Spring Break, they'll want to be there when they can enjoy the sun.

They fly to Oslo and stay at a swanky youth hostel with hot showers and no curfew, very luxurious. After Oslo, they get on the road with their thumbs out. These thumbs and all their other digits are soon numb with cold. They stand at the edge of highways stamping their feet and watching their breath make clouds in the icy air. Still, the skies are bright blue, the sun shines brilliantly on the snow, and there is no shortage of rides to take them through Sweden to Copenhagen.

From Copenhagen, she reports, they take a "short train ride" (the train ride is a fabrication) "to a beautiful little town where we went through a palace crammed with art treasures."

She finds Scandinavia a little too much like the Upper Midwest. Oslo and Copenhagen remind her of Milwaukee or Minneapolis and much of the countryside resembles the farmland of Wisconsin. Too familiar. Not quaint enough. But then they get into Germany at Christmas.

Fröhliche Weihnachten

They stay with a Frau Bökemeyer in a tiny village near Göttingen. The Bökemeyer home teems with relatives, friends, and friends of friends. Half the guests are sleeping on floors.

"We had the most old-fashioned Christmas imaginable! I got to help with stuffing and roasting a goose (!) and several of us decorated and built a Hansel & Gretel *hexenhaus* out of candy and cookies. At each meal everyone sang songs and held hands and greeted each other. It was all so folksy and traditional that we could hardly speak for the lumps in our throats."

As she writes, she can imagine her parents' delight for her, especially her father, who grew up in a German family.

Family Slope

From Göttingen the three of them hitch to the ancient city of Nuremberg where they stay in a castle turned youth hostel. Then on to Vienna and a performance by Rudolf Nureyev at the State Opera House. On New Year's Eve, she comes down with a twenty-four-hour flu. In the freezing cold youth hostel bathroom, compassionate Beth holds her head while she throws up, and afterward washes vomit and diarrhea from her nightgown.

From Vienna they pass through the beautiful medieval city of Salzburg, then on to the resort town of Igls where they'll have a chance to ski in the Tyrolean Alps. As usual, her friends are more adventurous than she is. On the babies' slope she takes a fruitless lesson from one of the ski instructors while virtual toddlers ski circles around her. Gracie and Beth, who have been on skis once before, take the lift to the top of the family slope.

After her lesson, she sits inside the warm lodge drinking hot chocolate and waiting for Gracie and Beth to return. They don't. It's late in the afternoon, soon to be dark. She's starting to get scared. She decides to take the lift up to try to find them. At the top she is momentarily stunned by the view across miles and miles of white peaks. But it's bitterly cold—10 degrees F—and she has no idea where or how to look for her friends. She takes the lift back down. When she gets to the bottom, there is Beth, skiing out of the woods, looking ghastly. She tells the story.

Starting down the "family" slope, Beth and Gracie realized that they couldn't turn back and would have to ski seven kilometers down the entire mountain. Beth tumbled, fell, slid on her rear end, and soon left Gracie behind.

Beth is utterly exhausted. She flops into a chair by the fire, trying to rub warmth into her hands.

Now she starts to panic. It's getting very dark. Has Gracie hurt herself or lost her way or frozen to death? She collars a ski instructor and gets back on the lift. Halfway up they get off and start walking back along the ski trail. In some places it's sheer ice. She has visions of Gracie losing control on a corner and flying into space.

Their voices bounce off the peaks as they shout Gracie's name. In reply there's only the sound of the wind sweeping across the powdery snow.

When they get back to the lodge, Beth comes running out to inform her that Gracie had finally found her way down ten minutes earlier. They're giddy with relief. Sitting by the fire, they giggle uncontrollably over Gracie's story. She had been so terrified that when she came to what looked like a road, she skied down it, hoping to walk the rest of the way, and suddenly found herself on an almost vertical drop. Men working nearby laughed as she slid by on her bottom. Finally a man turned up to help her the rest of the way down in the dark. He informed her she had been on the slope used at the 1964 Winter Olympics.

Gracie and Beth have bruises for days. It's a good thing she's not the adventurous type, she thinks. And although she may not have her own story to tell, she can always get a laugh with theirs.

Amsterdam

Houses, businesses, and churches in the Old City date from the sixteenth century or earlier and overlook hundreds of picturesque canals. Tall, narrow buildings with steeply pitched gables rise up shoulder to shoulder four or five floors high and are canted forward as if trying to get a look at their own reflections in the water.

Trash is routinely chucked into the canals. It amuses her to hear English-speaking tourists walking about with noses in guide books exclaiming, "And everything here is so *clean*!" Do they even *look* at the canals? But of course it is well known that the Dutch are good housekeepers.

Their student hotel is in the red light district, straight out of *Irma La Douce*. The prostitutes sit framed behind lighted windows. It's both fascinating and disturbing to pass these women, posing as living advertisements for the sale of their own bodies. She wonders what they think of all the tourists, some gawking, some, like herself, glancing sidelong a little ashamed for looking.

Indonesia was once a Dutch colony. They've heard that the Indonesian restaurants in Amsterdam are the best in the world outside of Indonesia itself. After being religiously frugal, they decide it's time to splurge and choose a pricey restaurant. They're seated by a window overlooking a canal. Reflected lights glitter on the water, the garbage obscured by the dark. When the waiter comes with the menus, they order the traditional *Rijsttafel*, for three.

Along with large bowls of rice, a two-foot-high, four-tiered tower of trays is set down in the middle of their table. It contains a vast array of colorful mouth-watering little dishes, maybe thirty or forty. Having gone light on lunch to save themselves for this meal, they're ravenous. They pile rice onto their plates and add spoonsful from four or five different dishes to start with.

Never in her life has she experienced such fire on her tongue and lips. Her nostrils are aflame, her eyes are tearing up. Within seconds after their first bites, she and Gracie and Beth are pouring water down their throats.

"How is everything?" the waiter asks.

What is there to say but, "Fine."

Doggedly, they keep trying to make a dent in the meal. It's hopeless. With this giant tower of food left on the table condemning their American wastefulness and unworldliness, they have to call for the waiter and pay the bill. Looking down, shamefaced, they leave large tips.

Brief Encounter

Gracie and Beth hitchhike up to Düsseldorf to catch their flight back to Manchester. Her flight to London leaves the next day. She lingers in Amsterdam, on her own for the first time since the trip began.

It's pleasant to stroll aimlessly along the canals, to poke her head in wherever she sees something of interest. She revisits the *Rijksmuseum* to admire again the Dutch masters' richly colored and naturalistic representations of domestic life. Passing by the building where Anne Frank and her family hid from the Nazis, she is uncomfortably reminded of herself and Beth and Gracie waiting with a mob of tourists for their turn to climb the stairs and gander at the place that symbolizes so much suffering.

That evening she returns to the student hotel to get a sweater. While there, she strikes up a conversation with a handsome French student about her age, maybe a little older. They go back out and wander the streets together. His English is almost perfect.

They talk about the Vietnam War and the culpability of both the United States and France. He laughs at her story of the *Rijsttafel* and of the starry-eyed tourists' persistence in believing that Amsterdam canals are clean. He takes her hand, and toward the end of the evening they stop occasionally to kiss.

At the student hotel, they climb the five flights to the communal room of cots under the eaves of the unheated garret. They are the only occupants tonight, Beth and Gracie having vacated. Shivering in the cold, they strip off their clothes and pull the blankets over themselves on her narrow bed.

Under the blankets they fondle and embrace. His body is lean and lithe, more muscular than David's. He smells salty and fresh. For a moment the action stops as he reaches for his trousers on the floor and pulls something from a pocket. She hears the tearing of a paper package and knows immediately what it is.

"No," she says. "We can't do that. We can do everything but that."

He pauses and pulls back a little.

A small window in the room lets in a bit of light from the street below. Her eyes have grown accustomed to the dark and she can see the puzzled frown on his face.

"Why?" he says. "I have protection."

"Well—" she starts.

"Are you a *virgin*?" he asks, in wonder.

"Yes."

"Oh." He puts the condom back in his trousers pocket and is silent for a few moments. "Okay," he says, "I guess we'd better sleep then." He retrieves his clothes, crosses the room naked, and descends the narrow stairs to his own cot on the floor below.

She lies there, thinking that she knew nothing about him when they picked each other up that evening. He could easily have raped her here in this room. That thought had not once crossed her mind. It seemed perfectly reasonable for a boy to accept a girl's expression of her sexual desire on her own terms. And, indeed, he has done just that.

The next day, she goes by train instead of taking the risk of hitchhiking alone to Düsseldorf. There, she catches the student flight back to London.

Home

She gets choked up as she emerges from the Archway Tube station, passes the familiar Highgate shops, and turns onto Cromwell Avenue. There is #27, her sweet little home, exactly like all the others on the street with their front steps and front "gardens," fan lights over the doors and Victorian brick facades.

Mrs. Lambert greets her with a hug, Hugo standing solemnly by her side. She remembers the day only four months ago when he looked up at her with those round, pale-blue eyes and asked, "Are you going on holiday?" The time is passing so quickly, and she feels tears rising at the thought that she will be leaving for good in another four months and never have London as a home again.

There is a great amount of mail to open. Letters from her parents, from David, from high school and college friends and many more, plus four copies of the Sunday *Daily Leader and Gazette* and a big box of Christmas presents.

She replies to her parents' letters first, telling them what a tremendously valuable experience her year abroad has been for her so far. "Thank you so much.

"I must have been a good girl to get all those fun little packages. It's amazing how you sense what sort of knick knacks I can use around the flat."

One of the letters in the pile is from Brent, the motorcycle buff. He announces that he intends to go back to the university. "I will not be able to build a house in the woods out of empty beer cans, so I'm going to cool the bars and save some money for school." He adds, "This letter writing isn't bad stuff. Wacked off a couple last week so I'm getting to like it." Is it possible that he absorbed her praise of his writing, or is he just sick of working an assembly line? She'd like to think she had an influence.

Shared Universe

Her second semester is all about psychology. She is taking seven different psych courses including Emotion & Motivation; Learning and Memory; and Psychology of the Abnormal Child, which includes six guest lectures by London psychoanalysts.

Meanwhile, her mother is in the same universe four thousand miles away, getting ready to take comps. "I'm using your Carroll textbooks to study from," she writes. "Your Intro book gives such a useful overview. But, gad, am I scrambling." She is exhausted from studying, entertaining, and working part time at the county hospital psychiatric department as a clinical assistant.

Her mother recommends Eric Berne's *Games People Play*, which she uses in counseling along with Transactional Analysis. "Very sensible and practical."

She runs to the college library and gets a copy. Not having to take exams as an Occasional Student, it's all reading, reading, reading. What could be better? This semester she reads almost nothing but books on child therapy, psychiatry and personality. She's trying to understand *The TAT and the CAT in Clinical Use* and is slogging through *The Handbook of Projective Techniques* and the Byzantine rules for scoring the Rorschach.

"I got a recent book called *Pavlovian Therapy* or something like that," she writes her mother, "so that I'll know what I've been sneering about when people mention the words 'behavior therapy.' I'm checking out books on non-directive counseling on your advice. It's so refreshing after all this Anna Freud, Melanie Klein malarky (a nine-month-old infant fantasizing about destroying the mother's breast with his feces, and so on)."

In late January, her mother passes her comps.

"I did the Rorschach well," her mother writes. "Got a blind Rorschach to score. I diagnosed the patient as a cyclothymic personality with strong possibility that he could become, or had been, manic depressive, manic-type. Made all kinds of guesses about impotence, distanciation, etc. Guess whose Rorschach it was? Herman Goering's! He took it during the Nuremberg trials. The psychologist who read my interpretation said after seeing it, he began to believe all the Rorschach gobbledeegook. Maybe this passed me because I did a terrible job on the analysis of variance problem." Her mother has the same statistics phobia that she has. "Now, on to the thesis and orals. If all goes well, I'll graduate with my MA on June 5th. Ted will graduate from high school the same day!"

Ivy League Blues

David is depressed by difficulties in understanding the high level mathematics he's studying at Harvard.

"I guess maybe I take these exams too seriously," he writes. "I'm glad I'm not going to a grad school where there's a lot of pressure (joke)."

As the year goes by, despite numerous successes, he focuses on his failures, in each letter expressing more self-castigation.

"Your letter helped me get over latest cumulative exam discouragement. I feel discouraged in a different way than last time. Things must be really bad when you get down to nuances of discouragement."

She realizes that she has never fully grasped the depth of his anxiety about academic success. Didn't he always end up getting A and A+ despite his gloomy predictions? She knows him to be brilliant in academics and in every other way and tells him so frequently.

"I'm so goddamned immature it's pitiful," he writes. "I wish I could live up to your somewhat idealized version of D. Kirschner."

As far as she's concerned her version isn't idealized at all. In spite of his grinding focus on his studies he still allows himself to read widely, to attend and show discernment about movies and plays. ("I find Ibsen so subtle and his sense of irony so keen." The film *McBird* is "a satire about Johnson and Kennedy, making a villain of harmless Mrs. Johnson.") He relieves his tension by playing on an intramural basketball team and hanging out with his genius pals. What is there not to admire about him?

His letters are always full of considerate questions about her life and her family. At the end of a string of such questions, he adds, "Do you still love me? (Just thought I'd sneak that one in inconspicuously)."

He is the ideal man. If only he didn't chew with his mouth open or kiss like a fish. If only her distaste for these insignificant flaws hadn't generalized to his entire physical being. Well, at least she tells him of her admiration, her respect, her awe. About that she's being truthful.

Psychoanalysis and the Prostate

The director of Harvard's Health Services does tests for David's chronic prostatitis and finds them negative. He thinks it might be psychosomatic. David agrees. He is referred to a psychiatrist and tells the doctor all his "deep dark inner thoughts."

The psychiatrist has tied together his sexual fantasies and feelings of inferiority, including a "facet of masochism and 'failure wish'" in his personality.

When she gets this letter, she shakes her head. He's got himself in the clutches of a psychoanalyst. She supposes it's to be expected since his family grew up steeped in the Freudianism of 1920s and 1930s Vienna. Among David's favorite dialogues in the Stan Freberg comedy album he used to play for her in the dorm:

> SAILOR: Watch yourself, Admiral. Natives. They may be hostile.
> CHRISTOPHER COLUMBUS: Well, we're all a little hostile now and then. Some of us are able to sublimate, others can adjust ... you know how it is.
>
> CHRISTOPHER COLUMBUS: That's why I've come here. To fulfill my dream.
> INDIAN CHIEF: You have a dream? Would you like to talk about it?

"Don't worry," he writes, "I won't let this guy psyche me out. He doesn't seem to have pre-conceived theories."

David enjoys free associating and remembering "all the significant traumas and sex fantasies" he's had in his life. She wonders if she has contributed to any of those traumas.

The next time, he writes that his sessions have taken a new turn, and besides himself his father is the real culprit. "It seems he's a somewhat Olympian figure to me and in trying to match his wittiness, intelligence, social poise, etc. I despair." She tries without success to imagine his homely, taciturn father as Olympian.

His prostate problems, having started when she and David began to have sex relations, are due to "sub-conscious guilty feelings about being an aggressor and showing masculinity when I was not sure of mine."

Didn't he say he wasn't going to allow this guy to psyche him out?

And then the psychiatrist decides this uncertainty concerning his masculinity is all about being surrounded by women (he has two sisters) and his mother being a good athlete.

Really? How does this jerk figure that being surrounded by adoring women is a *threat* to a man's manhood? Oh, of course! Because David's mother is athletic. Ah! *That* explains it.

Finally, a fear of success is diagnosed and accounts for his doing poorly on another cumulative exam.

Meanwhile, the prostatitis continues. "The sessions have become so much fun that I've forgotten all about it." The physical effects "haven't been as bad as sometimes lately, but the frequency is still above normal." Psychoanalysis. Grrrr.

Plans Afoot

Back in October it was decided that her parents and Ted would join her in England at the end of the school year and take a month-long European trip together. This is all pending her father's anticipated increase in salary. With the raise in the bag or not, he immediately draws up timelines and budgets, accumulates brochures and applies for updated passports.

In January her mother writes, "Did your Dad tell you he got a $4000 raise?" Her own wage at the hospital has also increased, to $3.75 an hour plus paid vacation. "Now sit down," she says, "while I rock your very foundations. Today I bought two, count them, two fur coats for the total sum of $800." It does rock her foundations. For her mother to buy even one fur coat is unimaginable. But then, she remembers how ashamed her mother had been in high school, living in a humble bungalow surrounded by the mansions of millionaires, her father out of work. And now there are the intimidating inaugural events coming up for the new university president, the city's elite attending. It's January. What's she going to wear? Her old wool coat frayed at the cuffs?

She replies, "First, allow me to congratulate you on your respective raises. I nearly choked when I saw the number $4000. Dad *didn't* write me about it & I have a pretty good idea why, but if he thinks *I* will become extravagant just because my mother goes around buying mink coats like penny candy, he is mistaken."

In her father's letters he rushes on with the plans. "Let me know *as soon as possible* the date you will be out in June. I want to get our plane reservations early." She can hear him getting into high gear, typical Dad, nothing left to chance. He proposes going to Paris after London and the English countryside, a car trip through the Loire Valley, Geneva, several cities in Germany, then Amsterdam and home.

Then a bombshell: his younger brother, rich Uncle Friedrich, wants them to interrupt their tour to join his family for a ten-day sail among the Greek islands on a hired yacht. Her father's yearning to do this is revealed by how much he downplays the possibility ("Cost will probably prevent it, but it's nice to dream.") and the disguised hope that Friedrich himself might actually intend to pay their way. ("I'm sure it will not be free and probably be far too expensive for us.")

Uncle Friedrich, it turns out, is not going to treat them to the experience. So their budget for the trip grows from $5000 to $7000. "Not sure where we'll get the extra money," her father writes. His raise amounts only to $2500 after taxes. He'll be paying for Ted to start college in September and has been partly subsidizing Nick as he makes his way in the jazz world. Good news, though. Nick has been hired to play in a band on a cruise ship for six weeks. She hopes he won't get queasy. Will it help combat seasickness to pound on drums and cymbals?

The yacht has been chosen—the *Sonia*—to sail out of Piraeus Harbor on July 16th.

From this time on her father's letters are taken up with constantly revised itineraries and requests for immediate information about the England sojourn she is cooking up for them. Every sentence reveals his immense excitement, and typical anxiety that everything go according to plan.

The More Things Change, the More They Stay the Same

She's in the choir again this term, singing Bruckner's Mass in F minor. "Can't wait to get together with the orchestra," she writes her parents. "I went to the Royal Festival Hall for a concert—'Changes' by Gordon Cross and 'Requiem' by Fauré. 1st very beautiful. 2nd stodgy."

Her professor will take the students in the Psychology of the Abnormal Child class to observe at Hampstead Child Treatment Center where they do children's therapy. "It's such a great opportunity."

Her mother writes to say her dad was a guest speaker at an alumni luncheon and was funny and interesting despite the topic ("University Financial Operations").

"I heard about the excellent speech you made for the alumni luncheon, Dad," she writes him. "You keep saying you're not good at public speaking, but I think that's a bunch of hogwash."

David continues to send lively and affectionate letters. Despite this, she writes him about her tryst with the French boy in Amsterdam.

He replies, "I wish you hadn't written that bit about Amsterdam. What would you think if I wrote you something like, Well, this girl & I were sexing it up but don't worry, I'm saving myself for you, etc.?" *What would she think, indeed?* "If you wouldn't feel some envy, jealousy or hurt, you're a better ~~man~~, woman than I am (a man)." He can even make this little joke about it! And he continues the letter in a friendly way, signing off with "Write soon & often. I miss you

Reasonable People · 217

very much. Love David." How much more forgiving he is than she.

As usual she has imparted this hurtful and unnecessary piece of information about the French boy to punish him because in a previous letter he had mentioned going on a double date. He adds that all the dates he's been on this semester have had the effect of increasing his affection for her. "Not having known too many girls when I met you, I guess I didn't appreciate how lucky I was."

And at the end of that letter he says, "Do you still care about me? Are you interested in spending any time with me this summer? Believe it or not, I am less of a cheapskate now that I have my own money."

Why did she give in to this compulsion to punish him after such a thoughtful and reassuring letter? How shameful her behavior is. How unfair, how mean-spirited and cruel. She herself has been dating since her first few weeks in London. Her double standard is especially perverse considering that she doesn't intend for the relationship to continue when she returns. Someone once wrote that the definition of evil is making someone else carry the insecurities that belong to you.

She tries to make it up to him by writing warmly and more often, but in the end this will only hurt him more. She's mired in hypocrisy. If she'd had any integrity, she would have broken it off before she left for England. But now, how heartless would it be to do it by letter? She can at least vow to herself never to punish him again. For what that's worth.

Unscathed

David isn't the only one to whom she reveals her encounter with the boy in Amsterdam. On her return to London she writes her mother, "Back safe & sound. I had a fairly unbelievable experience in Amsterdam which I can't relate to you since it had to do with a male, sex and the like, & you wouldn't approve. I came out unscathed and decided I'd better leave for Düsseldorf before my id completely overwhelmed my superego."

"Since you were 'unscathed,'" her mother replies, "and your super-ego remained in control, I think it would be unfair not to let your old Ma in on your Dolce Vita, Amsterdam-style, eh? I must say I no longer have the concern that your father's cautioning may have injured your sense of adventure."

She decides not to elaborate on the incident, since it had been far riskier than simply a sense of adventure.

Meanwhile, her father writes asking for advice on how to travel in Europe so inexpensively. She imagines her family traveling across Europe with their thumbs out. She tells him they took a student discounted flight to Oslo (true) and stayed at youth hostels for a pittance (also true). He seems to be satisfied with that.

And now she and Gracie and Beth are revving up for the spring trip. English school holidays are quite generous—another whole month to roam the Continent. This vacation will be sunshine all the way. No more frostbite. Even now her fingertips turn white when she's the least bit chilly. This time it's to be France and Spain, with a side trip across the straits to Tangier. On March twenty-third they leave for Paris.

Vive La France

She reports to her parents on the sights of Paris: "Notre Dame (fabulous gargoyles), Eiffel Tower (rusty-colored & looking like part of an erector set someone left out in the rain), The Louvre (Mona Lisa, Venus de Milo & Whistler's Mom). Champs Elysee & Arc de Triomphe. Best of all, the Seine." They stay three days.

Now they are hitching to Brittany where they will be guests at an actual chateau owned by the Marquis and Marquise Kergos. Monsieur Kergos served in World War II with the father of a friend of Beth's.

On the way to the chateau, they stop at the walled medieval town of Mont St. Michel. Like a mythical castle, it sits on an islet of granite in a bay half a mile from the mainland. Its narrow streets spiral up through the town to the foot of a massive, labyrinthine abbey, a statue of St. Michael seeming to balance at the tip of its soaring spire. At high tide, the causeway to the islet is under water, making it inaccessible.

The Château de Kergos is a magnificent stone castle with steeply pitched gray-blue metal roofs and many towers. They are warmly welcomed by the Marquis and Marquise, and their grown daughter and son. Madame Kergos and her daughter prepare the meals. Being impoverished aristocrats, they can't afford servants.

The chateau has two huge dining rooms, a gigantic kitchen, two living rooms, nine bed chambers and many more rooms they wish they could explore. One wing of the seventeenth-century chateau is a fifteenth-century chapel. She wonders how the Kergos family held on to the place during the French Revolution, but she wouldn't dream of asking.

On walks in the surrounding countryside, she sees thatched-roof stone houses and old women in large white coifs and black dresses with starched white collars. It's as if she's slipped back into another century.

Welcome to Spain

Hitchhiking down the Atlantic coast from Brittany into Spain, they view through the right-hand windows the dark blue ocean with white surf rolling in, while out the left the snow-capped Pyrenees mountains rise.

They are getting into cars driven primarily by Spanish businessmen on their way to Madrid. She is always the most suspicious of the three. Beth runs up to anyone who stops for them and hops into the front seat with a big smile for the driver. Gracie is a little more circumspect but generally amenable, while she stands by the vehicle, casing out the man, the car and its contents before reluctantly getting in. She does get in, though. So far, they haven't turned down any rides or met with any disasters.

Partway to Madrid, a middle-aged business man picks them up. After they've been on the road for a while, he tells them in quite good English that he'll need to stop off in Burgos to take care of some business before continuing. It will only take about a half hour. Her antennae immediately go up. What's this "business" and why didn't he tell them before? She frowns at Gracie, who shrugs. Beth is just enjoying the view.

In Burgos, he leaves them at a thirteenth-century cathedral and when he comes back offers to take them to a nice place he knows for lunch. Beth is delighted of course. Gracie is hungry and thinks it's a good idea. Her antennae go up again. Really? Just where does he plan to take them for this "lunch"?

They share a long truncheon table with other diners in the small restaurant. The waiter brings baskets of warm, home-made crusty bread with olive oil for dipping, wedges of locally produced goat cheese and a big wooden bowl of fresh salad greens and tomatoes. It is one of the best meals she's ever had. Their businessman will not allow them to pay.

He takes one more side trip, to the ancient town of Segovia so they can see the Roman aqueduct, whose lofty double tiers of arches, intact after two thousand years, span the old city and still carry water from a river ten miles away.

It is night by the time they arrive in Madrid on April 1st. He asks them if they have a place to stay; if not he could suggest a hotel. Here it comes, she thinks. The demand for a return on his day's investment.

She replies emphatically that they do have a hotel, pointing to an address on the marked page in their *Europe on Five Dollars a Day*.

He drives them there, helps them out with their backpacks, and shakes hands all around. "It was nice to meet you," he says. "I hope you enjoy Madrid and the rest of Spain." He gets back in his car and drives away almost before they can give him their profuse thanks.

The Bad with the Good

They spend two days in Madrid then head for the ancient city of Toledo.

In the El Greco Museum they gaze at the artist's soulful figures, weirdly elongated like martyrs of Spain's Inquisition after being stretched on the rack. It would be a pleasure to wander around Toledo's endless narrow streets, past intriguing doorways and courtyards if it weren't for the swarms of Spanish males who follow the three of them yelling lewd comments.

As they thread their way through a crowded indoor market, she sees in her peripheral vision two teen-aged boys starting to close in from behind. She's quite certain her bottom is about to get pinched and she feels a sudden rage. With her hand in a tight fist, she contracts all the muscles of her arm, and brings her elbow close against her side. The moment she feels the brush of a hand on the fabric of her pants, she takes a quick breath and slams her elbow straight back. The blow lands. There's an audible grunt and the sound of the boy stumbling backward. She walks on, gratified to hear the other boy laughing at his friend. By now she and Gracie and Beth agree they've had enough harassment and it's time to get the hell out of town.

On the way south, they're given a ride by two middle-aged workmen, or maybe farmers, driving a pick-up truck. They toss their backpacks in the bed of the truck and climb in after them. The truck turns off the highway and takes a dusty back road south. Leaning against their packs in the open air, they enjoy the grand views across the rugged, mountainous land.

Then, halfway across a bridge suspended high above a river, the truck comes to a halt. They turn to look through the window at the two men, who seem to be conferring with each other. The men get out of the truck and come around to the back. One of them says something incomprehensible, perhaps speaking a rural dialect or using some kind of slang Gracie never learned in her three years of high school textbook Spanish. The man's face is unreadable but certainly not friendly. Gracie asks him to repeat himself and now, though she's not sure, she thinks he is saying something about sex. The other man unlatches the tailgate.

They are in the middle of a bridge with a sheer mountain face rising on one side and a sheer drop of probably a thousand feet on the other. In panic, they grab their packs, jump out and start to run back across the bridge. The men saunter after them in leisurely pursuit. No other vehicles have come along this road for a good half hour.

There are only two of them, she thinks, and three of us, but they're strong, sturdy looking men, muscular from hard labor. They could easily lift up any one of the three and toss her over the bridge if they resist, or after the men get what they want. She pictures herself bouncing off the rocks like a rag doll all the way down to the river below.

It is at this moment that a car appears. The sedan comes around the bend from the direction the truck has been heading and slows down to pass them on the narrow bridge. Gripping their packs, she and Beth and Gracie run ahead, plant themselves in the car's lane and frantically signal for the driver to stop.

The sedan driver has no choice if she is to avoid running them down, and as soon as she stops, they rush the car, pull open the doors and to the astonishment of the passengers clamber onto their laps. Gracie points to the truck and tries in broken and panic-impaired Spanish to explain the reason for their intrusion. The driver and four passengers, dressed professionally—the two men in suits and ties, the women in dresses—seem to take the information in stride almost as if such a thing is routine on an isolated mountain road. She and Gracie and Beth turn to peer out the rear window as the farmers close the truck's tailgate, get back in and ease on across the bridge.

Local Color

The people whose car they've commandeered are young teachers, returning to their home town of Aranjuez after attending a conference. The driver, Liliana, teaches English, so there is no communication problem.

That night Liliana and her friends take them "pubbing" Spanish-style. This means they go to every bar in Aranjuez and buy glasses of cheap wine that come with unlimited free snacks (*tapas*). In the United States the *tapas* alone would have been as pricey as expensive hors d'oeuvres in a swanky restaurant: shrimp in garlic sauce, calamari, mussels, potato omelettes, pickled mushrooms, anchovies, olives.

The next day Liliana asks them to sit in on a small remedial English class she holds in her home. It reassures them a little about their own faulty language skills, watching the six teenagers struggle to leave off the *eh* before words starting with *s* (eh-school, eh-story, eh-stupid) and forget to add subject pronouns to sentences ("Am going to the museum," "Want to buy this fish, please") or pronounce the sound *h* ("'Ello. Ow are you?").

They divide into little conversation groups and she tells the students in her group the story of how she came to meet Liliana. She teaches them the word "hitchhiking." She's afraid she's being rather a bad influence. But at least they produce a lot of questions for her to correct ("Why went in the truck with the men?" "What think your mother and father about 'itch-iking?").

She writes to her parents, "We've experienced so much local color and—the icing on the cake—such kind and fun-loving people!" No need to go into the circumstances under which they met these kind, fun-loving people.

Earthy

Not being accustomed to rural life even in the Midwest where she grew up, she finds rural life in Spain unbelievably "earthy." She applies this word particularly to the place where they stay after Aranjuez, a partly converted shed on a truck farm. The beds are set on concrete slabs surrounded by sand. The shed is illuminated only by a kerosene lamp, with just basins and pitchers of water for washing.

Poor Beth has been stoically enduring constipation for the last week, and now, in the wee hours, her bowels hint that they are finally ready to loosen their grip. This might be Beth's only opportunity for who knows how long, so she springs from bed and gropes her way to the door and across the farmyard to the privy in the pitch dark, triggering an ear-piercing clamor of farm dogs.

She and Gracie sit up in bed with their fingers crossed hoping that the dogs are behind a fence and that Beth will make it back alive. The stress of all this pressure has clamped Beth's sphincter tight, and it takes her a good twenty minutes before she races past the penned, frenzied dogs once more and collapses on her bed, triumphant.

If anything could qualify as "earthy," this experience is surely it.

Madinah Mint

They make their way down through central Spain, then southeast to Seville and on to the southern coast. The people are kind and helpful when asked for directions or advice. Still, the country is crawling with men who have a one-track mind where women are concerned. She gets furious, but except for that one gratifying slam of an elbow into what she hopes was the boy's solar plexus or something farther down, she is careful not to lose her temper and anger these men. Gracie and Beth, too, are tired of being leered at and she's afraid she won't be able to restrain Gracie from screaming *"Chianga su madre!"* at the next passing truck driver who leans on his horn and laughs to see them jump.

They take the early morning ferry from Algeciras across the straits to Tangier, Morocco. After a rough two-hour crossing, they step onto the continent of Africa.

She can't believe anything could be earthier than Spain, but Tangier is easily the earthiest yet, especially the myriad of Old City market stalls, where you can buy everything from lamb's intestines to Berber rugs. "It's a pleasant change," she writes, "to have all these men after our money rather than our bodies. Somehow 'Come in ... no buy, only look ... I have very good things ... half price ...' etc. is not so infuriating."

A Moroccan man, probably in his forties and dressed in a Western style suit, asks if they would like to come to his house for tea. She, as usual, is appalled by the suggestion, but Beth immediately accepts, and they can't let her go alone. He leads them up and down a maze of alleyways so narrow they only allow for walking two abreast. At his house, from which they will never be able to find their way back, they enter through an ornately carved wooden door abutting the street and framed with blue and white tiles.

The man, inevitably named Mohammed, invites them to seat themselves in the living room on a circle of bright tasseled cushions and excuses himself, leaving them to gaze for a quarter of an hour at the colorful geometric and floral patterns and Arabic calligraphy of the wall hangings and pictures. He comes back with a large brass tray holding a silver tea pot, glasses, and small bowls of figs, pistachios, dates and pastries.

"This is a rather special mint tea imported from Saudi Arabia," he says. "Madinah Mint it's called." He pours the tea and adds sugar to each glass. They find it amazingly refreshing, better than any tea they've ever tasted. Mohammed is pleased when they ask for several refills and dig in to the snacks.

When it's time to leave, he gives them each a little cloth bag tied with ribbon and containing aromatic Madinah Mint tea leaves. Then he guides them back to the central plaza where they originally met, shakes their hands, wishes them well and says good-bye. She finally takes a full breath.

"Wasn't that fun?" says Beth. And once again, she is right.

One at a Time

Back to Algeciras by ferry, they continue up the coast of Spain, passing through Torremolinos, a terrible town famously infested with every rich alcoholic and drug-addicted ex-pat writer and artist in Europe and the United States, who loll about the beaches and taverns, smoking cigarettes and exhibiting conspicuous ennui.

After Torremolinos, they take a bus to Granada to wander through the Alhambra Palace, then back south to Almería to tour a Moorish Castle where an archaeological dig is underway. "From a turret we could see the archways they were unearthing. It was really a dream come true." She's glad she can provide her parents with the tidbit about taking a bus to Granada because now they are going to hitchhike halfway up the Gold Coast to Valencia and across France to Paris.

The roads are terrible, extremely zig zaggy through breathtaking mountains and cliffs overlooking the ocean. They must be, she thinks, the most spectacular and frightening roads in the world.

Halfway up the coast they're picked up by two skinny, teenaged German boys in a big American car with tailfins. Ensconced in the roomy back seat, they're well on their way along one of those spectacular and frightening roads before they realize the boys are drunk and playing a version of chicken, except that their opponent is themselves. *Ein! Zwei! Drei! Vier! Fünf!...* they shriek exuberantly, counting each hairpin turn they take on the inside of the road at maximum speed, the driver laying on his horn.

She and Gracie and Beth sit in back, gripping each other's wrists and closing their eyes before each curve. When a relatively straight stretch of road appears, she leans forward and taps the driver on the shoulder. In a carefully modulated calm and friendly voice, she says, "Excuse me, would you mind stopping here for a minute?"

The boy pulls to the side of the road in a cloud of dust. The three of them scramble out of the car clutching their backpacks. They wave good-bye and gesture for the boys to continue on. With a shrug and a boozy grin, they do.

For the rest of the almost thousand mile trip back, they adhere to a strict rule: never get into a car containing more than one man. This gets them from Alicante, Spain to Paris, France in one piece.

Beth's Trust

She and Gracie are ready to get back to England, but Beth decides to stay on for a few more days and go to Greece.

"You're going to hitch *alone*?" They can't imagine it after surviving their encounters with lecherous Spanish farmers and drunk German teenagers. Beth is nonchalant.

"I've always wanted to go to Greece," she says. "Especially Athens."

They aren't her parents, so what can they do but wish her good luck. They all three hitchhike out to the northern suburbs of Paris where Beth stops to put out her thumb. They put theirs out a few blocks away. Within minutes of getting a ride with a young married couple, they catch a glimpse out the car window of Beth whizzing past in a red convertible sports car driven by a handsome young man in sunglasses. Her hair is streaming out behind her and she's laughing at something he has said. At least there's only one of him.

She and Gracie spend all night on the boat train, playing cards and feeling queasy with two English schoolboys adorable in their sagging knee socks, crested blazers and caps. In London, Gracie takes the train to Manchester.

After a few anxious days, she gets a card from Beth, reporting that she got picked up in Greece by two Greek brothers who showed her around Athens, and then took her to their mother's home where she was fed and lodged and treated like a beloved sister. Oh Beth, she thinks. How do you do it? Trust? Is it just trust? Is it that simple?

One Does Not ...

She attends classes, reads her textbooks, digs into original sources and takes careful notes. When she gets back to Carroll, she will be prepared to justify the full number of credits Dr. Steiner has promised.

Miles Littlewood still asks her out, but she accepts less often, using various excuses, until he fades from her life and is replaced by Gareth Hawtry, a boy her age from the college. He, too, has access to his parents' car and drives her to Dartmoor, which she finds enchanting, right out of *Wuthering Heights* and *Return of the Native*. This is where she'll take her parents for their trip into the countryside when they come.

She and Gareth go to rugby matches, one of which he plays in. She wonders how these boys can play such a rough sport unprotected by the virtual armor that American footballers wear, and how they can come out of the match seemingly intact. Gareth is pleased by the question.

He compliments her, says corny things, even presents her with a cameo necklace on a little gold chain yet is quite satisfied with only a few tender kisses and a bit of hand holding.

"I can't figure him out," she writes her mother, "but I suspect he's another Bill Phelps. (Remember him? My Boy Scout boyfriend in high school?) I'm always standing around ready to jump him and indulge in some good-old fashioned passion. But I have to control myself and be demure, and the strain is getting to me."

After another trip to the country he takes her to the theatre and dinner afterwards. He always insists on paying. She feels squirmy at the amount of money he spends on her. He has to be as poor as any other English university student and in fact has let slip that he's the first in his family to attend college. There is something about the way he speaks that suggests a working class accent polished up and passing for posh.

Then one day Gareth takes her to see the sights at Kew Gardens in southwest London. It's a warm, breezy afternoon in May. They walk hand in hand. To feel the dewy grass beneath her feet, she slips off her sandals and dangles them from her fingers. Gareth lets go of her hand and puts a little distance between them. They continue walking, but he has become very silent.

"Is anything wrong?" she asks.

Icily, looking straight ahead, he says, "One does not go barefoot in the Queen's Botanical Gardens."

She looks around at people lounging casually in the grass. Aren't one or two of them barefoot? Without a word she leans down and puts on her sandals. They continue their tour.

That is the last time she lets him take her out.

Olé!

Toward the end of May David's school is about to be over for the year, and he is taking a Harvard friend home to meet his family and go with them to the Expo in Montreal.

"I don't know anyone back home now," he writes, "so I'm trying to badger Dad into getting us dates with girls from the college."

The sentence is like a matador's cape. But why? She's not a big dumb maddened animal and he's not a goddamned matador. He's not trying to provoke her. His letter begins with "Dear Sweetie." In all his letters he counts the days until he sees her again. What possesses her to go back on her word to herself: *I will not punish him.* And yet, she charges.

This time, she doesn't get away with it.

Her letter is waiting for him when he returns to Harvard from Montreal.

He replies: "My mind is in great turmoil due to one paragraph in your letter. I have been looking forward so much to seeing you in August with the expectation of the continuation (beginning?) of a mature, lasting relationship. But now my hopes are considerably dimmed. I was very hurt, first by the flippant tone of your beginning: 'You'll probably be appalled ... but here goes' and your insulting last sentence: 'Be honest, I expect it of you.' What is a relationship to be based on if not honesty? And you have the gall to ask me to be honest with you when you don't give your motive for your somewhat unusual question. From the evidence, your question and its timing (coming just before you're leaving England), I'm forced to think that probably you have found a man with whom you have had a good (I don't know what word fits) and warm relationship and with whom you would like to have sexual intercourse. Your decision will be based on whether I plead guilty or innocent to having done so myself. If this is the case, I wish you to make your decision in the context of the relationship itself, uncluttered by anything I say. I abstain from answering."

The final gut punch: "I'd prefer to marry a non-virgin who is warm, compassionate and sensitive than a virgin whose virginity in sex is matched by a 'virginity' in understanding human feelings and sensitivity."

A Ratio of Two to One

She doesn't actually see David's letter until after the semester ends and she returns from a two-week trip to Scotland with Janet Brown, an American post graduate studying English at University College London. Janet is the only American friend she has allowed herself to make.

The doors to the youth hostels are locked between nine a.m. and six p.m., which makes for miserable times on days when it rains. They stand beside the road dripping and shivering under dreary gray skies. On their way back to London, they get dropped off at a remote tea shop in the middle of the countryside with nothing but bleak hills and wet, dejected sheep in all directions.

Stepping inside the tea shop, they're instantly warmed by a well-stoked fire in a large stone fireplace. The tea shop is a half-timbered structure with low, wood-beamed ceilings and tables covered by lace cloths. They are among only three or four other customers. Shaking their heads in disbelief at their good fortune, they shed their dripping jackets and take a seat at a table snugged up against a bay window.

An elderly waitress in a gingham apron places on the table two translucent china cups and saucers, a tea pot kept warm by a tea cosy, a pitcher of cream and a bowl of sugar cubes. Scones arrive warm from the oven in a basket along with a plate of white country butter and a pot of honey.

For the price of one cup of tea and one scone each, the contents of teapot and basket, pitcher, bowl, plate and honey pot are replenished repeatedly until she and Janet, leaning back in their chairs and gazing out at the misty hills through rivulets of rain running down the glass, have become euphoric on caffeine and comfort.

After a while, when it sinks in that they are welcome to stay as long as they like, they pull out novels from their backpacks and lazily read their respective books—Janet's Agatha Christie, her Jane Austen—until hours later the rain stops, sunbeams stream from behind the clouds, and they can continue on their way.

Outside of Leeds they get a ride with a lorry driver going to London. What luck! They'll get into the city before dark. Then, twenty-five miles or so from Leeds, he pulls the truck off the highway and takes a back country road into a forest.

"Where are you going?" she says, realizing all at once that the no-more-than-one-man rule doesn't work anymore. The ratio on this trip isn't 3:1. It's 2:1.

He doesn't answer her question, and when they have come far enough into the woods to be out of sight of the highway, he stops and turns off the engine. He makes no bones about what he wants.

She wrenches open the door and pulls Janet out behind her. They start running back along the road, packs bouncing. It will take him some time to reverse on the narrow road and maneuver his semi-trailer truck in the right direction. They reach the open highway and cross it so that they're headed north. An old fashioned black Bentley pulls over and stops. At the wheel is a straight-backed elderly woman out of one of Janet's Christie novels. She's even wearing a long black dress with a high lace collar. A lap robe covers her knees.

"I've only stopped for you girls," she says, "because it's dangerous and foolhardy to get in cars with strangers. You don't know what kind of person might pick you up." She asks for their destination. "Well, I'm going to take you to the Leeds train station and you are to buy tickets and go back to London by train." If she only knew how happy they are to take her advice.

He Looked Marvelous

When she returns home, David's irate letter is waiting for her.

Flippant, immature, insulting, dishonest, a "virgin" in the understanding of human feelings and sensitivity, he calls her. And that's without even knowing the true nastiness of her manipulative desire to punish him for contemplating a harmless double date.

Now, at last, no more Mr. Nice Guy. David Kirschner has put up with it long enough.

He's right about everything.

Without the imagination to consider how truly hurtful her letter's impact would be, she has blithely been sending off friendly, affectionate postcards to him without any reference to her letter at all.

The most humiliating aspect of his response is the unstated but implied fact that she, training to become a clinical psychologist, appears to have neither empathy nor the remotest understanding of human nature.

Her chest feels heavy, her heart palpitates. She folds up David's letter and shoves it out of sight in a drawer. There is no need to read it again. Every word is burned into her conscience and mocks her self-esteem.

In the pile of unopened correspondence from her parents, there is another letter from David, dated only a few days ago. She puts it aside, afraid to open it, and reads instead the latest revision of her parents' itinerary—6/22 leave home, 6/23–6/30 London and English countryside, 7/1–7/3 Paris and Loire Valley, 7/4–7/8 Germany, 7/9–7/11 Rome, 7/12–7/23 Athens and the Greek Islands by yacht, etc. Then Geneva, Amsterdam. Back home on 7/30.

Her father thanks her for having planned their London visit so well. "Although you thought it might be cheaper for you to stay where you are," he writes, "I think it's going to be more fun and practical for us all to be staying at the hotel together." Her mother adds, "I can't believe we'll get to see you in only a few days."

She cries, thinking how little she deserves such loving parents. David has liked and respected them from their first meeting and they feel the same about him. On his long drive back from Montreal he went to the trouble to take a detour and visit them. He must be wondering how such nice people produced such a self-centered child.

"David came here on his way back East," her mother writes. "He looked marvelous, wearing a camel hair sweater I think you gave him, button-down collar shirt, good hair-cut."

She thinks, Poor Mom, she's really selling him. Her mother would never say so, but she probably hopes, and with good reason, that after all she'll marry David. He'd make a sterling husband.

Her mother has no idea that she can't marry anyone as long as she harbors this perverse character flaw.

Mr. Nice Guy

David's latest letter is sitting off to one side on the kitchen table in its stiff white envelope looking like a lawyer ready to wrap up the prosecution's case. With great trepidation, she opens it and at first scans it quickly to prepare herself for the worst before settling down to read. It is short.

"Dear Annie, I really appreciate the letter and frequent cards from your trip," he begins. "It is always reassuring to hear that the other member of a duo gives a damn, and you must care a little to waste all that good money on stamps as well as the time writing. I was thinking about my comments in my last letter, which you might not have seen before coming back to London." He has decided that the violence of his reaction was unwarranted although he was justifiably unhappy regarding the tone and content of her letter.

Her warm cards and letter have reassured him that her statements were "merely perfunctorily callous and not with malice aforethought (or a-afterthought). You were right, though, in assuming that I would be appalled. And all who know me were surprised at Kirschner's atypical unphlegmatic response. I'll write more on this subject soon. Gee whiz. It's less than two months until we see each other (knock on wood). Love, David."

Now she has to reply. She can do nothing to repair her *self*-image; the jealousy and compulsion to punish still lurk behind her facade. But she can try to repair her image with David. She can apologize, take blame, show appreciation for his forgiving nature and maturity.

"I'm sorry for my thoughtlessness," she writes. "I can see why you would be appalled by my asking such an 'unusual' question as you so generously put it and for asking it in such an insulting way. You're right to question my maturity. I'm afraid I've done irreparable damage to our relationship, and it's probably presumptuous of me to imagine you care now, but I do want to say that there is no man here that I'm even slightly interested in. My letter certainly revealed the depth of my insecurities, and I suppose I see you as so much more confident and mature than I am that I forget you can be hurt."

She goes on to list his virtues, easy to summon, there being so many. She quotes her mother on his looking marvelous. Perhaps she is laying it on too thick, but all of it is true except for her old standby use of the ambiguous word "insecurities," the term she's often employed to weasel out of giving the specific reason—jealousy—for her episodes of coldness. What is also dishonest is the fact that in spite of everything she has said and done out of "insecurity," including her reply to his letter, she doesn't intend to continue the relationship when she comes home. She simply isn't physically attracted to him anymore. Her letter is a sham. But she sends it anyway.

Found

She watches for them among the people streaming out of the plane, and suddenly at a distance, there they are, the three of them, beaming and waving. She rushes forward, wondering how it is possible that they've actually arrived, and on time. She has expected a worrisome delay or misconnection, something gone wrong, but they've traveled halfway across the country and all the way across the ocean and actually found her.

Their smiles are ecstatic as if they had taken a wrong turn and gotten separated from her somewhere and searched and searched until, rounding a corner, they've come upon her, here, in this place that's nothing like home. These three very familiar people are hurrying to meet her, smiling and smiling as strangers brush by.

Familiar and yet not quite the same people. Her parents look older than the last time she saw them, her mother slightly thickened in the waist, her father with bags under his eyes that she hadn't noticed before. And Ted! Ted has shot up to such a height. He must be six feet tall. Nine months ago he looked like a little boy. He still has the body of an adolescent who hasn't quite finished filling out, but now he's a handsome young man in a tweed jacket, with tousled Kennedyesque hair and high Lang cheekbones.

They rush together and hug and cry out endearments. How strange it is to hear their Midwestern American voices in this context. She hears her own accent in theirs and realizes it is only now that she can hear it.

She takes charge, knowing how to navigate the airport, knowing which exit to leave by and where to get a taxi, knowing not to tip a London cabby. The three of them stare and stare out the car windows, taking it all in as she did from the train last September.

She's twenty-one now. Twenty-one. Technically an adult, yet she feels, looking after her parents and brother, that she is an actor performing the role of an adult in a play. David's letter, still lingering in her mind, tells her that she still has not grown up.

Her father seems relieved, even grateful to be divested of his usual role of man in charge. For once, he has nothing to do but let her lead them around like children on a school excursion.

Their luggage is manageable among them; they're traveling light—due, no doubt, to her father's meticulous planning. She has booked them into The Devon House, a modest and pleasant hotel on a quiet street, centrally located near the college. For a while, they just collapse on the beds and relax and talk.

Tablecloth

She takes them to Speakers Corner where they mingle in the crowds of earnest orators, ranters, hecklers and hellfire preachers holding placards announcing The End is At Hand. There is a bit of excitement when two uniformed Bobbies try to subdue a young man who has gone berserk in some undetermined way.

They go to the British Museum and Buckingham Palace and the other famous places she visited in her first weeks. She shows them around her college. She takes them on London's legendary red, double-decker buses. Any sight they want to see she can get them to on the Tube, which impresses them with its efficiency and cleanliness.

Her father has sacrificed considerable luggage space for his movie and still cameras. These spend little, if any, time in a suitcase, however. They are permanent fixtures hanging from straps around his neck.

Finally, after all this sightseeing, she brings them to her neighborhood of Highgate. First she takes them to Highgate Cemetery and shows them Karl Marx's grave and the wonderfully eerie corridors of Victorian crypts overhung with holly vines. They view London spread out before them from the heights of Hampstead Heath where they have tea and meat pasties on a bench in the sunshine. Her mother endorses everything as "breathtaking." Finally, they make their way to Cromwell Avenue, to her bed sitter and the Lamberts.

It's quite sweet, this meeting of her parents and her landlords with cute little Hugo standing by all round-eyed and curious. Glynis and Adrian have unobtrusively looked after her for these nine months, and she's glad to present them to her appreciative parents. It is a pleasure to take them up the narrow stairs to her apartment and show them how cozy Glynis made it for her. Her mother notices with satisfaction the scouring balls she had sent months ago, coincidentally in colors matching the kitchen tablecloth that Glynis had provided.

For the first time, it hits her that in a few days she will leave not only England, but the Lamberts. She has grown very fond of them and their modest, unassuming ways, and it seems inconceivable but quite likely that she will never see them again.

White Knuckles

She has reserved rooms at a country inn for their day trips to Dartmoor, Stonehenge, and Salisbury. For these trips, they've rented a four-door Morris Minor. She herself has not driven a car since her failed, nerve-wracking lessons with her father. She is especially sensitive to the signs of tension in him as he negotiates the suburban London death traps called "roundabouts" while driving on the left side of the road.

At every turning on the winding country lanes she braces herself for a surprise flock of sheep or a bicyclist that will trigger her father's reflexes to do exactly the wrong thing. Then, when the road briefly straightens out enough to pass the farm cart ahead, and Ted shouts from the back seat ("Make your move now, Dad. Now! Now!"), her father's knuckles turn white on the wheel. ("There's a goddamn semi on my tail!")

He is concentrating so hard he barely speaks as her mother points out a thatched barn or cross-timbered pub or distant church spire ("Just like a Trollope novel!"), humming her unconscious hum of detachment, reflecting on the quirk of language that a girlish word like "lorry" could represent the ten tons of mannish steel that are about to muscle them into the path of a merging Mini.

In spite of his nerves, or maybe because of them, her father is incapable of driving slowly. She has both feet pressed on imaginary brakes during every mile and doesn't relax until they reach each destination and get out or when at last they pull into the driveway at nightfall and park in front of their comfortable eighteenth-century inn.

Dartmoor is just as wild and windswept as she remembers it and she's gratified by her mother's "breathtaking!" which in this case is apt, not hyperbolic.

She brings them to Stonehenge at sunrise and is happy to see that the peace symbol graffiti has been expunged since October.

A picturesque group of choir boys in black gowns and white ruffs walks in lockstep to the Cathedral at Salisbury. She has coincidentally brought her family there just as a service is about to begin. They sit in a back pew long enough to hear the Latin hymns echo from the high arched ceilings. As she listens, she wonders idly why, if the church likes these soprano voices so much, they don't just give the job to women or girls, but she supposes the custom began in the days when females were banned from doing anything of a public nature and, like so many things in England—the ridiculous wigs in courtrooms and the monstrous fur hats on the heads of the Queen's Guards—the tradition became sacrosanct.

Back in the Morris, her father pulls the car onto the road and she holds her breath and grips the seat back.

Nine Minutes, 426 Rooms

After England, they cross the channel and spend several days in Paris before renting a *Citroën* to tour some of the famous chateaus of the Loire Valley. Her father has consulted his brochures and chosen a very definite itinerary: "The Four Cs"—Château de Chenonceau, Château de Chaumont, Château de Cheverny, and Château de Chambord. He has allocated one day for the trip.

Now that they are in a country where people sensibly drive on the right side, there's no lollygagging on scenic back roads; instead he takes the perfectly straight, tree-lined, two-lane provincial highway that has apparently no speed limit. Compared to this sprint to visit four chateaus in one day, the white knuckle trips in the English countryside seem like lazy Sunday drives.

The magnificent Château de Chenonceau bridges a river. From its arched galleries they watch ducks gliding among the supporting columns and disappearing on one side of the castle to reappear on the other. Chaumont is flanked all around by massive round towers with peaked slate roofs that gleam black in the sunlight. Cheverny, on its vast grounds, stands elegant, symmetrical, and restrained. They could spend an entire day wandering through any one of these castles and not begin to see all the grand ancestral portraits, tapestries, gilded salons and bedrooms festooned with satin and velvet draperies. She and Ted and her mother linger as long as possible before her father taps his watch. There is one last chateau that he doesn't want to miss.

They pull into the parking lot. Between 4:46 and 4:47 p.m. they're racing after him across the broad green lawn toward the entrance. The gates are due to close at 5:00 p.m. He skids to a stop at the ticket booth. Already, in full flight, he's done the math and counted out the proper number of francs. He slaps down the bills for admission, snatches up the tickets and thrusts them in their hands, then takes the grand double helix staircase two steps at a time. He is out of earshot before the guard is able to utter the warning that the chateau is about to close.

"Come on, guys," her father yells. He disappears into the first vaulted gallery before they catch up with him.

The Château de Chambord has four hundred twenty-six rooms, seventy-seven staircases, two hundred eighty-two fireplaces, over eight hundred columns, and uncountable towers, turrets and chimneys. It's their fourth chateau of the day and her father is going for the gold. They have nine minutes.

When they emerge into daylight at 5:01 p.m. (French officials being surprisingly punctual), her father stands at the entrance gazing up happily at the facade of the chateau casting its massive shadow across the lawn. It is the first time in twelve hours he looks calm. All the day's deadlines have been met.

Friedrich IV

After France, they spend six days visiting Heidelberg and other medieval German cities unscathed by the war. This is a sentimental journey. In 1939 Opa's father died, and her father and his brothers, Friedrich and Karl sailed to Germany to spend their inheritance there since Hitler didn't allow Deutsche marks to leave the country. They took off a year from college and hung out with relatives in northern Germany followed by a ski trip in the winter, then a bike trip in the spring from Bremen down through Bavaria.

"Didn't you see what was happening in Germany at that time?" she once asked her father.

"We were oblivious," he replied, though they did spend a few hours in a local constabulary being detained and questioned by the *polizei* for unknowingly bicycling too near the vicinity of Hitler's Eagle's Nest.

In Rome she and her parents and Ted meet up with rich Uncle Friedrich, his Filipina wife Lucinda, his stepson Ernesto and their own son, Freddy. Rich Uncle Friedrich is rich because he became an executive at an importing/exporting company in the Philippines, where it's possible to live like a pasha with scads of servants who work for little more than room and board. He's also rich because he married Lucinda, a wealthy young widow and daughter of a Filipino senator. She is a famous beauty, treated as a celebrity ("La Luz") by the Filipino tabloids and Manila society. Friedrich and La Luz are part of Ferdinand Marcos's avaricious and corrupt strata. Luz probably has more shoes than Imelda.

On his business expense account, Friedrich goes around the world a couple times a year ostensibly to pick up antiquarian bargains for the company but mostly to buy and display them in the lavish compound he has built with La Luz's money. When he passes through the United States accompanied by his entourage, which includes a nanny for little Freddy, he stops at the homes of his brothers and sisters and at Opa's to show off his beautiful wife and opulent lifestyle.

Whenever he's due to arrive, the aunts run around Opa's house hiding the family photo albums, the *Stammbaum* (family tree), and portraits of ancestors. Friedrich is known to swipe any family memento he can get his hands on. He is a dynastic guy whose greatest regret is that he was born one year shy of being the first son. Her father, Erich Lang, has that honor, and according to the rigid Prussian rules to which Opa strictly adheres, it's the oldest son who will have dibs on all the stuff when the patriarch passes.

Friedrich has numbered himself The Fourth. He is Friedrich Helmut Wolfgang Lang IV, though there is only one other Friedrich Helmut Wolfgang Lang, a distant uncle, making Uncle Friedrich in fact the Second. Nonetheless, Freddy, his only child to be born in wedlock, is numbered Friedrich Helmut Wolfgang Lang V.

Despite all of Friedrich's posturing and his felonious character, her father gets a kick out of his younger brother. She suspects that, being such a strictly moral and restrained man, her father harbors some vicarious pleasure from Friedrich's sociopathic shenanigans.

In Rome they visit the Coliseum and other antiquities including the Catacombs, where Uncle Friedrich manages to steal a finger bone.

Strangers in the Night

On the evening before their departure to the Greek isles, they're in Athens, about to spend ten days on a boat together. They climb the hill to the Acropolis at dusk and wander among the columns and statuary, the Caryatids bearing the stone porch roof on their heads.

She goes off on her own for a while and sits on a boulder looking out across the city as the sun goes down. Very soon, the inevitable flock of teen-age boys approaches her. There are three of them, young Greek boys, giggly and almost shy. Standing off several yards as if she were a skittish fawn who might flee, they open the discussion by asking her what language she speaks. "You speak English?" She ignores them and continues to gaze at the sunset. "Sprechen Sie Deutsch?" She makes no response. "Parlez vous français?" In how many languages can they ask this question? It's beginning to amuse her. Then: "Strangers in the night?" And that breaks her up. She can't help laughing. They laugh with her. She gets up and walks off, leaving them with their little success.

The Sonia

The Sonia is a sixty-one foot motor sailing yacht with two masts, one mainsail, three jibs, four cabins, seven berths, two baths with showers, a saloon for eating and lounging, and a spacious deck. Its crew of three share a separate cabin forward.

Captain Dimitrio, fortyish, mustached, always dressed in khaki and a skipper's cap, speaks little English. There are two young deck hands aboard, Andras and Hektor. Andras doubles as a steward, whipping up three meals a day in a miniscule galley kitchen for eight people plus the crew. He has thick wavy black hair, dimples, and the muscular physique of a tanned Adonis. He often works shirtless. Though he understands some English, he usually expresses himself with body language. Tall, beak-nosed Hektor keeps his T-shirt on over his skinny chest and frequently slumps against the rigging, pallid with seasickness. He speaks the best English of the three but is usually not in a mood to speak at all.

Not surprisingly, it is Hektor she has a little crush on. She tends to gravitate toward skinny, beak-nosed men, poetic and sensitive-looking and a little morose. She can hardly bear to watch his stoic struggle to carry out his work while fighting the impulse to heave over the side of the boat. His travail must be especially difficult in light of Andras's sunny, enthusiastic hopping from task to task. Also, it's July, the very middle of the Aegean's Meltemi season when dry north winds are sometimes so strong and the seas so high, especially in the afternoon and early evening, that boats have to remain in dock for a day or two until the winds calm down.

The advantage of the Meltemi is that it cools the intense sun's heat which otherwise would broil them mercilessly. Wherever they go, on land and sea, their clothes and hair never cease to flap and flutter.

She and the rest of the family experience this Meltemi wind for the first time on their way out of Piraeus. It's down to their berths for her and Ted. The others, it seems, have all spent enough time sailing on choppy waters to be impervious. Her parents grew up on Lake Michigan and Friedrich's group has sailed on seas all over the world.

Freddy V

Freddy the Fifth is an interesting mix of La Luz's Chinese-Filipino and Friedrich IV's German ancestries with a longish nose in an otherwise petite face. A silent little boy. Between his father's overwhelming dominance and his mother's disinterest, he follows along like a shadow, easily unnoticed. At eight, he's now too old for a nanny and too young to enjoy the grown-ups' boring meanderings through the markets or their long lunches under the awnings of outdoor cafés and tavernas. Silently tagging along, he doesn't complain.

Uncle Friedrich likes to bring the young princeling on his trips as part of the entourage, but he seldom interacts with him or touches him except to move him around like a chess piece. There's no one for Freddy to play with. Twelve-year-old Ernesto, the youngest of Luz's four children, is the only one of them to come on the trip. His siblings have opted to stay in Manila to hang out with their friends. Nesto is as shadow-like as Freddy but seemingly because of a languid insouciance: I've got nothing better to do, I might as well sail around the Aegean.

After the first couple of days, she and Ted start to realize Freddy V's plight. The group has disembarked and is heading up the quay for an evening walk among the whitewashed stucco houses and shops and cafes of Mykonos. Freddy for the first time decides to stay on the boat. She turns to see him sitting alone on a pile of life preservers, staring at nothing, his legs dangling. She points him out to Ted, they look at each other, and in that moment know their duty. They turn back down the quay and come aboard. Freddy looks up.

"Did you forget something?" he asks.

"No," says Ted. "We thought we'd rather stay on the boat and hang out with you." The look of sheer joy on the little boy's face breaks her heart.

"With *me*?" he says, in bald disbelief. She can hardly keep from crying.

Ted goes to his cabin and comes back with a deck of cards. "Do you know how to play Seven-Up?"

They sit on the foredeck and play cards until the moon rises and the others return. From then on, she and Ted make a point of talking with Freddy, joking with him, throwing an arm around his small shoulders. He still doesn't have much to say, but his smile communicates everything.

Your Mother Swims?

Her mother carries her sweater over her arm, and whenever her father goes to take her picture, she uses the sweater to cover the slightly protruding middle-aged stomach that she tries to keep sucked in, giving her a strained, compressed smile as if she's not getting enough air. For as long as she can remember, her mother always wore her signature belted circle skirts that draped gracefully to mid-calf and showed off her slim waist. In this year she has switched to the shapeless sheath dresses in fashion for women of her age, presumably because she thinks her waistline no longer deserves to be on display.

And now she has to spend ten days in the forced company of La Luz, the sylph-like glamour queen who floats along the islands' whitewashed lanes in her tunic-length linen shirts, loose linen trousers and huaraches, her slender fingers and long manicured nails wrapped around the handle of a pink parasol to protect her perfectly smooth skin from the sun.

She cringes with empathy. This has got to be painful for her mother.

Uncle Friedrich, not to be outdone by his wife, poses in a yellow Speedo. He hangs from the rigging, nonchalantly sporting his tan and flexing his muscles, the products of a perpetually sunny climate and regular gym workouts. Her father seems utterly unconscious of his own pale skin, sagging pectorals, spindly legs and droopy swim trunks. He's just having a good old time with his cameras and an occasional dive into the transparent blue water to cool off.

Her mother has loved the water her whole life, and now, in spite of her dislike of herself in a bathing suit, she simply can't resist the pull of the sea. With her flowered cap to protect her hair and her one-piece skirted suit to hide her midriff, she dives in and swims gloriously. It's a triumph over the body shame of middle age womanhood.

Freddy V turns to her in astonishment. "Your mother swims?"

La Luz doesn't go in the water. In the whole ten days of the trip, she doesn't so much as dip a toe in. There is, presumably, too much danger of damaging her skin or ruining her celebrated coiffure. So. Her mother and La Luz, not so different, are both caught in the merciless snare of beauty standards.

Tile

They hop from one idyllic island to another—Mykonos, Naxos, Andros, Delos. Delos is especially fascinating. An archaelogical site, it has no inhabitants except a few caretakers and archaeologists with temporary permission from the Greek government. The ground is strewn with remnants of the past—mosaic tiles, bits and pieces of stone walls and columns. Everywhere there are signs warning: "By government order. <u>Do not handle or pick up anything on the island</u>! Violators will be prosecuted."

They tie up in a little sheltered cove and wander through the ruins. Later, they dive off the side of the boat and swim in the calm water. Uncle Friedrich spots a blue mosaic tile on the white sand at the bottom, about twelve feet deep. Ted has been floating belly down with his mask and snorkel on.

From the boat, Uncle Friedrich shouts. "Teddy!" Ted looks up. Friedrich points. "There's a mosaic down there. See it? Dive down there and get it for me." He'd do it himself but he has already showered the salt water off and is dressed for dinner.

Ted takes a deep breath, dives, paddling his big rubber fins, plucks the tile from the sand and emerges, holding it up in his fingers. Uncle Friedrich hovers over the side and reaches down to help Ted into the boat. But first, Ted dog-paddles in place while he carefully puts the tile in a little zip pocket on the inside of his swim trunks.

"Finders keepers," he says, grinning his boyish grin. Nothing Friedrich can say persuades Ted to hand over the relic, and he can't very well go rummaging around inside Ted's trunks.

Below deck, Ted gives her the tile to hide it in her Kotex box for safe keeping. Now she is complicit. But, she figures, better they than Friedrich. He owns enough stolen loot.

No Prescription

After Greece, they leave Uncle Friedrich and family and fly to Switzerland. It's quite a change from the Aegean to the Alps, but the altitude is so high and the sun so brilliant that even surrounded by deep snow, they barely need the lightweight trench coats they've brought along. Then they descend from snow-capped Mont Blanc to Lake Geneva, and it is in the city of Geneva, before they're due to fly home, that she slips away from the others and walks into a Swiss pharmacy to ask for birth control pills.

She can't remember who informed her that in European pharmacies you don't need a prescription for the Pill. Maybe it was Gracie. In any case, it's true. For a surprisingly low cost, the pharmacist hands over two boxes of six 21-day dial packs—a year's supply—and shows her how to use the round plastic dispensers that look like little clocks. You turn the dial and out pops a pill for the appropriate day of the week. How clever, she thinks, how convenient, how cute.

V

Hug Kiss Hold and Protect

She gets back to the United States at the end of July, three weeks before she and David are to meet. When he drives to her house, they will see each other for the first time in almost a year. Over these three weeks they exchange friendly letters and talk once on the phone. From Harvard he writes, "I enjoyed talking to you, too, and am looking forward to doing it with you (...uh, talking) in person. Wow, I'll see you in seven days. Love, David." All the while, scenarios for breaking up with him are going around and around in her head.

The bottom line is that she is not attracted to him anymore and hasn't been for a long time. How can she end it with as much honesty as possible without deeply wounding his self-esteem? The jealousy is another, unrelated matter. Need it be brought up at all?

Or is it unrelated? Did she lose interest in him because jealousy finally depleted her sexual pleasure, her affections? But then, did she ever feel affectionate toward him? She respected him, no question about that. She enjoyed his company. She liked it that she turned him on. She liked his sexual playfulness. She liked their orgasms. But affection? Does she even know what that emotion is?

She thinks of affection as what love must be all about. An impulse to hug and kiss and hold and protect someone because you love their essential being. When you see them, you want to pinch their cheek, nuzzle them, squeeze them, kiss the top of their head. And it's not contingent on they're being infatuated with you.

Does she feel this for anyone? She's never asked herself this question. It shocks her that the answer is: no, she doesn't, not for her parents or her brothers or any boy she's ever been involved with or any friend. She frequently feels empathy and sympathy, but affection? No.

Yet, if not, how does she know what it's supposed to feel like?

She feels it for cats.

Cats? That's all she can come up with? Hug, kiss, hold and protect? Yes, cats. She remembers the wild cat that used to attack her from the neighbors' weeds. It scratched and bit her over and over, yet it never made her angry. She would finally subdue it by gently kneading its neck. And what pleasure it was to feel the cat go all peaceful and happy under her hand. Pleasure at the cat's pleasure. No doubt this is what loving parents feel for their children. All they want is for the child to feel peaceful and happy.

The Talk

She explains it to him in every way she can so as to pin it on her own inadequacies and his strengths. It's a hodge-podge of self-deprecatory excuses. She has always felt insecure, she says, and being involved with someone so much more mature seems to have increased her insecurity. In high school her relationships were shallow and frivolous. This was her first significant relationship, and she became dependent on him for status and self-worth. She even felt resentful sometimes, as a hanger-on in his world of people who respected him so much. That's probably why often in the past she behaved selfishly and why her attraction started to dwindle, and now there's been too much water under the bridge for the attraction to be revived.

They have this one-sided talk while sitting at dusk by the reflecting pool of the Sylvan Museum of Modern Art, where she's taken him for privacy. As she explains the ending of their relationship, the Pegasus statue balances over them, the rider with arms outstretched, in a perpetual state of being flung off his flying horse. David's face crumples. He cries. She cries. He leaves for home an hour later.

With his usual generosity and humility, he doesn't blame her or lash out. The letter he sends when he gets home openly admits his pain but is forgiving, understanding, even sprinkled with bits of wry humor.

"Maybe I should have stayed at your house and talked things through, but it would have been very painful for me both to feel and display affection with no reciprocity and to have embarrassed your parents with tear-jerking scenes. I am quite relaxed now after practically setting the house afloat when I got home and again when Mom and my sister returned to find me there. The pain starts to ease until someone asks me what the story is—then all the memories rush back."

Unexpectedly his year in the clutches of the Freudian psychoanalyst provides him with solace even if it failed to cure his prostatitis. He writes again the next day: "I still have something to say—that is why you're getting another letter. I think it is possible (in the modest opinion of a physicist turned psychologist) that the fear of sexual intercourse may have had something to do with your coldness toward me—coming at a time when it was the next logical step. I am sad that it had to be the first relationship for both of us, thus minimizing the chances of success. That is why I wish you had had much sexual experience already. Then you might be more responsive to me.

"The above paragraph may be pure delusion and b.s., but as I found out this year, one's subconscious often works in strange ways relative to one's conscious mind."

He asks how she's feeling and "Oh, yes, a brilliant Freudian forget—I left my jacket at your house. Could you please send it or (preferably) deliver it in person? Love, David."

Why Not?

There are two weeks left to go before her senior year begins. Her mother has found her a job for August doing intake psych interviews at the county hospital outpatient clinic—no testing, just taking basic information. Otherwise, she's at loose ends since she ended it with David. Brent calls her for a date, and she thinks, why not?

He has thickened since last year, so she guesses he didn't lay off the beer after all. He proudly shows up in a sleek silver car he proclaims is a "1965 Chevy Malibu 66." It's not his, he's working on it for a friend. Now that there's no reason for him to express himself in print, she remembers how little they have in common. Even so, once again they fool around on a blanket in a secluded area of the park behind her house.

Since the end of July, she has been punching out those little pills from the clock-like dispenser and taking them as directed. On their next date, when she and Brent move to the backseat of the Malibu 66, she unzips him. There are no words, but he balances on one hand to remove his wallet from his back pocket and pull out a condom.

"Not necessary," she says. "I'm on the Pill."

"No kidding?"

"I got the pills in Switzerland."

"Whoa!" he says, "*Okay!*"

And they do it—awkwardly, since there isn't much leg room, or head room—but they do it. She's always a little wet, so there's no problem with his getting it in even though they haven't done very much beforehand to turn her on, and indeed she's not turned on. It's a stretchy feeling as he pumps away, but that's all. Not erotic, not stimulating, just kind of mechanical. When he withdraws, she grimaces in the dark at the feeling of slime on her thighs. Fortunately she has Kleenex in her purse.

"They all say it'll hurt," she tells him after they've both sat up and silently re-arranged their clothes, "but it didn't hurt at all."

He looks at her astonished. "Wait a minute. You're a *virgin?*"

"*Was.* Until now."

"Whoa." The news seems to have sobered him. "I didn't know. I mean, if I'd known ..."

If I'd known ... what? If I'd known, I would have enjoyed it more? If I'd known, I would have talked it over first? He doesn't finish the thought and she doesn't press.

When she gets home, she asks herself why she did it with him of all people. She concludes it was just because she could, just because she was curious, because it was time, because it was too late to do it with David and there was no one else on the horizon. She wasn't going to wait until marriage. She doesn't see herself getting married any time soon. Maybe someday in the distant future, if her jealousy problem has gone away.

And now she resents Brent. The thought of him disgusts her even though it isn't his fault that she has wasted the experience by doing it with someone she doesn't feel attracted to or in any way akin to. They never do it again; this is the last time she agrees to go out with him.

Major

She has been accepted as a graduate student in clinical psychology at her first choice university and intends to get a PhD, after which she believes she will become a college professor, a part-time therapist, and a writer of academic books. She will marry a professor in the sciences—chemistry or physics—where there are few women and she won't have to worry about her husband being seduced by undergraduates. They will have four children—with luck, two girls and two boys. She doesn't examine why she includes these potential daughters and sons in her plan when she isn't at all drawn to children.

Her mother had been surprised when she declared a psychology major at the end of her freshman year.

"Why are you surprised, Mom? You don't think I could be a good psychologist?" she'd asked.

"Oh of course you could, Annie. It's just that your interests have always been so different. Languages and theatre and writing. You're such a good writer."

"Psychology sounds like an interesting field, Mom, that's all." Why not?

License to Kill

She asks Dr. Steiner if she can sit in on group therapy sessions at a mental health clinic for her senior independent project. As usual, he comes through; he finds a clinic in the town of Barstow thirty miles away. She can reserve a college car to drive there. The catch is, she doesn't have a license. The good news is, all the college cars have automatic transmissions.

So now, finally, it's time to become a driver, but first she'll need to refresh the skills she learned in high school Driver Ed. Gracie knows a girl at Carroll with a car. She needs money and will give her a refresher for a couple dollars an hour. She still isn't too crazy about driving, but after a week of lessons she picks it up again.

The girl drives her to the county seat and waits while she takes the test. She passes the written part, and then, with trepidation, follows the license examiner to the car. He seems calm enough, not like her father when he taught her, but very business-like—no encouraging smile or small talk. She pulls out of the lot. He tells her where to drive.

She remembers to signal well ahead of lane changes and is gratified by his approving nod. What most scares her is getting on and off the Interstate, especially the part where you have to gauge when it's safe to enter a gap in traffic and accelerate on that short entrance ramp with cars zooming up behind you. She grips the wheel and cranes her neck fiercely, manages to get on without a collision and lets out her breath when he directs her to get off at the next exit.

After that, she feels more relaxed except when she takes a right turn on green and cuts in front of a woman crossing the street. The woman seems to have appeared out of nowhere. Back at the license office, she maneuvers the car smoothly into a parking space. For some reason she still has an aptitude for parallel parking.

She sits while the examiner checks off items on his clipboard. When he finishes, he turns to her and says, "You did quite well. I would pass you, but almost hitting a pedestrian is an automatic fail." He tears off the carbon copy of his report and hands it to her. "You can come back in a week and try again."

Having almost killed a pedestrian, she is, a week later, even more nervous than before. But this time she passes. Possibly forgetting the fact that it was his own anxiety as a driving teacher that discouraged her in the first place, her father writes, "Recently we drove to the northeast side to pick up a woman who does not know how to drive and I said to Jane how much I wished you would learn so you wouldn't be dependent on others, so I am most happy you got the license. Congratulations!" He encloses a check for the learner's permit ($3), instruction ($10), gas ($3), and license ($5), plus her monthly allowance ($25).

Tune in Next Week

Starting in October, every Wednesday after classes she drives to the clinic in Barstow. She's a little calmer behind the wheel now, but she's always reluctant to pass on the county road, even on stretches of straight highway. Perhaps passing brings back shades of her father driving white-knuckled in the left lane on English roads. Traffic backs up behind her, and as the days grow shorter, blinding headlights glare in the rearview mirror.

But it's worth it for the firsthand look at group psychotherapy in the real world. Her mother, herself a therapy group facilitator at the county hospital, is thrilled for her. "Fantastic experience for an undergrad!"

At her first session, Dr. Donahue, the clinical psychologist who leads the group, introduces her to the six women, who have given their permission to have an observer. She has been allowed to tape record the sessions on the condition that she hand over the tapes after she finishes her report at the end of the semester. The group members are White working- and middle-class women from nearby rural communities. They're all married with children.

There are long uncomfortable silences during the fifty-minute session. Everyone seems anxious. Dr. Donahue himself seems uncomfortable. She wonders if they don't like her being there, taping, taking notes, especially as she's so young, and whether he's nervous about making a good impression on a Carroll College student who will report back to her professor.

The group itself is fairly new. When they do talk, it is mostly about their financial difficulties and disagreements with their husbands over money. Her role is to sit in the background and listen. By the second session, her novelty seems to have worn off; she has become part of the furniture, and the long silences disappear.

The women, it turns out, have a lot to say.

Thirty-year-old Alice is indignant that she has to ask for money whenever she needs to buy something unexpected. "I have to account for every single penny! When I worked at the Stop and Shop," she says nostalgically, "I had my own spending money."

She wonders why Alice stopped working. Did her husband forbid it?

Miranda, forty-two years old and the mother of six children, is bewildered that she herself should have such depressed, anxious feelings even though her husband is so nice to her.

Connie resents the fact that her husband has taken little interest in an upcoming celebration of their thirtieth wedding anniversary which their children are planning for them. "It makes me feel worthless, or I guess I should say *more* worthless. I hate to cut cakes at church suppers. It's such a simple thing, but I never do a good job. The ladies kid me—'Oh that's the cake *Connie* cut'—I try to laugh along, but I'm so embarrassed."

"All my husband can talk about is Shriners, Shriners, Shriners!" says Trish. "Last night he took me out to dinner at the Turf and Surf on the highway—of his own free will, I didn't even ask him to—and then today he's griping because our budget doesn't allow for going out to dinner and going to the Shriners convention both. That's all he's interested in. He doesn't care for me at all."

Yet he took you out to dinner, she thinks. Why did he do that if he doesn't care at all?

The other two women have similar complaints.

They don't seem to be operating as a group but as individuals. Each waits her turn without listening to the others. She wonders why Dr. Donahue doesn't point this out or encourage them to respond and ask questions. But maybe it's too early in the group's life and he's waiting until they get comfortable with expressing themselves.

It's kind of like watching a soap opera. She looks forward to next week's episode.

Another Tome

That semester, fall '67, she takes History and Systems of Psychology and produces a twenty-page senior term paper—"A History of Psychosomatic Medicine." She has come to believe that her chronic insomnia, colds and migraines are psychosomatic, so in a way she might consider herself an expert on the subject. For the paper she uses nineteen sources and accumulates a stack of three by five cards six inches high, not unlike her sophomore tome: "The Effects of Four Educational Variables on Psychological and Intellectual Development." Once she's started, only the deadline drags her out of the library and brings the research to a halt. She's reminded of her ninety-page sixth grade report on birds complete with illustrations traced from bird books and colored with crayons. If she's unsure about quality, she goes for quantity.

L'Amant Militaire

In October Carroll College brings to campus the San Francisco Mime Troupe, a radical anti-establishment theatre company. She associates mime with the pathetic class she took in high school and almost doesn't attend the performance. But this isn't mime. *L'Amant Militaire* is performed in the style of sixteenth-century commedia dell'arte. Everything can be seen by the audience—the actors putting on their outlandish costumes and clownishly warming up; stage hands running around placing oversized props in odd places; each character being introduced with exaggerated flourishes; a puppet, Punch, interrupting to wreak havoc. And that is before the show even starts.

L'Amant Militaire is a biting, hilarious anti-Vietnam War satire, a broad mockery of the military-industrial complex and its self-serving pretensions, with disguised references to Lyndon Johnson's bankrolling of South Vietnam's corrupt dictators and generals. It's long—two hours or more—but it seems over in a minute and she wishes it had gone on longer. She feels cleaned out by laughter.

Afterwards, wading through the fallen oak leaves that blanket the sidewalk, she inhales the autumn air and wonders, for the length of her walk to the dorm, why she ended up eschewing theatre in favor of a major field that will doom her to sitting in groups and nodding thoughtfully as people complain about their husbands.

Olympic Gold

She has put off completing her two-credit Physical Education requirement until senior year. Without it, she can't graduate. Carroll requires both a major and minor sport. Looking over all the possible options, she hits on badminton for the major and bowling for the minor, neither of which she's any good at; on the other hand, neither of them is likely to make her perspire.

Bowling takes place once a week at the town lanes, where other un-athletic Carroll students take turns throwing their gutter balls and working toward a minimum average score of ninety to get course credit. She's only bowled once before this but finds it relaxing since it's not particularly competitive. It's also amusing. The bowlers look from behind like cats wriggling their bottoms before leaping at a bird. Once the ball is loosed, they scamper back in triumph if they manage to knock down more than one pin.

She gets her pass in bowling and the following semester takes badminton in the college gym. The instructor is the muscle-bound football coach, who asks her out after a few lessons. Apparently the college doesn't frown on this or at least turns a blind eye, and though she has no real interest in this coach, she hasn't been asked out by anyone else and she's flattered.

Derrick Hurt seems to embody her stereotype of a coach. He has nothing to say that isn't about sports, his chest is as hard as a Roman imperial breast plate, and there is, similarly, no give to the rest of him. Briefly, at a party, she sits on his lap. His thighs are like concrete. She thinks if she sits there too long she could end up with a bruised bottom.

After three dates, she turns him down the next time he asks, which rejection he takes without apparent disappointment and continues to coach her in badminton until she meets her requirement. At some point during that time he starts to date a junior named Carrie Kidder.

Carrie is known to have won pre-Olympic badminton championships. She keeps in practice by playing with Derrick even though he doesn't come near to her level. It's a joy to watch her. She drives Derrick up and down the court red-faced, snorting and perspiring like a beleaguered bull while Carrie, lithe and cool as an elegant matador, steps effortlessly back and forth, returning his desperate serves with ease.

She and Gracie along with plenty of others like to sit in the bleachers and watch the spectacle. The best part is after a match when Carrie hands Derrick a towel without needing to use it herself.

Then something horrible happens. Derrick and Carrie start dating. Within two weeks she loses a game to him. Within four weeks, she loses a whole match, and after that she no longer wins at all. He hasn't gotten any better. She's gotten worse.

She mourns over Carrie's losses. Discussing it, she and Gracie can't decide if Carrie is deliberately letting Derrick win or if it's an unconscious capitulation. Either way, the male ego comes out with the gold medal.

Good Old Kid

Gracie comes back to the dorm furious after serving sit-down dinner at the men's dining hall. She and her boyfriend Ethan have had a fight.

"I'm so pissed off at him."

Gracie and Ethan were planning to go to the Ides of March rock concert on Saturday, and now, out of the blue on their way back through the men's loggia, he tells her he doesn't want to go and she should ask someone else. He disparages the group as "Beatles wannabes from some Chicago suburb."

"Like I'm an unsophisticated low-brow for liking them. What a dick."

She considers this. "So it was right after you got off work that he told you this?"

"Yeah."

"Uh huh. Okay. So ... this argument has nothing to do with the Ides of March concert. Ethan is feeling insecure."

"What?! Why? *I* asked *him* to go to the concert."

"At dinner tonight, were you horsing around and teasing the guys at your tables?"

"Well, natch."

"Think about it."

She blinks, does a double take. "He's *jealous*?"

"Yes, he is."

Gracie rolls her eyes. "Nah. I always do that. He knows it doesn't mean shit."

"No special bantering going on tonight?"

Gracie thinks. "Just a lot of laughing. Jerry Smolek was being hilarious."

She nods wisely. "Okay. So I have a question for you. You've been seeing Ethan for quite a while. At this point, would you say you love him?"

Gracie looks away. "Well, yeah. Kinda."

"Have you ever said it to each other?"

"*God*, no."

"He definitely loves *you*. He's all moony-eyed around you."

"Well if he thinks I'm going to stop goofing around with the guys—Hell, I goof around with girls, too. I goof around with everyone."

"You don't have to stop goofing around with the guys."

She sits Gracie down at her desk and assumes her best stern parental look—not so easy since her own parents never give her such a look. "Here is what you need to do. Call him up and tell him you're coming over and you'll be there in ten minutes."

Gracie folds her arms across her chest. "*He's* the one who—"

"Be quiet. So, when you get there, say this: 'Ethan, I hope you realize that I love you.'" Gracie gasps. "I'm—"

"Shut up. Then you say, 'I am always going to goof around with the guys at work because that's what I do. It's not flirting, it's not sexual, it's not romantic, it's just me being goofy. *You* are the one I love. And you *are* going to The Ides of March concert with me on Saturday.'"

For a few moments Gracie just shakes her head. "But what if it's not about him being jealous?"

"Trust me. It is."

She's asleep when Gracie gets back that evening. The next morning she asks her how the talk with Ethan went. Gracie is doing some last minute reading for her econ class. She puts the book down and looks up at her soberly. She says, "Did anyone ever tell you you're a pretty good old kid?"

Presumed Guilty 'til Proven Innocent

She is asked out by Chris Connell, a senior who lives in McCollum House, David's old dorm. They've never met. The most important thing she knows about him is that last year he dated and broke up with Diane, a friend of Gracie's, and that Diane was bereft and still carries a torch for the guy.

Why he broke up with Diane she doesn't know but assumes it was because she wasn't glamorous enough for him. Though nice looking and amiable, Diane is by no means a glamor queen. But then she herself is no glamor queen, and he is asking her out without even knowing her. What does it mean?

Chris has that subtle air of superiority and confidence that she associates with Big Men on Campus. Gracie says he's been on the Dean's List since sophomore year and has been elected to Phi Beta Kappa. He's as athletic as you can get at a small college where athletics takes a back seat to scholarship, and intermural sports are played in a league of small colleges with tiny athletics budgets. He is good-looking enough—not ravingly handsome but well-proportioned, tall and square-shouldered with an engaging smile.

She agrees to go out with him, but the question is, should she? Gracie's friend still yearns for him. Wouldn't it be a kind of betrayal of another woman, even though the relationship is over and her own acquaintanceship with Diane is slight? Should she make an excuse and back out?

Since returning to Carroll after her junior year, she's only gone out casually with the coach. And now this BMOC has called her up. Against her instincts, prejudices and principles, she decides to go ahead with it.

They sit at a table in The Hub café and talk about the movie they've just seen, *The Graduate*, which has made her angry.

"Why do they make it seem like a woman is ludicrous and crazy for wanting to seduce a much younger man? Middle-aged men are constantly getting involved with women half their age and no one thinks a thing about it."

"Well, but it was her own daughter's boyfriend. I think that's the point."

She can't argue with that.

"But did you hear the music? The lyrics?" Her ears had pricked up as soon as 'Here's to you, Mrs. Robinson' began. "'We'd like to know about you for our *files*'? 'Help you learn to help your*self*'? 'Walk around the *grounds* until you feel at home'? It makes her sound like she belongs in an insane asylum for having being attracted to the boy."

"Hm," he says, "I guess I wasn't listening that carefully. I liked the part where the older guy comes over to Ben and says, "I have one word for you, are you listening? *Plastics!*"

She has her back up, but it doesn't seem to make him defensive.

A week later he asks her to the Brecht anti-war play, *Mother Courage and Her Children*, put on by the theatre department. Brecht wrote it in 1939 in response to the Nazi invasion of Poland. Like the Mime Troupe's *L'Amant Militaire*, it uses metaphors from another time and another war, the Thirty Years' European War of the seventeenth century. And like *L'Amant Militaire* it is long—two and a half hours. But there the similarity ends. In her opinion it is two and a half hours of unmitigated tedium, moments of humor undercut by so much grimness and pessimism. She is certainly not cleaned out by laughter when Mother Courage hitches herself up to her cart at the end of the play and carries on, having learned nothing.

"She's essentially a war profiteer," she complains. "There's nothing courageous about her."

"But that's the point," says Chris, sitting with her on a sofa in the McCollum House lounge. "War corrupts people."

"Well, yeah, I got that—about an hour and a half longer than I needed for them to bring the point home."

"It was pretty long."

Then she and Chris make out for twenty minutes or so before he walks her back to the dorm. Why do they make out? It's kind of automatic. He initiates, she reciprocates even though she feels no passion or excitement. Does he? Or is it just something obligatory for him too? Perversely, she still resents him for having broken up with Diane.

After that, he doesn't call her again. She's not surprised. In fact she feels a little smug that she didn't fall for him.

Frank Stika

She's introduced to Frank Stika by Ethan. They live in the same dorm, though they don't hang out together. Gracie has nagged Ethan to find her a date after Chris Connell and the coach didn't pan out.

Frank is a thin, pallid boy with the habit of passing a hand across his forehead to get his straight, rather greasy-looking bangs out of his eyes. When he smiles, he looks away as if smiling could get him in trouble.

He's a working class kid from Hammond, Indiana, the grandson of Czech immigrants. Everyone in his family for three generations has worked in Hammond factories and the steel mills of Gary. Since he was fifteen he has spent his summers on an assembly line of one sort or another. Last summer he got an easy job packaging soap at Lever Brothers. He is the first and so far the only member of his family to go to college and is on a full scholarship, so he must be very smart, however unentitled and humble he seems to feel.

Despite his somewhat lackluster personality and physical appearance there are a number of things to appreciate about Frank. He's serious, he reads widely, studies hard, and, if prompted, can hold intelligent conversations about the issues of the day. And maybe, if she's honest with herself, the big thing in his favor is that he seems to think he's hit the jackpot by dating *her*.

She would never admit to anyone and has only recently admitted to herself what her attraction to nerdy boys is about. In her mind she refers to it as her Beauty and the Beast Syndrome. Not because she thinks she's a beauty or that the boys she's drawn to are beasts, but that compared to the type of girl they might expect to win she's a catch, and because of that she feels relatively in control. But only relatively. It hasn't immunized her against her jealousy of the beauty queens, the Roz Cohens and Lily Robertses. She wonders, though, if in this respect she has something in common with Lily, who surrounds herself with a coterie of homely girls.

A Mother's Advice II

She has written her mother to lament the power differential between women and men, and how she instinctively punishes men, even innocent ones like David and Frank, by holding herself at a distance. It is the only way she knows to bring the power into balance. She understands she is cutting off her nose to spite her face, but she doesn't see a way out of the dilemma.

"Sweetie," her mother writes, "will you please put your good mind to the notion that men and women are complementary parts of a whole instead of totally separate rivals? You feel so angry with men because they feel superior. If you *knew* they were not, and really felt yourself to be their equal, it wouldn't bother you in the least. Stop feeling inferior. You're one of the best people I know."

Yes, yes. But how do you not resent what's all around you: the huge half-naked women on highway billboards advertising cars and cigarettes; the myriad television programs with all-male casts except for the "love interest" in the tight sweater; the thousands of little ways that a woman's self-esteem must be sacrificed to protect the man's.

She thinks of her father on vacations, driving for hours and hours until he finally has to pull over for a nap, while a perfectly qualified driver is sitting right next to him. What is so abhorrent about a wife in the driver's seat? And how exhausting is it to contrive never to let your husband see you without make-up?

Reluctance

Frank is ever so much safer than someone like Chris, but nowhere near as playful as David. Unlike David, Frank doesn't seem to consider the two hours of Sunday open dorm an opportunity for sexual frolicking. They usually spend it in Frank's room not hers, and he always leaves the door open. His pals feel free to wander in and out, chatting with her, teasing him.

She and Frank do plenty of handholding and kissing in Frank's room and elsewhere, but whenever she discreetly nudges his door shut and starts to move in on him, he seems strangely reluctant. He pulls back subtly or has some reason to get up from the bed where they've been half reclining and show her something or open a window. She recalls Bill Phelps, her Eagle Scout boyfriend in high school, who took it on his shoulders to be the one with the self-control. Maybe Frank is worried about going too far and getting her pregnant.

She considers how to bring up in casual conversation the subject of contraception.

"It's amazing how different things are in Europe," she says, off-handedly. "When I was in Switzerland, I just walked into a pharmacy and they gave me a year's supply of birth control pills, no prescription needed, no questions asked." She takes the circular pill dispenser from her purse and shows him. Quite obviously, the pills from July to the present have been punched out, with months remaining.

Still, nothing changes.

She's frustrated, not because she's in love with Frank and wants to be closer, but because she needs to know that he, as David used to put it, is "hot for her bod."

On a Sunday afternoon when they're studying together in his room, she leafs idly through his copy of the student newspaper. From inside the pages an 8 × 11 photo protrudes. It is a glossy of Roz Cohen, clearly the work of Frank's friend Harry Staley, a photographer for the college newspaper, who, she guesses, has handed out prints to all his friends. She quickly slips it back in.

For the next week, she wants very much to punish Frank by being cold and unavailable until he breaks down and anxiously asks if she's no longer interested in him. He loves her, he will say, but will understand her not loving *him*. She is sorely tempted to inflict this insecurity on him, but with a rare sense of fairness and compassion, for once she resists the temptation.

Vietnam

In February, a photograph, dubbed "Saigon Execution," appears on television and the front pages of every major newspaper. It is the image of a South Vietnamese commander shooting a Viet Cong suspect in the head. The point blank shooting takes place on a Saigon public street. The victim's hands are tied behind his back, so he is a prisoner of war. Somehow the photographer has caught the act at the instant the bullet has struck, distorting the man's face even before blood has had time to spurt.

The photograph is just one of many horrifying images to come out of this war, and it calls up the Nazi brutality word pictures that took root in her mind and afflicted her with pessimism when she was fourteen. What won't people do to each other if given the excuse?

She has never been an activist of any kind and isn't one now, but she despises what she sees as the faulty logic that started this war and the cynicism and face-saving political self-interest that prolong it.

"Vietnam finally throws off the French, and then the *U.S.* comes in to mess with their affairs!" she exclaims. "We prop up a sleazy, corrupt government, just in case the Chinese come in and take over. Do we think the Vietnamese want *any* other country taking them over? It's a *nationalist* movement, for Christ sake. Vietnam for the Vietnamese. Why do we support these fat cats in the South? How is bombing the hell out of the country and burning people alive with napalm, destroying villages, all that heinous shit, going to save that country from the communists? I guess the idea is there will be nothing left of the country when we get through with it. Problem solved."

This is her customary rant, delivered at the dinner table on visits home and professed to Gracie, Beth, Frank and others at school, but there's really no one to contend with. Her parents have essentially the same opinion, and she would be hard put to find a Vietnam War supporter at liberal Carroll College. If there are any, they keep it to themselves.

Ted will very soon be old enough to be drafted, but there are hints that a psychiatrist colleague of her mother's will get him a mental health deferment. Nick has already been classified 4F because of his eyesight. Even David got under the wire by being in graduate school before the graduate deferments were dropped. But with the changing draft rules, more of the privileged will be sitting on helicopters shoulder to shoulder with the poor and working class boys who, up to now, have been virtually the only ones getting shot out of the air over combat zones.

As irate as she feels about the war, she carries on with her privileged life, joining no movement, marching no marches, doing nothing. She feels guilty about this, but she continues to be more preoccupied with getting to the dining hall before all the French toast is gone.

In a Pup Tent

It's April, and now that the weather is getting warm, she proposes that she and Frank go camping over the weekend. It would be nice to take a break together, she says. Maybe his friend Harry could lend them his car and camping gear. She thinks that in the womblike intimacy of a tent Frank's resistance might be lowered.

He agrees, with what she senses is some reluctance, and then on Monday he stumbles and pitches forward on a stairway in the dorm and breaks his hand.

They put off the camping trip for two weeks. His hand is still in a splint, but Harry's car is an automatic and she can drive, so on Friday they go to a state park and pitch the pup tent. It's a beautiful, warm spring evening, still light at seven o'clock. They take a long walk through the woods, wade across a clear, rushing creek, and find their way to a bluff overlooking a lake. They get back to the campsite before it's too dark to find their way, and hunt around for twigs and branches to light a fire in the grill.

When the moon has risen, she leads the way to the tent and crawls in. There is just room for the two of them to lie close together on the outspread sleeping bag. She turns and presses against him. They kiss. She feels him getting hard. In the tight space she wriggles out of her clothes and helps him off with his since he's still operating one-handed. Now they're both naked.

There's a pause. Then, as if afraid of being overheard, he whispers in her ear, "I'm ... not sure what to do. I've never ... done it before."

Ahh! Finally it dawns on her. So *that's* what all the reluctance was about.

"Don't worry," she says, matter-of-factly. "I'll show you." And she rolls onto him, takes his erect penis, and guides it in. In seconds he is pumping away, and in seconds more, he has come.

"Oh," he gasps, "that was so fantastic! Thank you!" He clasps her tightly as his pulse and breathing slow down. "I was kind of scared," he admits. "When I broke my hand, I thought maybe I did it subconsciously so I wouldn't have to go on the camping trip. Thank you. That was so great." The relief and elation in his voice make her glad she has given him his first experience, and after sufficient time for him to recover, they do it again, the same way, avoiding the missionary position to spare his hand.

He falls asleep long before she does. She lies awake thinking how unstimulating and mechanical the act is without the Everything But part.

The Be-All and End-All

So sexual intercourse is supposedly the be-all and end-all of sexual experience. Well, it may be the end-all, she thinks, but it's certainly not the be-all. What she had gotten up to with Murray Tierney in high school and with David those two years they were together—those "Everything But" frolics—*that* was the be-all. Intense, intimate, experimental, prolonged—and with David, playful and fun.

As a child she was told by her mother that someday, when she was much older, the act of a man putting his penis in her vagina would seem "enjoyable." Then, when she reaches that age, and the act does sound like it might be enjoyable, her mother gently advises her against doing it before marriage so it will be special when the time comes.

But what if she and David had gone ahead and done it anyway, having obtained protection, of course, and done it as the culmination of one of their Everything But romps in her dorm room bed? How good would *that* have felt?

The act has not been the "ultimate in pleasure which male and female take in each other" as her mother claims but literally anticlimactic. She's struck by the irony of her mother's misplaced advice. Of all the men she should have done this renowned act with, it didn't need to be with some future husband, as her mother suggested, or the near stranger with his pick-up line about her blue eyes, or with Frank, whom she likes okay but doesn't love, but with David Kirschner, the boy who shot his wad in an arc like a rainbow and fondly referred to her breasts as her booby woobies. David, that's who she should have done it with, before she started being irreversibly annoyed by his oral habits.

Her mother, so kind and well-intentioned, had completely misguided her. Sexual intercourse is not the ultimate in pleasure which male and female take in each other, at least not for her. Apparently it is for men. And why is this one particular act labeled sexual intercourse? Isn't all of it sexual intercourse? In her virginal days with David, she had decided against doing something that couldn't be undone. The irony is that *not* doing it the first time with David, *that's* what can never be undone.

April 5th, 1968

She thinks, Why are White people indignant about the rioting? What in the world did we expect? After three hundred fifty years and still no end in sight, what would we do if *we* were the targets of violence and persecution despite doing everything humanly possible to peacefully, gradually struggle for equal rights and justice? Would our reaction be any different?

Her own reasoning condemns her. She's putting all the burden on Black people even as she defends them in her mind. Shouldn't she herself be so furious that she, too, takes to the streets? Shouldn't it be her burden as well? She thinks of the German pastor's famed words that she learned in Philosophy class just this year:

First they came for the socialists, and I did not speak out—
Because I was not a socialist.

Then they came for the trade unionists, and I did not speak out—
Because I was not a trade unionist.

Then they came for the Jews, and I did not speak out—
Because I was not a Jew.

Then they came for me—and there was no one left to speak for me.

In spring of her freshman year, after voting rights demonstrators were attacked by police, five students from Carroll went to Selma to report for the student newspaper on King's march to Montgomery. She would never have had the courage then and still doesn't. All she has is opinions.

The Group

She has sat in on Dr. Donahue's therapy group for many weeks now and, early on, he gave her their background information. It is woeful. Abandonment to cold, punitive relatives after a mother's death; a raging, terrifying father; rigid, hypercritical mothers; alcoholic parents; a mother arrested for prostitution.

The reactions they hold in common are depression, anxiety, headaches, suicidal thoughts.

Now that she knows more about the women, her compassion has been stirred. The sessions are more than soap opera episodes. It occurs to her that all six of them feel fundamentally alone and trapped in their solitude. Ideally the group members could act as mirrors in which they see their miseries shared and reflected back. Not just because misery loves company but because they can apply insights about each other to themselves. Ideally.

Dr. Donahue is mostly silent, on the assumption that they, not he, should drive the process. But so far it doesn't seem to her that he has found the right balance between leading and—in a non-directive way—helping *them* to lead. When he does take charge, he sometimes goes too far. Then they'll turn to him for a magic cure: "If I can learn to say 'no' to people, will that make me well?" "Is it true that all depressions are caused by anger?" Or else it shuts them up.

In the middle of April, Josie brings up the subject of sex. She says that she has hesitated to bring it up before because no one ever discusses sex in the group.

"I realize how much I've been kidding myself that my sex life is satisfactory," she says.

Connie exclaims, "I know what you mean, but I've never talked about it either because it's sure not something I'm proud of!"

Dr. Donahue is pleased that the forbidden subject has come out in the open at last. But only three members show up for the following session and none of them mentions sex. At the next session, when everyone is back, Donahue makes what she believes is a misstep. He says, facetiously, "Well, I'm glad to see everyone back today. Last time there were only three of you here. I thought maybe you got scared away by Josie's talking about sex." There is uproarious laughter and a brave protest by Connie: "Oh, I'm not afraid of *that*!" But the laughter quickly turns into a few nervous giggles, the subject is changed, and sex is not brought up again.

Having been assigned by her professor to analyze and evaluate the group process in her final report, she writes, regarding the incident:

> I think the flippant and rather abrupt way in which the therapist handled the silence about sex was premature. It might have been more effective to wait until a related subject was being discussed and use it to encourage Josie to mention sex again. Then perhaps the therapist might have asked, 'How do you all feel about discussing sex here in the group? Why do you think we haven't done it before?'

She wonders if her critique is presumptuous considering her own inexperience and Dr. Donahue's kindness in allowing her to sit in. But her professor writes "I think you're correct here."

All her reading to prepare for her end-of-semester report suggests that no studies have definitively shown group therapy to actually help. Most of the writing on the subject is anecdotal. Commonly, group therapy advocates assert that groups need at least a year, sometimes two or even three before they produce results. This seems inefficient and impractical. And how are results to be evaluated? She's come to realize that mental health is an elusive concept, difficult to measure.

Yet she produces a generally upbeat report on the independent project, concluding

> In time I hope to see training programs developed in the graduate schools and clinics which will help potential therapists gain the skill and insight necessary to master this excellent technique.

"You have profited greatly from this opportunity," her professor writes. "Excellent paper. Well-constructed, complete. Makes fascinating reading." It's a relief to think she's done something right at this demanding college

An Acquired Skill

With the days getting warmer, she's sweltering in her turtle necks and wool skirts. Beth can sew and keeps her small portable sewing machine on her desk in the dorm. In the last few weeks she's made herself some nice short-sleeved and sleeveless blouses, culottes and a pair of Bermuda shorts.

"You are so lucky!" she tells Beth. "What I wouldn't give to make my own clothes."

"Well, why don't you? You're welcome to use my sewing machine."

"Oh, I can't sew," she says. "My mother doesn't sew either. We don't even own a sewing machine." She and her mother can thread a needle and sew a hem by hand, and she dimly remembers making an apron back in seventh grade Homemaking, but that's the extent of it.

"Well, I'll teach you," says Beth.

"Teach me? Oh, I doubt it."

"What do you mean?"

"I mean I doubt if you could teach me. I just don't have a knack for that sort of thing."

"For what sort of thing? Sewing? How do you know if you've never tried?"

After classes that day, Beth insists that she come with her to the sewing section of the Ben Franklin store downtown. It's a world of craft that she must have seen many times in the store without noticing. Now she is introduced to the bulky pattern books—Butterick, McCall's, Vogue.

"Find something that looks good to you," says Beth.

She pages through the McCall's book and picks a sleeveless dress with a narrow waist and flared skirt. Beth directs her to the pattern drawers and stands back to let her search for the one she's chosen, size twelve. Then they look over the bolts of fabric until she finds a color and material she likes.

She carries the heavy bolt to the cutting table, and rolls it out. While the clerk cuts it, Beth shows her how to read the back of the pattern. "These are all the things you're going to need," she says and sends her on a quest for notions—seam binding, zipper, facing, straight pins, matching thread—while following silently behind. The whole process is a bit like a supervised scavenger hunt.

Back in the dorm, she opens the pattern, unfolds the tissue paper pieces and, under Beth's guidance, cuts them out, pins them on and cuts the fabric. Before she can start sewing, Beth teaches her how to wind the bobbin, thread the machine, raise and lower the foot, and choose the stitch size. Beth makes her do each of these tasks twice. She practices on a cloth scrap. It takes her a while to press the knee lever so the stitches don't take off and race away, something like when she was trying to learn to drive on a stick shift, but Beth is nothing like her father; she stands back calmly and utters the occasional encouraging word.

Once she starts working on this dress—drapey cotton with navy and white polka dots—she works on it continuously, forgetting to eat dinner or go to the bathroom, and has just finished when Beth and her roommate return from studying at the library at 10:30. She models the dress for them. It fits perfectly.

"You don't have to have a knack," says Beth. "You just have to follow directions." She turns to her roommate. "Annie thought you had to be born knowing how to sew. From the womb." They laugh. They all three laugh.

"Good, Though Somewhat Discursive"

Spring semester of senior year she takes History of the Far East and reads twelve required books altogether, including four on Chinese Communism and Maoist thought. Her memory is drawn back to Highgate Cemetery where Karl Marx, possibly disgruntled by the Stalinist and Maoist distortions of his theory, glowered with fierce indignation from his marble pedestal.

After so much reading of history and literature in England and all the papers she's written during almost four years of college, her writing is finally receiving more praise than condemnation. She receives As and the adjective "interesting" on her final history papers, "Peasant Nationalism and Communist Power" and "Examining *The Political Thought of Mao Tse-Tung*."

For her "Analysis of the Characters in *Point Counter Point*" in her Major British Writers course, she gets an A minus ("Good, though somewhat discursive"). She has to look up "discursive" in her Merriam Webster's and finds this definition: "moving from topic to topic without order, rambling." However, a second definition claims the opposite: "proceeding coherently from topic to topic, marked by analytical reasoning." Hm. She thinks this paper should have been judged "Good, very discursive." But what does *she* know?

Little Arlington

She steps out of her dorm into a mild, sunny day in late April, 1968. Carrying her books and binders, she strolls across the railroad tracks, rounds the side of The Hub, and comes in sight of central campus. Here she halts. The great square of spring-green grass has, overnight, been planted with hundreds of small, identical white crosses, symmetrically lined up in perfectly diagonal rows.

After only a split second of bewilderment, she gets it. She draws closer and walks slowly along a row, bending to peer at the small crosses, and finds that the names of the graduating senior men are written in precise block lettering on many of them. The cross at the apex has the name of the Marine Corps captain who has come to campus to recruit.

Amazing, brilliant.

Other early risers are standing and staring or walking through the faux cemetery, reading the names.

So far she has had no involvement with the radical students at this ultra-progressive liberal arts college. Of course she has known of their existence and agrees with their disgust at the imperialist politicians and generals who think nothing of bombing a people into submission. But there's something about the activists themselves she has found objectionable, these young "rebels," most of whom live communally off-campus. Without knowing any of them personally, she knows *of* them and of their pretensions to nonconformity—the long hair, the ragged clothes, the contempt for the conventional uniforms of "straight" society, when in fact, they wear uniforms of their own.

She sees them as smug, superior show-offs. Maybe that's it more than anything—the showing off. She herself tries not to show off, though she often fails, so it may just be projection on her part. Probably she shouldn't feel this way about these activists because she does agree with their goals and with the notion that people must take a stand if they want to confront the abuse of power. But she's sure she wouldn't like them personally.

Still, how did they lay out this symbolic cemetery—so meticulously designed, so geometrical—in the middle of the night, in the dark, while the rest of the campus slept? Now that she looks closer, she sees that there are upward of a thousand crosses. The protest says so much in such a simple way—among other things that the new military draft rules no longer allow the privileged to sit back and enjoy graduate deferments while society's poor are required to do the fighting and dying for an immoral cause.

She can't help admiring the designers of this particular spectacle, whoever they are, show-offs or not.

Dove

She graduates May 24th. Commencement is held on the commons in front of The Hub, folding chairs having replaced the white crosses. A breeze pushes puffy clouds along in the bright blue sky and flaps her black graduation gown against her legs. Her father is weighed down by filming equipment—the movie camera, a camera loaded with slide film, a camera bag holding rolls of print film. He snaps numerous pictures of the commencement speaker, a renowned environmentalist and nuclear disarmament advocate.

Sixty students have refused to wear a cap and gown in protest against the Vietnam War. It is a surprise to her. Among these, no doubt, are the same students who live off campus and planted the crosses on central campus.

If she'd known about this commencement protest, would she have taken part? She could remove her gown even now. But there her parents are, her mother looking thrilled and a little tearful, her father with his cameras at the ready. He slips into the aisle and starts filming as she, Frank, Beth, and Gracie go up one by one to receive their diplomas and return to their seats. At home, he will put up the screen and play back the ceremony and she will groan at her purposefully nonchalant walk and self-conscious smile.

What he fails to capture, because it is completely unexpected, is the most dramatic moment of the event. The last student to come on stage takes his diploma from the President, turns to the audience and opens his gown. A white dove bursts out and soars to the top of the great oak that shades the ceremony. Then the bird flies out of sight into the clouds. She thinks of the dove, how frightened it must have been, held against the boy's chest. But what is the distress of a single bird in light of the millions devastated by an unjust war?

Three hundred caps are flung in the air according to tradition, and she feels guilty that hers is among them.

Fear

Her parents help her haul her belongings down to the car. The dorms and the college are emptying. The trees of central campus are in full leaf, the grass dense and green, but though it's spring, there's an autumn feel, as of things thinning out, as of a season of life dwindling.

Beth gives her a hug and a hurried good-bye; her parents have come all the way from Pittsburgh and they're antsy to get back on the road. Gracie and Ethan she'll see at their wedding in June, which makes the parting feel less abrupt. And now Frank is at her side, having seen his parents off. He has proposed earlier that the two of them stick around for the rest of the day and take the train to their respective hometowns that evening. When he gets back, he'll immediately go to work at another factory job, and they won't see each other until the end of summer. Her parents have no objection—young love and all that.

She and Frank wander hand in hand along the converging sidewalks and loggias and in and out of empty classroom buildings. They roam around the abandoned dorms and dining halls. Housekeepers and janitors will soon descend to prepare for alumni reunions in June and July, but now they have the place to themselves. The door to Frank's room is unlocked, the bed stripped, shelves and closets empty. By mutual unspoken assent, they enter and shut the door behind them.

For her, more than an act of passion, it's a novelty, a kind of prank, to do it in a room that is now off-limits. There's no way they could find that door unlocked and *not* do it. A leftover towel hangs from a rack in the bathroom. They lay it under them to keep from staining the mattress.

As they're putting their clothes on afterward, she stifles a gasp, struck by the sickening realization that she has forgotten to take her birth control pill that morning.

She says nothing to Frank about it. They sit at the depot waiting for their trains headed in opposite directions. They kiss good-bye and promise to write. On the train, in dread, she stares out the window, seeing nothing.

Her period, always regular as clockwork, should start a couple of days later and doesn't. The horrendous scenario takes up all the space in her mind: finding an abortionist—who would she even ask?—undergoing the painful and dangerous procedure at the hands of someone who makes a living by breaking the law.

Having a baby is out of the question. She doesn't want to be a mother—not now, maybe never. She pictures herself in a house where in no room would she be free from another person's needs. Tied to a dependent child indefinitely. The claustrophobia of such a life.

She waits and waits for the blood to come. Five days pass. She has been too anxious for rational thought until it finally occurs to her to pour her heart out to Planned Parenthood.

"So you've been taking the Pill?" the woman on the phone asks calmly, matter-of-factly. "For how long?"

"Almost a year." It is some relief just to be talking to an authority.

"And how late is your period?"

"Five days. But it *always* comes every twenty-eight days. It's *never* late."

"And this is the only time you've forgotten to take the Pill?"

"Yes, I've never missed one until now."

The woman's voice becomes gentle, motherly.

"It would be virtually impossible for you to get pregnant from missing just one pill after all this time. The drug stays in your system for quite a while even after you stop taking it. Your period is late because of fear. Hormones are very sensitive to anxiety and stress. Don't worry. It'll come after you've calmed down."

She bursts into tears of relief. "Oh thank you, thank you," she chokes out, barely able to speak.

After she gets off the phone, in an incandescent euphoria she floats outside and down the path to the ravine. The rustling leaves, a scampering squirrel, the spring wild flowers beneath her feet—all strike her as profoundly beautiful. The next day, she doesn't even take aspirin for the dull ache in her low abdomen—she savors it. And the bright red stain on her underwear, it is the scarlet of royalty.

June 5th, 1968

It happens again. Now in her lifetime three public figures have been assassinated, two in the last month and a half. Bobby Kennedy had finally begun to commit himself sincerely to the things she believes in—civil rights, an end to the war, social justice. Recently he had met with Martin Luther King and actually listened. Is this what motivated the assassin? But no, she hears that the man was angry about Kennedy's support of Israel.

She hadn't planned to vote for Kennedy in her first election since coming of voting age. Eugene McCarthy is her candidate—a humble Midwesterner, not a privileged rich boy like Bobby. Even more in his favor, Gene McCarthy, years before, had confronted and ridiculed the despised other McCarthy—Joseph—in a face-to-face debate, and later supported her parents' favorite intellectual, Adlai Stevenson, when he ran unsuccessfully for president.

But she would have supported Kennedy if he had won the nomination. He had probably had a greater chance than McCarthy of beating Nixon or—god forbid—Reagan. It would have meant some progress at last after Johnson had abandoned the War on Poverty by pouring money into the actual war. And now Kennedy is gone. It seems it takes courage to put yourself in the public eye. There's no telling who will pick up a gun and shoot you.

So she decides to get involved in a political campaign for once. She doesn't do much, just stuffs envelopes at Democratic headquarters and runs errands. She shrinks from calling people to solicit campaign contributions or going door-to-door. The most she will do of that kind of thing is hand out flyers downtown, but even this makes her cringe and she does it for only a day.

When Gene McCarthy comes to town she gets to go with other campaigners and meet him, which she knows she doesn't really deserve. At the airport she reaches out and he shakes her hand. "I'll never wash it," she jokes. But she feels ashamed of her so-called involvement, thinking fleetingly of those Carroll College students freshman year who joined the D.C. march against the Vietnam War, and the student newspaper reporters who went to Selma to write about Martin Luther King's march to Montgomery. She can't even bring herself to make a few phone calls.

Intake

Her mother again gets her a summer job doing intake interviews at the county hospital's mental health clinic. This time she's considered qualified to interpret personality tests.

The Rorschach is scored using an elaborate and bewildering coding system devised by obsessive zealots who apparently didn't know when to quit. Patients are shown ten cards in succession and asked what they see in the inkblots. Responses are then coded depending on whether the person responds to the whole blot (W), a cut-off whole (W\), a normal detail (D), a rare detail (Dr), a normal fragmentary detail (Df), a rare fragmentary detail (Drf), an original response where form quality is accurate (O), and so on.

This doesn't include the even more fastidious identification of which *part* of the blot or white space is described (anywhere from 1 to 58 areas, depending on the card) and whether it's presented upright, inverted or sideways. So, if, for example, Card III is presented in an inverted position, and Patient X, pointing at area 1, says, "I see a child cannibal's head," the score is V 1 D F+.

These are just a few of the code categories. There are thousands and thousands of permutations, all laid out in 274 pages of tortuous charts.

And that's just the coding. Attempts to turn any of these codes into a valid and reliable evaluation of personality makes her sophomore tome "The Effects of Four Educational Variables on Psychological and Intellectual Development" seem simple and elegant, and the practice of Phrenology downright scientific. The Thematic Apperception Test is not much better. Thus, she thinks, is the influence of Freud. How is it that Freud got away with all that unsupported speculation and became lauded as the most significant theorist of the twentieth century?

She resorts to making up the Rorschach interpretations based on her own intuition and what the patient tells her in their half-hour session. She gathers her mother does much the same.

There It Is

Her graduation present was a sewing machine. Fabric and patterns and notions are cheap, and she spends most of her leisure time this summer churning out clothes. Making something practical from scratch with her own hands is highly addictive. Every time she picks up the scissors to cut out a pattern, she silently thanks Beth. She will start graduate school with more clothing than she's ever had in her life.

In late June she attends Gracie's wedding as a bridesmaid. It's all very traditional. Gracie looks pretty in her wedding dress and self-conscious as she poses with Ethan for the photographer. They're fully-fledged grownups now. It seems right on schedule. They've graduated from college and will both go on to graduate school as a married couple.

She can't imagine it for herself. In theory, yes. She gripes to her parents about not having found Mr. Right, becoming an old maid. But in reality it's hard to picture being a loving partner to someone. She's too selfish, she thinks. And there's the jealousy although it wasn't so bad this year. Maybe she's growing out of it.

In mid-August, she and Frank give up their jobs so they can spend one last week together before she goes off to her clinical psychology program and he to law school, or possibly to Vietnam courtesy of the United States Army. His number could come up at any time.

He arrives by train and they borrow her father's car to take her things down to the University. The tiny basement apartment she has rented sight unseen costs fifty dollars a month including utilities. After unloading her things and sleeping uncomfortably together on her single bed, they take off for Crater Lake in Arapahoe National Forest. For five days they camp in utter solitude by a bracing stream.

After they part ways, he writes from law school that their trip was one of the best times he ever had in his life and only regrets it wasn't longer and that he didn't talk more. "There were a lot of things I wanted to discuss, but as usual I didn't. I do think that I expressed my feelings, though. I miss you, sweetheat." In her reply, she teases him about the risqué Freudian slip.

One of the things he wanted to discuss was the idea of his going to Canada to avoid the draft. He writes to ask point blank if she would be willing to marry him and come with him. No, she replies, equally point blank. She can't make that sacrifice. He doesn't push, and it seems he has become resigned to the inevitable.

For the time being, he's an official student of law and loves it despite the enormous workload. He feels stimulated as he never has before. Any day now, though, he'll have to give it up.

The call comes in late October. In November 1968, he ships out to Fort Leonard Wood and after that Fort Knox for more training. "It's a miserable life," he says. But by a miracle he ends up stationed in Frankfurt, Germany, for his two-year stint, though apparently not because of his high level of education. For a reason known only to the Army, his intellectual gifts are put to use on routine clerical tasks.

"Life is so short," she writes her parents. "It seems incredible to be forced to waste two years of it because a bunch of morons in Washington made a lot of mistakes and can't bring themselves to admit it."

They correspond regularly. In spring of 1969 he comes home on leave, which they spend together, but she explains that there is no future for them, as much as she cares for him. They part in tears. From New York, on his way back to Germany, he writes, "I just don't know how to tell you how much you have meant to me and how much I appreciate everything you have done for me. I still love you, Annie, but I won't obsess." Once again she has withdrawn from a good man. It's a terrible thing to hurt someone like that, but there it is: she doesn't love him.

EPILOGUE
August, 1980

Off and on for the last half hour she has been peeking through a gap in the curtain. The audience has been pouring in and now the auditorium is packed. Five minutes to show time and her parents still haven't arrived. She has put reserved signs on seats for them in the sixth row, close enough for a good view but not so close they'll have to crane their necks to look up at the stage. Their seats are still empty.

She's worried that they might have had an accident. Her father was determined to make the trip. They haven't seen her perform yet, and this venue isn't so many hours from home—a convention center in Kansas City. She told them not to come. There would be other opportunities. Three days ago he had surgery to repair a detaching retina. And now he's driving. At dusk. She knows him—even with only one functioning eye, he'll insist on being the one to drive. And, anxious about arriving late, he'll be speeding.

Then, to her relief, there they are, being ushered down the aisle and directed to their seats. She watches them settle in. Her mother lays her purse on her lap. Her father unfastens the buttons of his sport coat. They look attentively toward the darkened stage.

She's still worried. She has counted the number of men in the audience. Including her father, out of some three hundred people, there are three men, and the other two are sitting toward the back where he might not have seen them, so he probably thinks he's the only man here. How does he feel? It's the National Organization for Women's annual convention. She's getting a decent fee, and she can expect a good reception. Probably a great reception. But still.

It's time to start. She signals for the house lights to go dim but not too dim (she likes to see the faces) and the stage lights to come up. The chair is down center facing the audience, her baskets and the coat tree scattered upstage behind it. She takes several breaths and walks on.

She is wearing a floor-length Quakerish dress. It's a hybrid she made from the top of a black, long-sleeved taffeta gown and a skirt of a brown tweed material, adding a modest bit of white lace at the wrists and neck. Her wig, parted down the middle and fashioned in a bun, is streaked with gray. She carries a small, old-fashioned carpet bag by its wooden handles.

Her walk is slow, erect, and a little stiff, to suggest age. She stops in front of the chair and stands for a beat, looking out. Then she reaches into the bag and removes a child's plastic bottle of soap bubbles. Taking her time, she unscrews the cap and pulls out the wand, eliciting titters from the audience. Then she holds it up to her lips and slowly blows a long stream of bubbles that almost reaches the front row. The titters turn to chuckles and a few outright laughs.

Now she returns the wand to the bottle, recaps it and puts it back in the bag. She straightens and takes a step forward, proffering her hand to an unseen interviewer.

"Good afternoon," she says, in a slightly creaky old woman's voice but with perfect nineteenth-century diction. "My name is Susan B.— for Brownell—Anthony. I am here to apply for the job of receptionist/ secretary that was advertised in the paper? The advertisement said you were looking for someone 'mature' ... and 'bubbly.'"

Two hundred ninety-seven women roar and applaud at the punch line. Possibly the two men, also, she can't see. And her parents? She sneaks a glance. Her mother is laughing and clapping, her hands at the prayerful level of her chest. Her father's head is thrown back in classic Lang-silent-laugh position and he is vigorously slapping her mother's knee.

She goes on to play out the imaginary job interview, ending by rising from the chair and pulling a pamphlet from her bag.

"Would you like to have one of these flyers explaining how the federal government is prosecuting employers for failing to hire older people?" She holds it out. Pause. "No? Well, I'll just put it on your bulletin board as I leave." She shakes the interviewer's hand. "Thank you again, and I'll be waiting for your call."

During the applause, she turns and walks upstage still in character. Then she tears the Velcroed back of her dress apart, takes it off, removes the wig and tosses them into the tall basket. Now she's standing with her back to the audience, stripped down to her basic costume: a white tuxedo shirt and black pants with satin ribbon down the legs. Her hair is an inch long all over to accommodate wigs.

From the coat tree she removes and dons an orange faux-velvet tunic and a piece of orange headgear with bobbling silver balls attached to antennae. When she turns to the audience the words "SPACE CAPTAIN LANG" are visible, spelled out across the tunic in silver sequins on a black background. She places a music stand downstage bearing a large poster board card:

EARTH EXPLORERS' TRAINING PROGRAM
INSTRUCTOR: SPACE CAPTAIN LANG

The sketch is a reverse role piece in which Martian astronauts are being prepared for the illogic and absurdities they'll encounter on Earth as they try to grasp the concepts of female and male. The training message of Space Captain Lang is delivered in spacey, laid-back Valley Girl-uptones:

"Remember that earth beings, instead of creating themselves from like conscious will, like we do? are created by these little teeny microscopic worms that stick together in pairs shaped like X's. Can everybody make an X, please?" She models the X with crossed fingers. The real audience complies. "Oh wow, that's really good." Laughter.

The speech is illustrated on the poster boards, one after another, with hand drawn cartoons—a female figure with a fat X on her lower half, a male figure with a Y.

"You might wonder ... like why do we need to know the sex of human beings? Like who cares? Well, we wouldn't need to know except that to male human beings it's really, really important. Male human beings base their social structure, their government, language, economic system entirely on the fact that they're missing a worm." She waits for the audience to stop laughing. "See, they don't feel good about it. So they try to set up everything to look like it's the *women* who are missing the worm." The Martian chuckles at the irony.

It goes on in this vein. The audience is eating it up. But she wonders how her parents are taking it. With a surreptitious glance she sees her father still slapping away at her mother's knee, and her mother's shoulders shaking with laughter.

After the first six sketches, she announces an intermission. As women leave their seats to chat with friends or head for the restrooms, she slips from behind stage, makes her way into the fifth row and leans across the back of a seat to talk with her parents.

They are beaming.

"Oh Anne," her mother exclaims, "it's wonderful!"

"And what a turnout!" her father says.

"How was the trip? How is your *eye*?"

He ignores the second question. They were almost late, he says, because a semi jackknifed on the interstate and traffic was tied up for half an hour. "We didn't think we were going to make it."

She has to get back on stage to move a few props around for the second set, but as she's withdrawing, a woman sitting to the left of her father turns to him and says, "Do you *know* her?" Her father nods and, with a note of boastfulness in his voice, replies, "That's our *daughter.*"

It is nine years since she stepped off the path she thought she had chosen—the path that would have given her parents the same bragging rights as their professional friends, whose accomplished offspring have produced precocious grandchildren. If her parents are disappointed that her path is not what they would have wished, they hold their disappointment close to the vest. And if in the future she diverges onto still another path, she is confident that they will continue to accept and embrace her because ultimately they respect the fact that their children don't belong to them, that their children belong to their own beloved and unique selves.

ACKNOWLEDGMENTS

Once the first draft of *Reasonable People* was complete, Caryl Lyons, my close friend of thirty years, kindly agreed to put her considerable editing skills to work on the book. As usual (she has improved the quality of all my other books) her comments made perfect sense. Except for my obstinacy in keeping a couple of obscure, possibly archaic words, I implemented most of her suggestions. Thank you, Caryl. You are a wonder.

I always figure a manuscript needs a perusal by at least two outside observers. The second one I turned to was my cousin Margaret Hawkins, a brilliant writer, writing teacher, and editor. Almost as if she were psychic, without my prompting, she zeroed in on every part of the draft where I had asked myself *Does this work? No. Yes. I'm not sure. Maybe. Okay, I'm leaving it in.* She also gave me permission to let go of a vast number of unnecessary details. In each case she saw what needed to be done. When I did it, I saw she was right. Any faults are my own.

Caryl's and Margaret's astute comments are like advanced master classes. I will take the lessons learned into future writing projects.

In this memoir, I've changed the names of people, places and institutions to protect their privacy (even—somewhat absurdly—my own name, which is right there on the front cover for all to see). This concern for anonymity prevents me from listing the actual people and institutions that provided me with documents and information. Suffice it to say there were many, and I thank them all.

Excuse me for thanking myself as well. I thank me for being the extreme saver that I am. Don't get me wrong. I don't hoard. When I moved from a house to a one-bedroom apartment I blithely gave away or tossed eighty percent of my household belongings. (Well, who knows exactly what percent it was. Trust me, it was plenty.) Whee! Who *needs* this stuff?! But. Where diaries, grade school essays and report cards, junior high class photos, college papers and every letter ever sent to me were concerned, the only criterion for KEEP or DON'T KEEP was: *Might I someday want to write about this?* Ninety-five percent of these went straight to the KEEP boxes. So, thank you, Anne Lang—that is, Kate Kasten—for thinking ahead.

KATE KASTEN lives and writes in Iowa City, Iowa. In an earlier phase of her life, she wrote, performed and toured a solo act—*Kate Kasten Comedy Theatre*. After a decade of portraying eccentric characters on stage, Kasten switched to fiction and is the author of four novels, a book of fairy tales for adults and two short story collections. *Reasonable People* is her first work of nonfiction. She is currently working on a second memoir, *A Certain Time*, covering the years from 1969 to the early 1980s when she was deeply immersed in the women's liberation movement.

www.ingramcontent.com/pod-product-compliance
Lightning Source LLC
Chambersburg PA
CBHW051748040426
42446CB00007B/272